The Art of
Derek Walcott

The Art of

Derek Walcott

Edited by Stewart Brown

SEREN BOOKS

Dufour

SEREN BOOKS is the book imprint of
Poetry Wales Press Ltd
Andmar House, Tondu Road,
Bridgend, Mid Glamorgan

British Library Cataloguing in Publication Data

The Art of Derek Walcott.
1. Trinidad. English poetry
I. Brown, Stewart 1951-   II. Walcott, Derek 1930-
811

UK ISBN 1-85411-021-7
UK ISBN 1-85411-027-6 pbk

Published in the United States of America by Dufour Editions Inc,
Chester Springs, Pennsylvania 19425-0449

Library of Congress Cataloguing-in-Publication Data
The Art of Derek Walcott / edited by Stewart Brown
      p.   cm.
      Includes bibliographical references (p.) and index.
$35.00
      1. Walcott, Derek – Criticism and interpretation.   I. Brown,
      Stewart.
PR9272.9.W3Z55 1991
811–dc20   90-3799 CIP

US ISBN 0-8023-1290-X

*Poetry Wales Press acknowledges the financial support of the
Welsh Arts Council*

Cover painting, 'The Death of Gaugin' by Derek Walcott

Typeset in 10½ point Plantin by Megaron, Cardiff
Printed by Billing & Sons, Worcester, U.K.

Contents

INTRODUCTION

How does one approach a body of work like the poetry of Derek Walcott? Is it enough to say that these are poems written in English in the second half of the twentieth century and assume that the trans-Atlantic critical orthodoxy which might allow a reading of, say, Ted Hughes or Gregory Corso, both his contemporaries, would be adequate to deal with Walcott's work? To an extent the answer is obviously yes, for just as we might amend our 'standard' methodology to accomodate Hughes' muscular mythologies or Corso's urban demotic we might adjust the tolerances to allow of Walcott's exotic landscape and his obsession with a 'marginal' history. What those distinctive voices share, in terms of the language and culture-of-the-poem, is more significant than their many differences. But such a position reads poetry as hamburger, as supra-cultural glop. As Geoffrey Hill remarked about Marvell – a not irrelevant comparison – "in order to empathise with a poet we need to understand him *in* his world . . . otherwise the meaning of the words on the page may elude us." The particular and peculiar circumstances of Walcott's work – and although his reputation in the U.K. and the U.S. is primarily as a poet, he is perhaps better known in the Caribbean for his plays (and as the essays in this volume demonstrate he has also been active as a cultural critic and as a painter) – demand careful contextualisation if its achievement is seriously to be assessed and understood.

But which contexts? Walcott's work *is*, now, part of that International Hyperculture; he takes jets between continents as easily as he once took the row-boat ferry across Castries harbour. So to understand the poems in *The Arkansas Testament* and *Omeros*, his most recent collections of poems, it is crucial to have some sense of where the poet has come from, and how; not just biographically but in terms of the Caribbean's social and cultural history. In particular, we must understand where he stands in terms of the fundamental shifts in

attitudes towards personal and national/regional identity that the
people of the Caribbean have experienced during Walcott's lifetime.
Such a context informs our reading of the poems; it becomes apparent
that the acerbic middle aged voice mocking, through the weary wit of
the *Spoiler* persona, those West Indian politicians who:

> . . . .promise free and just debate
> then blow up radicals to save the state,
> who allow, in democracy's defence,
> a parliament of spiked heads on a fence

has its genesis in the idealistic, optimistic, verse of a schoolboy patriot
punning his critique of St. Lucia's bastard Colonial "aristocracy":

> The inheritors of manners and manors,
> the lords of cane and acre

in 'Letter to a Sailor' from *25 Poems*, his first pamphlet collection,
privately published in 1948.

The problem of establishing an adequate context for a discussion of
his work is compounded by the fact that Walcott has always cultivated
his ambiguities, his complexities – refusing to simplify himself or his
art. He has appropriated Senghor's cunning self-assessment as "the
mulatto of style" and developed his own theory of influence, of
assimilation, which sanctions his (or any New World poet's) drawing
succour from whatever cultural sources he feels are relevant to the
task in hand. In his essay on Walcott's prose in this book, Fred
D'Aguiar draws attention to a lecture Walcott gave at the University
of the West Indies in the early '60's – when he was working through
the Crusoe metaphor – in which he writes of making a bonfire of the
influences that have washed up on his castaway's shore. It is, he
implies, part of the Caribbean condition that he should be at once so
isolated, so distinctive, and yet so wholeheartedly open to influence.
Walcott's own experience bears that out – on the one hand the St.
Lucia he was born into in 1930 was just a speck on a map of the British
empire, a colonial backwater, a place cut off from the main currents of
world events. On the other hand history had conspired to make that
island a kind of hinge between cultural worlds; French and English,
North and South, Latin and Anglo-Saxon, Amerindian and Afro-
American. St. Lucia was both virginal New World and the site of
some of the worst atrocities of slavery days. In his own time Walcott

was aware of both isolation – he was not black enough, not poor enough, a Methodist in a Catholic community, a precocious intellectual, an artist – and a communality, a shared colonial angst, a sense of being called to 'speak for' a generation, for a whole experience that was not heard in their (the metropolitan world's) books. In the several accounts, both in poetry and prose, of his boyhood, what stands out is Walcott's sense of himself as someone 'chosen', singled out by his 'gift' to address those apparent contradictions, to make something new, whole, distinctive from – to appropriate the term he applies to his inheritance of the English language – "the spoils of history". So, while not denying the importance of his personal experience and vision, the explanation of Walcott's work as the extraordinary achievement of an extraordinary man doesn't take adequate account of the complexities of his situation as a West Indian poet and the extent to which his 'individual voice' has been an expression of that cultural/regional experience. Even his poems of 'exile' in the more recent collections speak to a fundamental Caribbean concern: at one level indeed as the *defining* experience of Caribbean sensibility – just about all the people of the region are migrants in that sense – but perhaps growing out of that is a deep seated sense of rootlessness, of a willingness to dare to try to make 'another life' 'elsewhere'. Even if he's become a 'fortunate traveller' the literary celebrity jetting first-class across the globe can never escape that sense of a responsibility – albeit self-appointed and arguably self-serving – to, in some sense, represent the 'Mass Man'.

So despite his gradual accomodation, and 'domestication' as an American poet, those cultural complexities that *produced* Walcott continue to be both source and subject of his work. To read his work chronologically – as the essays in this book do – is to follow, not so much the 'development', but the ways in which his attitudes towards those central issues of Caribbean identity modify and change over the almost half a century of his writing career. Those changes are not always a matter of the overt subjects of his work but reveal themselves in the cast of his language, and in the formal and stylistic variety of his art.

For all that Walcott's status as a poet and playwright of international stature is undoubted – certainly his work speaks to all sorts of people in all sorts of circumstances – all the essays in this book begin from an understanding of Walcott's commitment to the idea of his 'place' in the West Indian cultural landscape, and a belief that the context, finally, which enables us to approach "the meaning of the words on the page" is one which sees Walcott emerging from, engaging with and returning to

> The midsummer sea, the hot pitch road, this grass, these shacks that
>   made me,
> jungle and razor grass shimmering by the roadside, the edge of art;
> wood lice are humming in the sacred wood,
> nothing can burn them out, they are in the blood.

Stewart Brown

The Apprentice:
25 Poems, *Epitaph for the Young*, *Poems*
and *In a Green Night*

The Apprentice:
25 Poems, *Epitaph for the Young*, *Poems* and *In a Green Night*

Walcott's poetry has always echoed with "Other men's voices / Other men's lives and lines."[1] This freely acknowledged willingness to appropriate styles, cadences, even attitudes from other poets has been variously explained as characteristic of a mind still culturally colonised or, on the other hand, as representing the humility of a major poet able and willing "to draw on the total heritage available to him as an alert and enquiring human being."[2]

There are grounds for both these views. As an English commentator notoriously observed at the time, "derivativeness, even pastiche, [was] common enough to be characteristic" of West Indian poetry right up to the period of Independence in the early '60s.[3] That urge to imitate was not, as that critic seemed to imply, some sort of congenital condition but was the cultural expression of a deeply ingrained and perhaps inevitable colonial outlook, which valued only that which had first been sanctioned by the 'mother country'.

The structuring ethos of the society was self-negating, dismissive of anything indigenous or locally instigated, especially if it were associated with folk values or a positive racial consciousness on behalf of the black population. The 'postcard verse'[4] collected in the early anthologies of West Indian poetry is characteristic of that mentality. The mellow fruitfulness of Vivian Virtue's Jamaican landscapes,

> Mid the rusted brown of the star-apple boughs
> How the light south wind leaps and soughs
> In the gay days of March, the glad days of March,
> When the sky is a stainless violet arch,[5]

is typical of the genre, poets still, "imaginatively expatriates,"[6] as
O.R. Dathorne put it, looking away from the West Indies for their
mentors, their metres and their audience.

Any poet who would aspire to break the colonial die was taking on
more than just literary tradition then. For the formally educated
young colonial, effectively alienated by that education from such
alternative traditions as his 'folk' society could provide, working in a
language inextricably tied to the literature of the colonial power, and
lacking any kind of intellectual community that might understand and
support experiments in expressing a sense of national consciousness
in forms and language appropriate to those concerns, the task must
have seemed impossible. This was more or less Walcott's situation in
the St. Lucia of his childhood, though in some ways he was fortunate,
having that small band of "self civilising",[7] artistically inclined people
– friends of his parents and a few of his peers – who were at least
willing to listen to and discuss his ideas. More importantly his
imagination was genuinely fired and sustained by his classical
education and the literature it introduced to him. It was an education
which, he was to assert later,

> must have ranked with the finest in the world. The grounding was rigid
> – Latin, Greek and the essential masterpieces, but there was this elation
> of discovery.[8]

Such a relish for the classic literature of Europe, supplemented by his,

> voracious appetite for literature . . . you know you just ravage and
> cannibalise anything as a young writer . . . [9]

which devoured first the 'moderns', then the Metaphysicals and
subsequently Latin American, Russian, North American literatures
constitute his access to that "total heritage" to which Mervyn Morris
referred. Of course this cosmopolitan range of reference was more
than just literary anthropology; it reflected his sense that history, such
an encumbering and inhibiting force in many ways, had "made him a
citizen of the world".[10] His family background and his island's history
provided tangible links with many cultures and sanctioned his sense
of legitimate access to the literatures of those cultures.

Much later in Walcott's career Joseph Brodsky, trying to
understand the sweep of cultural reference in the body of Walcott's
work, has argued that beyond such historical self-justifications,

Walcott's ultimate claim to the empire of the world's literatures is his absolute commitment to poetry. That his sense of a "sacred duty to the Word",[11] beyond ties of race or political allegiance or personal love, bonds him to "Homer, Lucretius, Ovid, Dante, Rilke, Machado, Lorca, Neruda, Akmatova, Mandelstam, Pasternak, Baudelaire, Valery, Apollinaire . . . "[12] Indeed, Brodsky asserts, "These are not influences – they are the cells of his bloodstream."[13]

In much of his early work, however, those cells sometimes threatened to clot into thromboses of ventriloquism. Just as in his early attempts at painting

> my hand was crabbed by that style,
> this epoch, that school . . .
>   . . . this classic
> condition of servitude.[14]

so most of the poems in *In A Green Night* and the three self-financed, locally published booklets, *25 Poems* (1948), *Epitaph for the Young* (1949) and *Poems* (published while he was a student in Jamaica in 1951) are blatantly 'in the style of' various masters. The quest for a language and forms adequate to both his lived experience and his – seemingly contradictory – determination to make a poetry "legitimately prolonging the mighty line of Marlowe and Milton"[15] drove the young Walcott to test out the voices of his acknowledged masters as a means of identifying what styles might best serve the trauma of his situation:

> The whole course of imitations and adaptations was simply a method of apprenticeship. I knew I was copying and imitating and learning . . . I knew I had to absorb everything in order to be able to discover what I was eventually trying to sound like.[16]

The journeyman apprentice, indentured to a particular artist or mastercraftsman whose techniques and mannerisms he would learn by a process of meticulous copying, only very gradually allowing anything of his own to enter the work, was a character familiar to Walcott from his study of painting. It is just such a relationship that he so lovingly recalls in 'Another Life' between Harry Simmonds, the eccentric, bohemian St. Lucian artist and his two art-besotted pupils, Walcott and 'Gregorias'– Dunstan St. Omer. The transference from one art to another was natural enough and was sanctioned anyway by his equally beloved classical tradition in literature, which held imitation of master poets to be one of the routes to artistic fulfilment. Walcott seems to have taken to heart the advice of Longinus who declared that such imitation should not be "merely a copy of devices of arrangement and style but a positive emulation of their [the great poets'] spirit."[17]

So although there were no local literary masters the young Walcott would wish to emulate, the school anthology poets were "immediate experiences" and the technique of the apprentice – that working 'in the style of' – was both a challenge and a channel for the young poet's talent. Much later in his career Walcott offered one of his typically self-justifying prescriptions for the humility appropriate to a young poet by recalling his own apprentice period:

> Young poets should have no individuality. They should be total apprentices, if they want to be masters. If you get chance to paint a knuckle on a painting by Leonardo then you say "Thank God!" and you just paint a knuckle as well as you can.[18]

Just so the young Walcott had seen himself entering:

> . . . the house of literature as a houseboy,
> [who] filtched as the slum child stole.[19]

Such a self-conscious apprenticeship constituted, in itself, an enabling mask which sanctioned the inevitable derivativeness of any young colonial writer's poetry[20] but at the same time furthered Walcott's career as the poet, the man of letters, in a society which placed small value on poetry as an end or art for itself but appreciated the spectacle of a local prodigy flaunting his colonial education and drawing praise from the metropolis or its representatives.

The real value of the early, colonially derivative Apprentice role lay in the distance it created between the poet – the mask wearer – and what the mask said. In a sense, of course, all writing is produced through such a mask, the I of a first person narrative is not even Barthes' "instance writing"[21] but an invention, a selection, a self-conscious – if sometimes self-deceived – projection of a character the writer invents to stand for himself. But the willed adoption of a distinctly other mask signifies something more cunning, more artful. As a strategy for dealing with the complexities of the Caribbean's on-going history which would inevitably be the poet's theme if he was to write anything more than the postcard scrapes he so despised, the Apprentice persona allowed the young man to try out different positions on that history as well as different styles. Indeed the two were inextricably linked. Echoing Eliot's Prufrock, who must defend his vulnerability by making time "To prepare a face to meet the faces that you meet"[22] Walcott gives notice, in 'Prelude', the opening poem of *In A Green Night* and a survivor from his first collection *25 Poems*, that he will adopt the masks expected of him in the world from which the "steamers which divide horizons" came and to which he must, seemingly inevitably, direct his "accurate iambics":

> I go, of course, through all the isolated acts,
> Make a holiday of situations,
> Straighten my tie and fix important jaws.[23]

By accepting the role of Apprentice the historic pain which is his essential subject in the early verse – "the pain of history words contain"[24] – is deflected onto the various 'masters' and the young poet can examine it, manipulate it, start to come to terms with it almost in the way that a playwright investigates and manipulates his characters.

These words, "the pain of history words contain", encapsulate many of the historical and cultural contradictions of Walcott's situation in the St. Lucia of his youth. The dilemmas out of which Walcott wrote are metaphored precisely by the antagonism between his commitment to the language of English poetry – with all the cultural baggage that implies – and his similarly absolute commitment to the world he felt bound to recreate in his writing – the street and peasant life he could not enter except as an observer because he was not "black or poor" enough, which lived by a different language but which, none- the-less, provided the rhythms which constituted the "pulse beat of [his] wrist."[25] It is his determination to learn the means by which he might do justice to that other life that is the heart of his apprenticeship, which distinguishes even his most derivative pastiche from the 'postcard verse' of his forbears in West Indian poetry. For above all else Walcott was determined to capture:

> the *feel* of the island, bow, gunwhales and stern as jealously as the fisherman knew his boat, and, despite the intimacy of its size, to be as free as a canoe out on the ocean.
> That apprenticeship would mean nothing unless life were made so real that it stank, so close that you could catch the changes of morning

and afternoon light on the rocks of the Three Sisters, pale brown rocks
carious in the gargle of sea, could catch the flash of a banana leaf in
sunlight, catch the smell of drizzled asphalt and the always surprisingly
stale smell of the sea, the reek of human rags that you once thought
colourful, but, God give you that, in rage, a reek both fresh and resinous,
all salted on the page . . . [26]

It is an aspect of that "life" – albeit a measured, tranquil, "Sabbath
afternoon" aspect of it – that is evoked in 'A Sea Chantey', in *In A
Green Night*, which pivots around the lines:

> Now an apprentice washes his cheeks
> With salt water and sunlight[27]

That "apprentice" is both the "ship boys" and, by implication, the
poet himself – an identification which is Walcott's metaphor for his
avowed commitment (as poet) to the life 'A Sea Chantey' celebrates.
Embracing the Apprentice role and so making a virtue of his
inevitable imitativeness frees the young poet from the immediate
problem of finding a form and a language for the pain of that
commitment; the master in whose studio he was apprenticed has
decided that for him. For the Apprentice then, "maturity" will begin
once he has completed "the assimilation of the features of [his poetic]
ancestors".[28] What I want to do in the rest of this essay is, very briefly,
to identify some of the "ancestors" to whom the Apprentice was
indentured in the early poems, and more importantly, to try to
understand why those writers were so attractive to Walcott at that
stage of his career, why he chose to use them as models in his self-
conscious – and thus hardly 'derivative' – apprenticeship.

To list all the authors that critics have heard echoing in Walcott's
early work is to compile a literary encyclopedia – from Matthew
Arnold to Wordsworth and Yeats via Hart Crane, Dante, Hopkins
and Shakespeare. But most of these are only mannered echoes,
passing allusions. There are, it seems to me, three distinct levels or
intensities of influence evident in Walcott's work as a whole,
categories we might call; 'Literary Echoes', 'the Colonial Apprenticeship' and 'the Workshop Contemporaries'.

Literary Echoes

At one level there are these many voices that echo just occasionally in
odd lines or cadences throughout his poetry, reflecting his

"innocent"[29] literariness, or, more often, an acknowledgement of a debt, a way of paying respects to authors he has learnt from. For example, the echo of the opening lines of 'Piers Plowman' in the first line of 'The Schooner *Flight*', was, Walcott says, "put there deliberately: 'as this reminded me of that, so let it remind you also.' "[30] So, "In idle August, while the sea soft"[31] pays tribute to, and invokes the associations of, "In a somer seson, whan softe was the sonne".[32]

The Colonial Apprenticeship

Walcott's allusiveness was not always so discreet however; in the second published volume of juvenilia – the long poem *Epitaph for the Young* – (hereafter referred to as 'Epitaph') other writers' lines, hardly amended, intrude into the narrative merely, it sometimes seems, to flaunt the young poet's knowledge of them. Walcott has said of 'Epitaph', that it was in many ways a conscious exercise in imitation, "all the influences are there: I mean visible, deliberately quoted influences."[33] It is the classic example of the second degree of imitation in Walcott's work; those poems written with another poet – or poets – providing more or less "the complete formula".[34] But even in these poems the 'masters' were not chosen arbitrarily; they all spoke to Walcott's ambition and situation in various ways.

The Colonial Apprentice's first master, T.S. Eliot[35] was *of* the establishment and yet his work was experimental; he was both admired and suspected by the cultural masters at Walcott's school and in the literary world to which the young poet aspired. Eliot had broken the genteel, degenerate tradition of verse writing in his time but was also clearly in awe of Tradition; he was an 'outsider', a 'colonial', yet had somehow captured the imaginative centre ground. A radical in terms of his poetic methods and effects but beneath the bristling style essentially conservative in his attitudes, he had dramatised a personal anguish of faith against imagery drawn from what was traditionally considered an 'unpoetic' environment. In all these ways the appeal and relevance of the poetry and the man to the young Walcott's felt situation is clear.

The temperamental comparison between the two poets is underscored by biographical details included in a letter Eliot wrote to Sir Herbert Read,

> Some day I want to write an essay about the point of view of an American who wasn't an American, because he was born in the south with a nigger

drawl, but who wasn't a Southerner in the south because his people were Northerners in a border state and looked down on Southerners and Virginians, and who therefore felt himself to be more a Frenchman than an American and more an Englishman than a Frenchman and yet felt that the USA up to a hundred years ago was a family extension.[36]

That schizophrenic self-image anticipates Walcott's sense of isolation – "part white and Methodist"[37] in a community overwhelmingly black and Catholic, but yet not comfortable in any other society, caught between worlds with a language which set him apart and a dramatic sense of himself as the outsider, the castaway. And just as that dislocation is basic to the cast of Walcott's poetry so Eliot's sense of unease, of *outsiderness* may be crucial to the view of the world that informs his poetry. His vision of 'The Waste Land', one might infer, germinated in that very unease about his *place* in the world.

True to his role as the Colonial Apprentice, Walcott adopted and adapted Eliot's embattled world view. In 'Epitaph' Walcott was consciously trying to make a 'Waste Land' of and for the Caribbean, transposing the landscape of his burnt out cities, after the fire of 1948, with Eliot's broken, haunted images. Chunks of various Eliot poems loom like proverbial icebergs throughout the poem; as well as 'The Waste Land', 'Ash Wednesday' echoes in 'Canto V', which moves from the shipwreck – a faith become a "Broken three-master on the reefs of reason" – through the humiliation of human vanity – "Man's only time of grace is utter weakness" – to the belligerent reconciliation of the prayer to "Our Lady of Fishermen", which is very reminiscent of section four of 'Dry Salvages' in 'Four Quartets':

> Protector and Maker of the weak
> Prevent us the necessity of coming to Thee
> Or the coming to Thee from necessity.[38]

But where 'The Waste Land' coalesces into a coherent vision, 'Epitaph', for all its ambition and for all that it caught " the frustration of youth in the Caribbean, the narrowness of island life and the deadening lack of opportunity . . ."[39], remains "a heap of broken images" that never quite come together.

After *Poems* and 'Epitaph', Eliot's influence on Walcott's poetry is much less apparent; the apprentice had moved on to other masters. The influence persists, though, in the bleak imagery and allusive technique of the *The Castaway* poems and I suspect that Eliot's domestic sonnet 'Aunt Helen' may have provided a model for 'Tales of the Islands'. But after 'Epitaph' Eliot is essentially absorbed, has become one of the masters in the mature poet's archive of imagination.

Eliot, of course, had his own influences and some of these were adopted in turn by his apprentice. The most important was Baudelaire, whose sense of himself as being both *outside* the commonweal by virtue of his education and calling, yet crucially attracted to that milieu as the authentic life of his society, mirrors Walcott's feelings very well. Poems like 'Le Crépuscule de Soir' observe and understand the life of nineteenth century French society's outcasts without either pity or condescension:

> A travers les lueurs que tourmente le vent
> La Prostitution s'allume dans les rues;
> Comme une fourmilière elle ouvre ses issues;
> Partout elle se fraye un occulte chemin,
> Ainsi que l'ennemi qui tente un coup de main;
> Elle remue au sein de la cité de fange
> Comme un ver qui dérobe a l'Homme ce qu'il mange.[40]

> [Across those lights the wind tortures
> Prostitution is ignited in the streets;
> Like an ant-hill she opens her escapes,
> Spawning all over a secret path,
> Like an enemy's sudden attack;
> She stirs on the breast of the city of dung
> Like a worm that steals his meals from Man.][41]

That poem recalls some of the description of Castries low life and characters in 'Another Life', but more specifically it offered itself as the model for 'Kingston-Nocturne' in *25 Poems*.

> The peanut barrows whistle, and the ladies with perfumes
> And prophylactics included in the expenses
> Hiss in a minor key, the desperate think of rooms
>   With white utensils.

> Walking near parks, where the trees, wearing white socks
> Shake over the illicit liaison under the leaves,
> Silent on the heraldic sky, the statue grieves
>   That the locks

> Have still to be tested, and stores shut up their eyes
> At the beggars and hoodlums, when the skin breaks
> From the city and the owls, and maggots and lice,
>   Strike alight the old hates.[42]

Just as Baudelaire's poem has its companion piece in 'Le Crépuscule du Matin' so the Apprentice has his 'Kingston by Daylight'.

The other aspect of Baudelaire's work that spoke directly to the young Walcott was his honest exploration of the contradictions in his personality, particularly the antagonism between his "idealistic aspirations and a sinful nature".[43] Baudelaire's perverse relationship with his mulatto mistress Jean Duval also mirrors – with a nicely Walcottian irony – the young poet's relationship with Anna, his first love so affectionately recalled in 'Another Life'. Both women obsessed their respective poet's imagination and generated a self-consciously betraying art, and at the same time as both poets were celebrating the purity and fidelity of their love they were also indulging the baser aspects of their passions in the bars and brothels of their respective cities. So the pollen of the *Fleurs du Mal* blossoms in 'Letter to Margaret', in *Poems*,

> Pluck from the root
> This flowering evil of those divided by coins[44]

and in Chapters II-V of 'Tales of the Islands'. The guilty exploration of the 'dark' side of Baudelaire's nature provides the models for the most *explicit* passages of adolescent bravado or "confession" in 'Epitaph'. When, in 'Canto IX', which is prefaced by a quotation from Baudelaire's 'Le Voyage', the questing persona declares:

> I kick heels away from the white hairs of remission, am
> Divided between desire and dissolution,
> Between the advice of the red hag and the piety-pilfering sea[45]

he is embracing Baudelaire's "infernal experience"[46] as an adolescent rite of passage. Indeed the metaphor of the voyage of discovery, the central motif of 'Epitaph', is clearly derived from 'Le Voyage', the opening stanza of which is used as an epigraph to the whole poem. If Eliot and 'Four Quartets' provide the technical model for 'Epitaph', then Baudelaire and 'Le Voyage' emerge as its spiritual guides.

Baudelaire's influence, like Eliot's, is much more subtly manifested in the later work but the abiding influence seems to have been the particular significance of 'Le Voyage' for Walcott's imagination. Echoes of it are heard in several of Walcott's mature journeying-towards-truth poems. In 'The Gulf', for example, and particularly in 'The Schooner *Flight*', Shabine's soul is "a brigantine seeking its Ithaca"; he is another for whom:

> Chaque ilôt signalé par l'homme de vigie
> Est un Eldorado promis par le Destin:[47]

> [Each little island sighted by the look-out man
> Becomes another Eldorado, the promise of Destiny:][48]

But for him too,

> L'imagination qui dresse son orgie
> Ne trouve qu'un récif aux clartés du matin.[49]

> [Imagination, setting out its revels,
> Finds but a reef in the morning light.][50]

One wonders if that "l'homme de vigie" didn't resonate in the young man's imagination – himself a 'Man of Vigie', in Castries – whose vocation as a poet seemed to make him a kind of "look-out man".

That kind of punning would have been recognised by the third master of 'Epitaph for the Young', James Joyce, whose pubescent hero Stephen Daedalus provided a model for the kind of literary self portrait of the artist as adolescent rebel that is the narrative thread of the poem. Walcott recalls that at seventeen he was attracted by:

> the blasphemous, arrogant Stephen Daedalus . . . my current hero . . . [because] . . . in the struggle and wrestling with my mind to find out who I was, I was discovering the art of bitterness. I had been tormented enough by the priests . . . like Stephen I had my nights of two shilling whores . . . and silently howling remorse. Like him I was a knot of paradoxes.[51]

So the poem contains passages of unashamed pastiche, flaunting "puns in the Joycean manner" as in the opening of 'Canto IX':

> In Buck Mulligan's mad tower, bulwarking all winds,
> Or stale as the flat sea repeating its wet vows, I
> Stephen, tremble at the drying hand of the withered sun,
> That is too old a hag to bother about the weather.[52]

Joyce – whose stature in Walcott's pantheon of great writers is acknowledged much later in his career in the poem 'Volcano'[53] – was in fact only one inflection of an Irish voice that constitutes a school to which the Colonial Apprentice was indentured. The other accents of that voice are those of Yeats and, in the early verse dramas, Synge. Walcott explained his identification with the Irish writers in an interview he gave in 1980:

> I've always felt some kind of intimacy with the Irish poets because one realised that they were also colonials with the same kind of problems that existed in the Caribbean. They were the niggers of Britain. Now, with all that, to have those outstanding achievements of genius whether by Joyce or Beckett or Yeats illustrated that one could come out of a depressed, depraved, oppressed situation and be defiant and creative at the same time . . . [54]

If Joyce and Synge are openly 'cannibalised' by the Apprentice, Yeats' influence is less direct. In fact although one critic has spoken dismissively of Walcott's "theatrical borrowings" from Yeats and felt a crippling disjunction between a perceived racial anguish and "his harmonious pentameters, his stately rhymes, his Yeatsian meditations,"[55] it seems to me that Yeats serves more as a model of purpose and pose than of poetic technique. For although we know that Walcott had read Yeats keenly as a schoolboy there is little, apart perhaps from the Yeatsian self-dramatisation of the *hero* of 'Epitaph', in the three books of juvenilia that reveals anything substantially reminiscent of Yeats' several styles – and, as we have seen, the Colonial Apprentice was not shy to announce his imitations.

What Walcott seems to have drawn on in Yeats was, on the one hand his determination to create a specifically Irish literature that embraced the island's folk traditions, and on the other the idea of transposing – by an act of willed imagination – his own 'provincial' circumstances to a Classic other life; Yeats' work clearly legitimises Walcott's practice, Castries becoming Troy and Anna its Helen. And, in the context of Walcott's remarks about the resonances between the Irish and the West Indian experience, the compassion that could comprehend the beauty and capacity for good in the great houses of Ireland and their 'alien' aristocracy, in poems like 'Meditations in Time of Civil War' or 'Upon a House Shaken by the Land Agitation', can perhaps be seen to inform Walcott's controversial 'humanism' in 'Ruins of a Great House' and 'A Far Cry from Africa'.

Other early influences were less subtly assimilated. The two writers whose voices are most clearly emulated in *25 Poems* and *Poems* are

W.H. Auden and Dylan Thomas. In his review of Walcott's first collection, broadcast on the BBC's 'Caribbean Voices' programme in 1948, Roy Fuller identified these two masters as the presiding influences on the apprentice work and made what was to become the conventional judgement, that of the two the example of Auden's "images drawn from contemporary experience; a verse that is capable of satire as well as love, flippancy as well as seriousness, ease as well as difficulty" might be beneficial to the young writer but that Thomas's "romantic . . . stylised rhetoric" was a dangerous dead end.[56]

Just a generation older than Walcott and both intense, ambitious literary prodigies, acclaimed as poets of importance while still in their teens, Auden and Thomas were perhaps the most natural models for the Colonial Apprentice. Their opposed techniques appealed to distinct but equally fundamental aspects of his nature. Auden's classicism and technical virtuosity, made to serve the self-conscious image of himself as the rebellious intellectual, a spokesman for a disgruntled generation, tied in very neatly with Walcott's view of his own situation, as 'Epitaph' makes obscurely clear. In different ways Dylan Thomas shared many similarities of circumstance and personality with the teenage Walcott. Most importantly Thomas and Walcott shared a sense of being both *provincial* and yet uncomfortably distanced from the roots of the culture they felt to be their particular – provincial – inheritance. That distance was measured by the felt dislocation between the language of their poetry and a language that would be true to the experience of that culture's inner life and mythology. The provincialism bred in Thomas (as later in Walcott) a conviction never overcome that – notwithstanding the fame and the critical acclaim – he would always be an *outsider*, an intruder in the hallowed halls of metropolitan culture. So, trapped between two worlds – the Welsh-speaking heartland and the literary centre – and bespeaking an awe of God-in-nature that chimed true to the adolescent Walcott's spiritual self- shriving, the emotional appeal of Thomas's poetry is easy to understand.

Basically, then, the 'Audenic' apprentice-pieces are 'of the head' while the 'Thomasonian' are 'of the heart'. This head/heart opposition is exemplified by the two poems most often cited as evidence of the influence of Auden and Thomas on Walcott's early work, 'A Country Club Romance' and 'A City's Death by Fire'. Auden's sharp suburban ballads 'Miss Gee' and 'Victor' are obvious models for 'A Country Club Romance':

> They were married early in August,
>   She said; 'Kiss me, you funny boy;'
> Victor took her in his arms and said;
>   "O my Helen of Troy."
>
> It was the middle of September,
>   Victor came to our office one day;
> He was wearing a flower in his button hole,
>   He was late but he was gay.
>
> The clerks were talking of Anna,
>   The door was just ajar;
> One said; "Poor old Victor, but where ignorance
>   Is bliss, et cetera."[57]

though despite their wry social commentary neither carries quite the edge of personal pain that informs the satire of Walcott's poem. 'A Country Club Romance' is a witty, cutting treatment of a very serious theme, and one close to Walcott's experience as a "high brown" man of the Carribean middle class (one who, in 'Another Life', recalls his boyhood prayers that when he awoke he would be white![58]). That theme is the "spite of shade" prejudice that poisoned West Indian society and made such outcasts of individuals who defied it.

The example of Auden's quirky and rather mechanically formal ballads, distancing the teller from the subject whose tale is told – in very matter-of-fact language and with a dry superior humour – provided the Apprentice with a vehicle that enabled him to keep the anger that clearly fires the poem under control and yet make his point most effectively:

> The Club was carefree as Paris,
> Its lawns, Arcadian;
> Until at one tournament, Harris
> Met her, a black Barbadian.
>
> He worked in the Civil Service,
> She had this job at the bank;
> When she praised his forearm swerve, his
> Brain went completely blank.
>
> O love has its revenges,
> Love whom man has devised;

They married and lay down like Slazengers
Together. She was ostracised.[59]

Of the several poems of overt social commentary or criticism in the juvenilia only 'A Country Club Romance' survived the ten years of consideration that informed Walcott's selection for *In A Green Night*. (The poem first appears as 'Margaret Verlieu Dies' in *Poems* and is considerably revised for the much smoother version in the major collection.) The particular reason why Walcott felt that this poem had enough in it to be rescued for the full collection while poems like 'O My Shameful, My Audacious', 'The Sunny Caribbean', 'The Cracked Playground' and 'Montego Bay – Travelogue 11', did not relates, I suspect, to that control of tone and emotion which Auden's handling of the ballad form demonstrated; for while the rage and anguish which characterises those discarded poems rings genuine enough, it also rings raw and naive against the restrained artfulness of 'A Country Club Romance'.

The borrowing from Dylan Thomas most often cited announces the debt in its very title; 'A City's Death by Fire', a survivor from *25 Poems* recalling Thomas's 'A Refusal To Mourn the Death, by Fire, of a Child in London'. But although the central issues of the two poems are similar the Apprentice echoes lines from all over Thomas's work to construct his poem, for example the lines,

the hills were a flock of faiths
. . .
All day I walked abroad among the rubbled tales
. . .
Loud was the bird-rocked sky, and all the clouds were bales

all chime in Thomas's distinctive cadences. The justification of these overt borrowings is less apparent than that of the Audenesque style of 'A Country Club Romance', although perhaps the echoes of pulpit oration which sound in Thomas's poem might have been felt to be appropriate to Walcott's theme. The overall effect, however, is to distract the reader from what is otherwise a moving and important statement of personal dedication and renewed faith.

But it is in the nature of the role of the Apprentice that he suffers such lapses of judgement and it is too easy, with the advantage of thirty years hindsight, to underestimate the effect of Dylan Thomas's poems on a generation of impressionable, intense adolescents – there

are certainly many worse sub-Dylan pastiches in the metropolitan
journals and anthologies of the late 1940s and early 1950s. Dylan
Thomas is in fact the master in whose school the journeyman
apprentice seems to have tarried longest; 'In A Year', 'At Break of
Mist', 'The Yellow Cemetery','As John to Patamos', 'Notebooks of
Ruin' and 'Choc Bay' all owe much to Thomas's sonorous diction and
distinctive mannerisms.

If Thomas's influence was the most pervasive in the early work,
Auden's was the most meticulously copied. The classic expression of
the Colonial Apprentice technique is certainly 'Berceuse' from *Poems*,
which while it may be, as Frank Collymore judged, "as charming as
one could wish for",[60] is such a straight take from Auden's famous
'Lullaby' as to induce schizophrenia of the inner ear in the reader!

> Darling as you bend to sleep,
> May your mortal breath remain
> Poised between the extreme deep
> Of the silence, or the pain.
> A bed and breath alone divide
> The body from the soul's release,
> In their dark judgement they decide
> Six feet of flesh, six feet of peace.[61]

In addition to 'Berceuse' and 'Margaret Verlieu Dies', poems like
'The Sunny Caribbean', and 'We Exiles' all bear Auden's imprint,
one way or another. It is a nice irony, then, that a decade later, when
Walcott was selecting his "poems 1948-60" for *In A Green Night*, that
only one of the Audenesque poems was kept while four of the
Thomas-school pieces survived.

Eventually the Apprentice must begin to *invent* his masters, to
delineate the features and inflections of a style enunciated in voices
which will be his own. Those voices are informed by a controlling
intelligence still voraciously open to influence (though no longer
prone to mimicry) by great literature whenever it is encountered, for
Walcott has always contended that "maturity is the assimilation of the
features of every ancestor", and in the "timeless, yet habitable
moment" his great contemporaries are included among those
"ancestors". So Neruda, Cesaire, Brodsky and Lowell are all
"ancestors" as much as Marvell, Donne, Mandelstam and St. John
Perse are.

In that context Walcott's apprenticeship was both inevitable and
purposeful – a duty for one who aspired to be a great poet. He asserts

in 'The Muse of History' that "Fear of imitation obsesses minor poets" but that:

> . . . in any age a common genius almost indistinguishably will show itself, and the perpetuity of this genius is the only valid tradition, not the tradition which categorises poets by epochs and by schools. We know that the great poets have no wish to be different, no time to be original, but that their originality emerges only when they have absorbed all the poetry which they have read, entire, that their first work appears to be the accumulation of other people's trash but that they become bonfires . . . [62]

The Contemporaries

The voices that crackle in the bonfire that is Walcott's major poetry constitute the third level of influence bearing on his mature imagination, what we might call the Apprentice's 'workshop borrowings' from his contemporaries in that timeless yet habitable moment. For just as in a well established poetry workshop one member will – both consciously and unconsciously – borrow ways of seeing and saying from another member, so the mature Walcott has borrowed from those poets – alive and dead – whose work he both admired and drew a particular energy from. The image of the poetry workshop derives from some of Walcott's remarks about his relationship with these great poets. For example, when he says of his introduction to the Classic poets of his education that they evinced an,

> elation of discovery . . . Shakespeare, Marlowe, Horace, Vergil – these writers weren't jaded but immediate experiences. The atmosphere was competitive, creative[63]

he might be speaking as a member of the best kind of poetry workshop where the writers' ideas, approaches and techniques spark off and inspire each other. Later in his career we might nominate such figures as Neruda, Pasternak, Marquez, Mandelstam, Lowell and Brodsky as members of this elite workshop, but in *In A Green Night* the influence of Yeats, as we have seen, and, I would argue, Marvell are best understood in these terms.

Much has been made of the parallels of personality and circumstance that link Walcott and Marvell and as we have seen Walcott was keen on such 'connections' but he 'discovered' Marvell and the Metaphysicals quite late on in his student career, as part of his undergraduate studies at the then University College of the West Indies in Jamaica. He was, by then, beyond the stage of making straightforward 'imitations' and he draws on 'The Bermudas', which provides the images around which 'In A Green Night' weaves its spiritual meditations and is a model for the language of several Walcott poems in that first full collection, in much more selective and subtle ways. 'In A Green Night' is by no means an apprentice work in the way that 'Prelude', 'A City's Death by Fire' or 'A Country Club Romance' are. It is, though, a mannered, highly wrought construction in the Metaphysical tradition; ambiguous, eliptical and dense with meanings that the reader must puzzle out or abandon. Helen Gardner's account of the problems some readers have always had with Metaphysical poetry has a familiar ring when we remember some responses to Walcott's early poetry in the Caribbean,

> It confuses the pleasures of poetry with the pleasures of puzzles . . .
> [and] . . . frequently employs curious learning in its comparisons. It
> makes demands upon the reader and challenges him to make it out. It
> does not attempt to attract the lazy and its lovers have always a certain
> sense of being a privileged class, able to enjoy what is beyond the reach
> of vulgar wits.[64]

It was the Metaphysicals' technique of using metaphor as the prime vehicle of shape and meaning in their poetry that seems to have so greatly impressed Walcott, who has always, in Edward Baugh's words, "moved in metaphor as in his natural element."[65] The extended metaphors developed in poems like 'A Lesson for this Sunday','A Letter from Brooklyn', 'Laventille', 'The Gulf' and of course 'Another Life', owe more than a little to the Metaphysicals' manner of argument but are distinctively Walcott's in their language and movement.

Walcott is continually adding voices to the list of those 'workshop contemporaries', asserting his status as one of the "great poets" who refuses to be obsessed by "fear of imitation". That determination was apparent even in those early works in which the young Walcott was consciously adopting a particular writer as his master – Eliot, Auden, Dylan Thomas – and attempting to produce poems in the style of those masters as a way of acquiring the tools and techniques that would equip him for his chosen career as the poet who would be both true to his place/people and to himself. That humility of spirit, that willingness to learn – to retain the apprentice's awe of his masters –

also resonates in the mature poet's adaptation of the vision and techniques of peers – Lowell, Cesaire, Neruda, Brodsky – whose poetry seemed to him to deal most adequately with contemporary experience. These latter 'Workshop Contemporaries' are not crudely mimicked but subtly assimilated as resources of a voice that is, always, confronting the most serious and profound issues of his time. Overall, the humility of the Apprentice role enables the poet to indulge and *justify* his instinct, acknowledged in 'Midsummer VIII' to:

> . . . let the imagination range wherever
> its correspondences take it.[67]

NOTES

1. Walcott, *Another Life*, p.106.
2. Mervyn Morris, 'Derek Walcott', in Bruce King (*ed*), *West Indian Literature*, London, 1979, p.144.
3. R.J. Owens, 'West Indian Poetry', in *Caribbean Quarterly*, Vol.7, no.3, December 1961, p.121.
4. Walcott, in Edward Hirsh, 'An Interview with Derek Walcott', in *Contemporary Literature*, Vol.20, no.3, 1980, p.283.
5. 'March Days' in J.E. Clare McFarlane (*ed*), *A Treasury of Jamaican Poetry*, London, 1949, p.68.
6. O.R. Dathorne, Ed. *Caribbean Verse*, London, 1967, p.9.
7. Walcott, in 'Meanings', in *Savacou*, no.2, 1970, p.45.
8. Walcott, 'Meanings', op.cit., p.51.
9. In Edward Hirsch, 'An interview with Derek Walcott', op.cit., p.282.
10. P.N. Furbank, 'In A Green Night', in *The Listener*, Vol.68, no.1736, 5 July 1962, p.33.
11. Walcott, 'A Letter from Brooklyn', in *In A Green Night*, p.53. (While this reference refers directly to the Word of God, elsewhere Walcott uses the phrase to refer to his sense of vocation as a writer.)
12. Joseph Brodsky, 'On Derek Walcott', *New York Review of Books*, 10 November, 1983, p.39.
13. *ibid*.
14. Walcott, *Another Life*, p.59.
15. Walcott, 'What the Twilight Says, an Overture', in *Dream on Monkey Mountain and Other Plays*, p.31.
16. In Edward Hirsch, 'An interview with Derek Walcott', op.cit., p.282.
17. See Gerald F. Else, in Alex Preminger (*ed*), *The Princeton Encyclopedia of Poetry and Poetics*, Princeton, 1971, p.379.
18. In Edward Hirsch, 'An interview with Derek Walcott', op.cit., p.419.
19. Walcott, *Another Life*, p.77.
20. In his review of 'Young Trinidadian Poets' (*Sunday Guardian*, Trinidad, 19 June 1966, p.5), Walcott commended the apprentice mentality in some of those whose work he was reviewing and advocated that all serious young poets should go through a period of consciously imitating the masters of the past, just as he had.

21. Roland Barthes, 'The Death of the Author', in *Image, Music, Text*, London, 1977, p.145.
22. T.S. Eliot, 'The Lovesong of J. Alfred Prufrock', in *Collected Poems*, London, 1974, p.141.
23. *In A Green Night*, p.11.
24. Walcott, 'The Schooner *Flight*', in *The Fortunate Traveller*, p.12.
25. Walcott, 'What the Twilight Says, an Overture', *op.cit.*, p.15 /16.
26. *ibid.*, p.65.
27. Walcott, *In A Green Night*, p.65.
28. Walcott, 'The Muse of History', in Orde Coombs (*ed*), *Is Massa Day Dead?*, New York, 1974, p.1.
29. P.N. Furbank, 'In A Green Night', *op.cit.*, p.33.
30. In Nancy Schoenberger, 'An interview with Derek Walcott', in *The Threepenny Review*, Fall, 1983, p.17.
31. Walcott, 'The Schooner *Flight*', in *The Star-apple Kingdom*, p.3.
32. Line 1 of 'Piers Plowman'.
33. Robert Hamner, 'Conversation with Derek Walcott', in *World Literature Written in English*, Vol.16, no.2, November 1977, p.411.
34. Keith Alleyne, 'Epitaph for the Young, a poem in XII cantos by Derek Walcott', in *Bim*, Vol.3, no.11, 1949, p.267.
35. Although Eliot's influence is chiefly evident in 'Epitaph for the Young', which was published after *25 Poems*, it was in fact begun when Walcott was just 16, three years before the publication of *25 Poems*.
36. In Alan Tate (*ed*), *T.S. Eliot, The Man and His Work*, London, 1967, p.15.
37. Walcott, 'What the Twilight Says, an Overture', *op.cit.*, p.15.
38. Walcott, *Epitaph for the Young*, p.27.
39. In Stanley Sharpe, *A West Indian Literature*, an unpublished MA thesis of the University of Leeds in 1952, p.140. Sharpe was a contemporary of Walcott's and his fascinating thesis is the first sustained account of West Indian literature.
40. Baudelaire, *Selected Poems*, New York 1974, p.80.
41. *ibid.*, p.81.
42. Walcott, *Poems*, p.26.
43. Edith Starkie in the Introduction to her edition of Baudelaire's *Selected Poems*, *op.cit.*, p.19.
44. Walcott, *Poems*, p.26.
45. Walcott, *Epitaph for the Young*, p.27.
46. Edith Starkie in the Introduction to her edition of Baudelaire's *Selected Poems*, *op.cit.*, p.19.
47. Baudelaire, *Selected Poems*, p.96.
48. *ibid.*, p.97.
49. *ibid.*, p.96.
50. *ibid.*, p.97.
51. Walcott, 'Leaving School', *op.cit.*, p.13.
52. Walcott, *Epitaph for the Young*, p.26.
53. Walcott, *Sea Grapes*, p.62.
54. In Edward Hirsch, 'An interview with Derek Walcott', *op.cit.*, p.288.
55. Helen Vendler, 'Poet of Two Worlds', *The New York Review of Books*, 4 March 1982, p.23.
56. Roy Fuller, cited by Collymore, in his 'Review of *Poems*', in *Bim*, Vol.4, no.15, p.224.
57. W.H. Auden, 'Victor, a Ballad', in *Selected Poems*, Harmondsworth, 1958, p.48 /49.

58. Walcott, *Another Life*, p.6 /7.
59. Walcott, *In A Green Night*, p.31.
60. Frank Collymore, 'Review of *Poems*' *op.cit.*, p.224.
61. Walcott, *Poems*, p.23.
62. Walcott, 'The Muse of History', p.25.
63. Walcott, 'Meanings', *op.cit.*, p.51.
64. Helen Gardner, *The Metaphysical Poets*, Harmondsworth, 1957, p.17.
65. Edward Baugh, 'Metaphor and Plainness in the Poetry of Derek Walcott', in *Literary Half-Yearly*, Vol.11, no.2, 1970, p.53.
66. Helen Gardner, *The Metaphysical Poets*, *op.cit.*, p.23.
67. Walcott, 'Midsummer VIII', in *Midsummer*, p.218.

Katie Jones

Land and Sea: *The Castaway*
and *The Gulf*

Land and Sea: *The Castaway* and *The Gulf*

Not the least of Walcott's achievements is his contribution to the resurrection of 'landscape poetry'. Since Eliot, poets have tended to shy away from any landscape not barren, urban or infernal; a different approach would have been regarded as anachronistic or merely self-indulgent. Misfits like Edward Thomas (to whom Walcott writes an impressive homage in *The Gulf*) who wrote challenging landscape poetry focussed upon a sharply-observed, solid natural world, have thus until recently been neglected or maligned as nostalgic Romantics. What Walcott admires in Thomas, the elm-like hardness, the indissolubility of lines which at first appear tenuous, is what he seeks in his own poems of landscape: plainness, grittiness. In 'Islands' (*In a Green Night*, 1962) Walcott makes this aim quite clear:

> I seek
> As climate seeks its style, to write
> Verse as crisp as sand, clear as sunlight,
> Cold as the curled wave, ordinary
> As a tumbler of island water.[1]

It is in his next two volumes of verse, *The Castaway* (1965) and *The Gulf* (1969) that Walcott begins to achieve this style, through which, as he puts it in 'Homage to Edward Thomas', "topography delineates its verse".[2] The very titles announce the poems' island landscapes, and hint also that Walcott, the "diarist in sand", is evoking and transforming literary landscapes.

In the autobiographical poem *Another Life* (1973), Walcott tells of his youthful vow never to leave his island until he has "put it down" in words. One of his earliest impulses, then, is that of the chronicler, the recorder, the diarist, writing of a new and unexplored world. In this way, and in his sense of isolation, the poet is like the mythical figure of Robinson Crusoe.

Crusoe is the literary figure who lurks in the background of *The Castaway*, as the title itself suggests. Crusoe's island, in Defoe's novel, is topographically similar to Walcott's, and both are, using Defoe's vague geography, near the mouth of the Orinoco. Crusoe's situation, as lonely Castaway, is similar to Walcott's, as a lonely and embittered poet. The castaway figure in the volume is also Defoe, the maker of Crusoe, as Walcott is of his castaway persona. They share a God-like power, as Crusoe does, over their domain, their literary landscape.

Walcott is not parading his literary allusions for self-aggrandise-ment. His use of the Crusoe myth as an underlying pattern for *The Castaway* is the first step in a series of reworkings or re-inter-pretations of classic European literature. In adopting this technique, of course, Walcott is not alone among modern post-colonial writers. Rewriting the classics for politically subversive as well as literary ends is a growing trend among both African and Caribbean writers: two instances very close to Walcott's home are Jean Rhys's *Wide Sargasso Sea* (1966) and Aimé Césaire's *Une Tempête* (1969), reworkings of *Jane Eyre* and *The Tempest* respectively.

Robinson Crusoe is not just a novel but a myth. The character of the castaway, his resilience, humanity, inventiveness, industry, have come to represent a European ideal of civilisation in the face of barbarism. The novel unwittingly enacts the process of colonialism: Crusoe saves Man Friday from death at the hands of cannibals (barbarism) but he also proceeds to make Man Friday his slave (colonialism).

This other character in the Crusoe story also figures in Walcott's poetry: the poet, with his mixed ancestry, is both Crusoe and Friday, master and slave. As a West Indian, the poet can be seen as a castaway from both his ancestral cultures, African and European, stemming from both, belonging to neither. To salve this split, Walcott creates a castaway who is also a new Adam (*Robinson Crusoe* being "our first book, our profane genesis"[3]) whose task is to name his world. Walcott's castaway is thus a poet who creates and gives meaning to nothingness. In this complex way, literary, mythical and real characters and landscapes become one in Walcott's book.

In an unpublished lecture called 'The Figure of Crusoe' Walcott has described the many-masked figure of his Crusoe like this:

> My Crusoe . . . is Adam because he is the first inhabitant of a second paradise. He is Columbus because he has discovered this new world, by accident, by fatality. He is God because he teaches himself to control his creation, he rules the world he has made, and also, because he is to Friday, a white concept of Godhead. He is a missionary because he instructs Friday in the uses of religion . . . He is a beachcomber because I have imagined him as . . . some derelict out of Conrad or Stevenson . . . and finally (because he writes his journal) he is also Daniel Defoe.[4]

That Defoe is also alligned to Walcott as writer is hinted at by the words the poet chooses to describe Defoe's style: "plain", "bare", "as odorous as raw wood".[5] This is perhaps analogous to the "style past metaphor" that Walcott, in 1965, was still aiming for in his own poetry. Similarly, Crusoe's struggle to tame and manipulate his world is like the poet's struggle with the language. If these poems can be interposed as chronicles of colonial history, they can equally be seen as a charting of the poet's life in the realm of art. Art and history are brought together in Walcott's synthesizing vision of landscape.

In 'The Almond Trees'[6] Walcott demonstrates how both art and history are implicit in the landscape; in this case, in a clump of almond trees near the beach. The "twisted, coppery" trees are identified with the sunburnt bodies of women lying on the beach, and in the poet's imagination become the seared writhing bodies of slaves brought from Africa. The dense texture of the poem is further enriched by the allusion to the myth of Daphne, who metamorphosised into a laurel tree. The association of images appears quite natural and unforced, but has a concentrated effect of great richness: the limbs of the women sunbathers resemble the colour and shape of the branches: this similarity brings Daphne to mind: the story of her attempted rape and metamorphosis, together with the fiery heat of the sun on the beach, brings to mind the sufferings endured on the middle passage. Yet such suffering was unlike Daphne's – aesthetic, appealing to generations of artists, fictional – rather it was savage, unappealing, real, and therefore ripe for amnesia. Thus the whole poem becomes a veiled reply to the detractors of the West Indies – the Froudes and the Naipauls – a negation of the idea that there is "no visible history" there. Walcott asserts that everything is a silent witness of the past, even "this stand/ of twisted, coppery sea-almond trees."

The allusion to classical myth in 'The Almond Trees' is not untypical of either *The Castaway* or *The Gulf*. In *The Gulf* Walcott refers ironically to himself and his schoolfellows as being "like solemn Afro-Greeks eager for grades", learning about Helen and "the shades/ of borrowed ancestors".[7] The Greek myths, *Robinson Crusoe*, Shakespeare's plays, and so on, provide the poet with images to enrich his landscapes, images to be used ironically or to illuminate the actual with the light of "another life" – the life of art and artist. One could enumerate Walcott's influences but to no avail: the significance of his allusiveness is that it signals his maturity as an artist, his lack of what Bloom calls "the anxiety of influence". *The Castaway* and *The Gulf* are in fact crucially important stages in Walcott's poetic development because they demonstrate his willingness to pare down his exuberant style and his talent for imitation, to establish a definite 'voice', and yet to make unashamed use of all his sources – literary, historical, personal, topographical.

The Castaway contains a few poems which might be seen to belong to an earlier, more highly metaphorical Walcott style. 'The Flock' and 'The Prince',[8] for example, both crafted in highly-wrought iambic pentameters, seem stylistically out of place in this plainer atmosphere. Yet 'The Prince', Hamlet, is a companion piece to 'Goats and Monkeys', a much finer poem about Othello, with its emblematic contrast of white and black, which in turn complements the Crusoe/ Friday poems. 'The Flock', too, revolves upon a black/white image: black birds migrating southwards from the snowy north, which is identified with the poet's task of filling his white page with the black, bird-like symbols of his writing. The poem seems to have been written, like several others in the collection, in the United States, a wintry landscape, where the poet's isolation is intensified by exile, by homesickness for a "lost fire".

The poet is consistently alienated, detached, like a castaway on his native island, like a foreigner in the north. He expresses this separation in 'A Village Life':

> And since that winter I have learnt to gaze
> on life indifferently as through a pane of glass.[9]

In these lines, as in many others, I hear a deliberate echo of Wordworth's "For I have learned/ To look on nature, not as in the hour/Of thoughtless youth."[10] The echo is self-derogatory and bathetic: Walcott is well aware that his statement is as pessimistic as

Wordsworth's is optimistic, and yet the "pane of glass" which separates him from human contact implies also a clarity of vision, a solidity. There is no mysticism in Walcott's vision of landscape, unlike Wordsworth's, but there is a constant metamorphosis whereby the ordinary becomes extraordinary by the quasi-magical power of art and the synthesizing power of the poetic imagination. For Walcott there is no call for "a sense sublime/ Of something far more deeply interfused";[11] instead, "there's terror enough in the habitual,/ miracle enough in the familiar."[12]

In 'Crusoe's Island'[13] the poet's synthesizing vision is at its strongest. Like 'The Almond Trees', it has an almost palpable atmosphere of intense, fiery heat, here used as a metaphor of forging: God's forging of the earth and man, the poet's forging of language and memory into art. It culminates in an image of sacrificial burning: the artist is released from his clay prison by the fire of inspiration, a conventional image transfigured by Walcott's verbal dexterity:

> Art is profane and pagan,
> The most it has revealed
> Is what a crippled Vulcan
> Beat on Achilles' shield.
> By these blue, changing graves
> Fanned by the furnace blast
> Of heaven, may the mind
> Catch fire till it cleaves
> Its mould of clay at last.[14]

Yet this release is hoped for, not achieved: poet and castaway are isolated in their self-built Eden, yearning for love, companionship and fulfillment yet denied them by their loss of simple faith and by the "mania" of their art.

The landscape of the poem is immediate, present, yet conveyed overwhelmingly by atmospheric effect rather than descriptive detail: the church bell tolling, the castaway's lengthening shadow, the troop of little girls going along the beach to church. These images create for us Crusoe's island; they also map out the mind of the island's creator. Walcott's landscape is not a Romantic pathetic fallacy, not an illustration of Byron's dictum that "every landscape is a state of mind". Walcott's mind and his landscape in these poems are indivisibly forced together, "welded in one flame": only here perhaps is it possible to achieve that blessed unity which is the escape from loneliness.

Thematically, though, the strongest message of *The Castaway* is one of division, especially self-division. Even in 'Crusoe's Island' there is a split between the poet and the church-going childhood self he remembers at the prompting of the bell's toll. The sense of division is made particularly explicit in the bitter final poem, 'Codicil'[15], which describes the poet as "schizophrenic, wrenched by two styles". The hesitancy of this last poem counteracts the confident statements of the opening poem, 'The Castaway':

> Godlike, annihilating godhead, art
> And self, I abandon
> Dead metaphors.[16]

The self reasserts itself though, startling the castaway with its lengthening shadow, forcing the poet into bald statements: "I am nearing middle-/ age." This is one of the most appealing aspects of Walcott's mature poetry: when 'the artist' begins to take up a melodramatic pose, his other voice speaks up and deflates his pretentions. In *The Castaway* this voice can be devastatingly caustic:

> Once I thought love of country was enough,
> now, even I choose, there's no room at the trough.

Even the figure of the castaway, Crusoe, is a mask, a guise, fulfilling "the wish to dramatize/ ourselves at nature's cost".[17] In the final poem, the guise is thrown off, and the poet is revealed as himself, like the onion of Peer Gynt's riddle, all layers peeled away, leaving nothing – "a blank page".

This is not quite as despairing as it might seem. A *tabula rasa* is there to be written upon, or, as Walcott has said: "If there was nothing, there was everything to be made."[18] Ultimately, he must throw off the mask of Crusoe for, as he explains in 'The Muse of History': "The shipwrecks of Crusoe and of her crew in *The Tempest* are the end of an Old World . . . For us in the archipelago . . . arrival must be seen as the beginning, not the end of our history."[19]

Walcott quotes a passage from *Robinson Crusoe* as an epigram to 'Crusoe's Journal'; the passage ends with Crusoe's words "and well might I say, as Father Abraham to Dives, 'Between me and thee is a great gulf fixed' ". Defoe uses the Biblical reference to convey Crusoe's feeling of unreality, of separation from life. It is this gulf which gives Walcott's next collection its title and its dominant theme.

The gulf in Derek Walcott's poems is geographical, historical, psychological. Having thrown off his Crusoe mask, the poet is revealed as himself but with an even stronger sense both of self-division and of alienation from others. In 'Mass Man' the poet is cut off from the communal festivities of Carnival: in 'Homecoming: Anse La Raye' he finds himself a stranger on returning to his home; in 'Cold Spring Harbour' he feels the alienation of exile; in 'Love in the Valley' the cold, perfect world of art is, like Keats' urn, an unenterable refuge, intensifying his isolation.

If *The Castaway* emphasizes the lone individual's life on the island, *The Gulf* shows him embarking on his self-built ship, travelling, and in exile. The traveller figure is always the outsider, the detached observer. The gulf he crosses is often, quite literally, the Gulf of Mexico, to enter the United States; it is also a gulf separating two worlds, almost as sharply demarcated as the realms of life and death in Crusoe's Biblical allusion.

The Gulf begins a pattern of Odyssean imagery in Walcott's mature poetry. In poems such as 'Homecoming: Anse La Raye' the returning Odysseus receives a disillusioning 'welcome', but in later works, such as 'The Schooner *Flight*' in *The Star-apple Kingdom*, the poet's Odyssean persona is more resilient and fortunate in his travels. It must be said that *The Gulf* is one of the most despairing and self-questioning of all Walcott's collections. It seems to enact a crisis in the poet's life when he is "nearing forty", alone, dissatisfied with his writing, embittered by politics, wandering, and in exile. It is fitting, then, that the dominant images of the volume are not those of landscape but of seascape and incessant journeying. Only at the very close of the volume does the poet proclaim "*hic jacet*": an end to his fruitless, internal quest, the dreary "treadmill" he travels along in the first poem, 'Ebb'.

The landscapes evoked in poems such as 'Cold Spring Harbour' and 'Love in the Valley' [20] are, appropriately, alien, snowy scenes witnessed in exile or in memory only. Unlike the intensely present, felt heat of the island in *The Castaway*, the icy cold of these landscapes is imagined, distanced, literary, but nonetheless real. As Walcott says in 'The Muse of History': "Like any colonial child I was taught English literature as my natural inheritance. Forget the snow and the daffodils. They were real, more real than the heat and the oleander, perhaps, because they lived on the page, in imagination, and therefore in memory." The real snowscape in 'Cold Spring Harbour' reminds the poet of "an old Christmas card/ turned by a child's dark hand", of his own childhood fascination with the "card/ of a season, forever foreign". The unselfconscious awe of that child is long gone, and the adult poet is now aware only of his cynicism and his isolation, even from his own children.

In 'Love in the Valley' Walcott takes an imagined journey through a fairy-tale childhood landscape:

> I ride through a white childhood
> whose pines glittered with bracelets,
> when I heard wolves, feared the black wood . . .

His memory and imagination are unremittingly literary, drawn always to the perfect, cold worlds of art – the women in the novels of Hardy and Pasternak, whose love is tragic, ideal, everlasting. *The Gulf* is full of disillusionment with drab realities and consequently has a special fascination with the other, ideal world of art and the idealised memory of childhood. Art and childhood inhabit similar inviolate realms: they, unlike all else, are immune to cynicism. In this journeying collection, the image of the schooner on the horizon recurs: it is far away in Walcott's memory of his boyhood self gazing at the schooner, longing for escape and adventure. But the boat is "out too far", "that silvery freighter/ threading the horizon like a toy";[21] the memory is too insubstantial to console sufficiently the anguish of now, the reality of the "starved, pot-bellied children" who crowd around him, begging.

These are the children who make the poet realise, in 'Homecoming: Anse La Raye' that "there are homecomings without home". One of the best poems in the volume, this movingly expresses the poet's embitterment, evoking the two worlds which represent his self-division. Patterned upon the homecoming of Odysseus, the poem opens with ironic echoes of Homer: "the coconuts' salt-rusted/ swords", "the seacrabs' brittle helmets" and "this barbecue of branches, like the ribs/ of sacrificial oxen on scorched sand". The synthesis of actual and literary landscape is succinctly put when the poet talks of "this well-known passage", which is both an avenue under the coconut trees along which the returned exile walks, and a favourite passage of Homeric verse, perhaps the return of Odysseus.

This synthesis is abruptly destroyed towards the end of the first verse paragraph, when the poet seems to draw himself up, offering two versions of a line:

> whose spindly, sugar-headed children race
> whose starved, pot-bellied children race . . .

The children are the same: at first seen 'poetically' from far away, and then realistically, from close up. The bitterness of this 'welcome' is expressed directly in the lines: "They swarm like flies/ round your heart's sore". Having begun the poem with a light-hearted, communal "we", perhaps thinking specifically of his childhood friend Dunstan St. Omer, to whom the poem is dedicated, Walcott now resorts to the distanced, isolated "you", referring to himself and his failed ambition: "you . . . hoped it would mean something to declare/ today, I am your poet, yours".[22] This is a recurrent technique in *The Gulf* in which the poet is often divided into "I" and "you", dramatising his self-division in a Yeatsian manner. Yet this poem does not overdo the drama: it ends quietly, disconsolately, with an image of fishermen aimlessly playing draughts, "eating their islands". That one has the "ignorant sweet smile" of a politician indicates one of the sources of Walcott's bitterness: the islands, abused by politicians, are seen as insignificant as toys, not like the prodigious, magical islands of *The Odyssey*. And as for their poet, he is mistaken for a tourist, sworn at, abused.

Despite all, the poet carries on: "someone must write your poems."[23] The references to Walcott's audience in 'Homecoming: Anse La Raye' and in 'Mass Man' ironically intensify the poet's isolation. He is writing for his own people but they are not listening. In 'Mass Man' they are obsessed with the metaphors of Carnival and its manic, communal festivity. Only the poet and the child are cut off from the revelry, weeping instead of dancing. There is again something distinctly Yeatsian about Walcott's commitment to his art and his people – "my mania is a terrible calm".

Even in a poem as disillusioned as 'Nearing Forty', in which poet and dreary rain are identified, the close expresses continued commitment, the compulsion of the poet to write on, just as the rain needs must fall:

> you will rise and set your lines to work
> with sadder joy but steadier elation,
> until the night when you can really sleep,
> measuring how imagination
> ebbs, conventional as any water-clerk
> who weighs the force of lightly-falling rain,
> which, as the new moon moves it, does its work,
> even when it seems to weep.[24]

Playing with the word "conventional" ("this year's end rain/ which, as greenhorns at school, we'd/ call conventional for convectional")

Walcott summons up the poetic convention of the moon as the poet's muse, moving the waters of his imagination. But he disguises its literariness, linking it instead with the "guttering rainspout", "the plain . . . bleaching bedsheet". Walcott thus combines the ordinary with the elemental in a conversational manner which conceals his natural taste for metaphor. This poem, for instance, works as a complex metaphorical pattern of contrasts between water and fire, reduced to everyday dimensions – "a damp match" or "the dry wheezing of a dented kettle." This shows his growing confidence in a plain style. In another poem in *The Gulf*, 'Moon', we find him writing in his former, more elevated and elaborate style and he proceeds to chastise himself: "Haven't you sworn off such poems for this year, and no more on the moon?"[25]

His plain style is perhaps best displayed in the title poem of *The Gulf*.[26] Here the poet's perspective is again distant, like his view of the schooner on the horizon, but on this occasion he looks down on the landscape through the "cold glass" of an aeroplane window (a "casket hole"). From this distance everything looks new, healed and perfect, like the works of the "great dead" which "shine on our shelves." We feel that the detachment of the poet here is self-protecting, sorrowing: he reflects on the bloody divisions of the American South which "felt like home" and which yet treated him as a "secondary soul". Violence simmers beneath the surface, and the poet's voice turns prophetic, warning of the night when the "stalking, moonlit panthers" turn on their prey. Meanwhile, the poet takes refuge behind glass, and in the prose of Borges, a "stalking moonlit tiger". No more on the moon?

Violence erupts in 'Blues'[27] where the flippant tone disguises intense fear, sorrow and disgust. The naive poet "figured we were all/ one, wop, nigger, jew" but he gets beaten up as reward for his belief in such solidarity. The laconic style ("Yeah . . . forget it") is what gives the poem its strength – its subject is ripe for melodrama but Walcott resists the temptation and instead achieves a blues-like poignancy. Like most blues songs, this poem is a social criticism as much as a personal confession:

> I did nothing. They fought
> each other, really. Life
> gives them a few kicks,
> that's all. The spades the spicks.

If the castaway looks inward, into his inner-self, into history, the poet of *The Gulf* looks outward, at other people as well as at his estranged self, even though it may be through "cold glass". There is a growing concern with his audience, his people, his society, with injustice, even with politics, which later develops into such direct 'protest' poems as 'The Lost Federation' in *Sea Grapes* and into the eloquent vituperation against "all o' dem big boys" in Chapter 19 of *Another Life*. Walcott seems to acknowledge this change of focus in the Wordsworthian tones of lines in 'Nearing Forty', when he speaks of setting his lines to work "with sadder joy but steadier elation". The poem brings echoes of Wordsworth once more not only because of its anxiety over waning inspiration ("whither is fled the visionary gleam?"[28]) but also because of its dogged avowal to carry on. He does carry on, and the personal crisis represented by *The Gulf* is relieved by the therapeutic autobiography of Walcott's next work, *Another Life*, where "all in compassion ends". [29]

NOTES

1. Derek Walcott, *Collected Poems*, New York, 1986, p.52.
2. Walcott, *The Gulf*, London, 1969, p.25.
3. Walcott, 'Crusoe's Journal', in *The Castaway*, London, 1965, p.51.
4. Quoted in Robert D. Hamner, 'Aspects of National Character: V.S. Naipaul and Derek Walcott', in Satendra Nadan (*ed*), *Language and Literature in Multicultural Contexts*, Fiji, 1983, pp.179–188.
5. Walcott, 'Crusoe's Journal', *op.cit.*
6. Walcott, *The Castaway*, p.36.
7. Walcott, 'Homecoming: Anse La Rave', in *The Gulf*, p.50.
8. Walcott, *The Castaway*, p.14 and p.29.
9. *ibid.*, p.17.
10. Wordsworth, 'Tintern Abbey'.
11. *ibid.*
12. Walcott, 'Ebb', in *The Gulf*, p.10.
13. Walcott, *The Castaway*, p.54.
14. *ibid.*, p.57.
15. *ibid.*, p.61.
16. *ibid.*, p.10.
17. Walcott, 'Crusoe's Journal', *op.cit.*, p.52.
18. Walcott, 'What the Twilight Says: An Overture', prologue to *Dream on Monkey Mountain and Other Plays*, New York, 1970.
19. Walcott, 'The Muse of History', in Orde Coombs (*ed*), *Is Massa Day Done?: Black Moods in the Caribbean*, New York, 1974, pp.1–27.
20. Walcott, *The Gulf*, pp.61 and 64.
21. Walcott, 'Homecoming: Anse La Rave', *op.cit.*, p.50.
22. Walcott, *The Gulf*, p.51.
23. Walcott, 'Mass Man', in *The Gulf*, p.19.

24. Walcott, *The Gulf*, pp.67–8.
25. *ibid.*, p.12.
26. *ibid.*, p.27.
27. *ibid.*, p.34.
28. Wordsworth, 'Ode on Intimations of Immortality'.
29. Walcott, 'Ruins of a Great House', in *Collected Poems 1948-1984*, London, 1986, p.21.

Nana Wilson-Tagoe

History and Style in *Another Life*

History and Style in *Another Life*

There is a memory of imagination in literature which has nothing to do
with actual experience, which is in fact, another life . . .
                                                'The Muse of History'

> . . . I am nearing forty, nearer the weak
> vision thickening to a frosted pane,
> nearer the day when I may judge my work
> by the bleak modesty of middle-age
> as a false dawn, fireless and average,
> which would be just, because your life bled for
> the household truth, the style past metaphor
> that finds its parallels, however wretched
> in simple, shining lines, in pages stretched
> plain as a bleaching bedsheet under a gutter-
> ing rainspout;
>   'Nearing Forty' *The Gulf*

In spite of its dilemmas and anguish, Walcott's engagement with
history has had a far more complex effect on his themes and style than
has often been credited. Although he was perceived in his early work
as a poet of 'landscape', as the 'poet's poet', 'the private poet',

the humanist poet, involved in the Western tradition of humanity but
evolving a humanism that relates to the West Indian condition, [1]

with the publication of *Another Life*, in the collections which followed
it the form and direction of his poetry had to be re-examined. Some
relationship needed to be established between his developing concept
of history[2] and the direction of his poetic style. In my view, the
relationship is so close that an attempt to trace Walcott's progress

towards a concept of history is also revelatory of an important shift in his conception of style.

As a recapitulation of Walcott's memories of his past: his past of home, landscape and personal experience, *Another Life* exemplifies the contradictions and paradoxes of Walcott's personal development as artist and man. The very progress of the poem, the dramas of its various sections and the styles of representation reflect the varied, often conflicting backgrounds of the poet and his attempt to fuse them into a creative whole without obliterating the distinctiveness of each one.

In his modes of representing this past Walcott re-enacts the seemingly conflicting pulls of history and art: the historical need on one hand, to record and transfix experience and the creative poetic urge the other, to illuminate and extend what is real. In their complementary relationships these two modes reflect the inter-relationships between Walcott's historical vision and his conception both of the imagination and of poetic style.

Another Life marked the climax of Walcott's obsessive engagement with Caribbean history. Very often, ideas on history raised and argued in the essays 'What the Twilight Says' and 'The Muse of History' are reflected not only in the themes but also in the very art of the poems' composition and styling. The young poet's vision of history as amnesia, his rejection of historical time and the mature poet's vision of man in the New World as elemental, all have repercussions in the language of *Another Life*.

"The sense of history in poets lives rawly along their nerves",[3] said Walcott in 1970, distinguishing between history as time, motive and expiation, and history as elation and invention.

> It is this awe of the numinous, this elemental privilege of naming the new world which annihilates history in our great poets, an elation common to all of them, whether they are aligned by heritage to Crusoe and Prospero or to Friday and Caliban.[4]

For Walcott a vision of history rooted in elation encompasses not the ethnic order and movement of a particular time and place but the recreated vision of an Adamic man, beginning afresh to name his landscape and his world, not with the naive innocence of a noble savage but with the memory and experience of an Adam with a past.

For Walcott's 'Adamic' man the past of motive and event is not as crucial, not as creative a force, as his renewed vision and elation in the

New World. Rather than a creature riveted to his past, he is a man capable of inhabiting any historical moment unencumbered by time, and because he is absolved from the histories of the old worlds he is able to recreate the entire order from religion to the simplest domestic rituals. This was the transforming and creative process by which the New World slave had yielded his own past, invested the acquired Christian tradition with a new feeling and faith and began the new naming of things in the New World.

By this act of imagination the slaves had created an oral poetic tradition whose inner language and inflexions were distinctive. For Walcott this effort of creation, with its force of revelation and its particular sensibility, is the essence of history in the West Indies. "The truly tough aesthetic of the New World", he argues, "is the aesthetic that refuses to recognise 'history' as a creative or culpable force".[5] It is one that moves beyond expiation and revenge to capture that elation, faith and feeling with which the New World man had invented his world.

As an inheritor of this tradition the poet of the West Indies, in Walcott's view, had a duty to both "purify the language of the tribe", and to make with it a literature that achieved the essence of the people's lives. So he aspired to a poetry in which:

> That life were made so real that it stank, so close that you could catch the change of morning and afternoon light on the rocks . . . could catch the flash of a banana leaf in sunlight, catch the smell of drizzled asphalt and the always surprisingly stale smell of the sea, the reek that chafes in the guts of canoes, and the reek of human rags that you once thought colorful . . . a reek both fresh and resinous all salted on the page . . . that dark catalogue of country- shop-smells . . . folded round the proprietor, some exact magical woman who emerges from the darkness like history.[6]

Having extended the meaning of 'elemental' in this way to cover landscape, people and language, Walcott then faces a dual engagement in *Another Life*: the reconciliation of two stylistic modes: the apprentice poet's crabbed style, steeped in metaphor and echoes of the 'great tradition', and the Adamic, elemental "style past metaphor".

In Chapter 7 of the poem, which culminates in the epiphanic vision in which the nature and direction of the poet's vocation are made clear, the tension between the two styles is powerfully evoked. It is a section which Walcott devotes entirely to different modes of perceiving reality on the island and comes on as a transition from the young poet's pseudo-epic rendering of island characters:

> remember I beheld them at knee-height,
> and that their thunderous exchanges
> rumbled like gods about another life . . .

>   . . . Remember years must pass before he saw an orchestra,
> a train, a theatre, the spark-coloured leaves
> of autumn whirling from a rail-line,

>   . . . then pardon, life,
> if he saw autumn in a rusted leaf.
> What else was he but a divided child?[7]

Here Walcott establishes a relationship between the child's psychology and his perception of reality, pointing to the divided consciousness, the split between an alien colonial perspective and the starkly real world of poverty and degradation. He recalls the symbols of his father's world: the stuffed object reminiscent of England's literature, culture and religion which were the door of his father's vision and the sum of his belief and faith.

> I saw, as through the glass of some provincial gallery
> the hieratic objects which my father loved.[8]

The older Walcott's judgement is operating here, a negative judgement implied in the image of the stuffed birds, the "dark nightingale" and the bead-eyed, snow-headed eagles. That clearly belonged to another life. The discovery of the child's own Word, and through it his capacity to name and 'make' his world, is heralded by an overflow of excitement and emotion in the poem, but the limits and dangers of this discovery are also suggested by the poem's ironies:

>   . . . . .this new Word
> was here, attainable
> to my own hand,
> in the deep country it found the natural man,
> generous, rooted.
> And I now yearned to suffer for that life,
> I looked for some ancestral, tribal country,
> I heard its clear tongue over the clean stones
> of the river, I looked from the bus-window
> and multiplied the bush with savages,
> speckled the leaves with jaguar and deer,

I changed those crusted boulders
to grey, stone-lidded crocodiles.[9]

In spite of its being inspired by the rooted man in the deep country,
the poet's imagination rambles, unrooted.

The crucial transition in the poem represents the epiphanic
moment of the poet's real coming to being as an artist, and the
moment is enacted almost as a mystical experience, a kind of
transfiguration in which the young child's sensitivities and emotions
seem stretched to the point of extinction. In spite of the mystical
suggestions there is a clear sense of place established which is crucial:

At the hills edge there was a scarp
with bushes and boulders stuck in its side.
Afternoon light ripened the valley,
rifling smoke climbed from small labourers' houses.[10]

The entire section is a powerful dramatisation of the elements of the
creative imagination, the kind of imagination that can create the style
past metaphor as an expression of Walcott's new vision. It is a
celebration of life, of the senses' capability to be affected and
stretched, a celebration, also, of identity with people and place. The
"nothing and everything" that is echoed later in Chapter 22 is the
total possession which the older, renewed poet, purged of the burden
of historical time, enacts in a celebration of life.

Here, for the first time, the poet's new relationship to land and
people is enacted in the language of the poem:

. . . I climbed
with the labouring smoke,
I drowned in the labouring breakers of bright cloud,
                    . . .
I wept for the earth of the hill under my knees.[11]

Now, it is the poet's imagination that must seek out the people, taking
its cue from the light that still shines in their hovels like "litmus".

. . . in that ship of *night*, locked in together,
through which, like chains, a little *light might* leak,
something still fastens us forever to the poor. [12]

                                        (my emphasis)

The poet's doubts, fears and conflicts are also enacted as part of the evocation, and the entire chapter works through its conflicts to a final resolution. The fears appear as "unheard avalanches of white cloud" and the conflicts are summed up first in those words of doubt which creep into the evocation from the poet's memory: "darker grows the valley, more and more forgetting", and later in the poet's fascination with the retreating colonial order, with its "Roman arches, Vergilian terraces and its tiered, ordered colonial world"

> where evening, like the talons of a bird
> bent the blue jacaranda softly . . . [13]

By the end of the section however, the poet's resolution has been made. He is aware of his imagination and his choice. In spite of his fascination for the retreating colonial order his commitment is to the "blare noon" and not to the "twilight"

> It was then
>   that he fell in love, having no care
>
>   . . .
>
> that he fell in love with art,
> and life began.[14]

Thus, this final claim, which when considered out of context, seems almost blasphemous and selfish, can be interpreted now in relation to the affirmation which Walcott has just celebrated: art is a celebration of life; life takes on extended, heightened dimensions as it is evoked by art. So the central dilemma bound up in the crisis of style that the early parts of the poem explored ("which was the true light?/ Blare noon or twilight?"[15]) has been resolved. Walcott has chosen the blare noon, the sun, symbol of life and of renewal and he receives its benediction: "Noon,/and its sacred waters sprinkle".[16]

Because this particular evocation of the poet's imaginative awakening occupies a pivotal place in *Another Life* it has reverberations not only on the other perceptions in the section but also on the entire range of Walcott's poetry. "Noon", "Blare noon", "The afternoon light" that finally emerges as the 'truth' and which blesses the poet in this section, is the same symbol to which the older poet dedicates himself at the end of the poem. It is also the "fierce acetylene air"[17] that singes the almond trees in *The Castaway* and in a similar connotation relates to the "sunburnt body" of the girl acknowledging the past and its own metamorphosis.[18] The Sun which appears here as the symbol of the 'truth', as the source of the poet's creativity and the element of his imagination, now becomes an all-embracing symbol of 'history', not of linear history or of a tiered, ordered, artefacted history in a conventional sense, but the human history of endurance and survival which is the poet's inheritance.

In some respects, though not explicitly stated, the symbol's life-asserting quality establishes it in opposition to the mesmerising, petrifying power of the moon, the dominant symbol in the early sections of *Another Life* and in Walcott's early poetry. The sun that ripens the valley, whose image characterises the epiphanic moment of the poet's transfiguration and which finally blesses him at the end of Chapter 7, can now be seen in opposition to the moon that arrests the village in one photographic still "As if a sudden flashbulb showed their deaths" or to the moon-milk "that x-rays their bodies,/the bone tree show[ing]/through the starved skins".[19]

As an image of contrast and opposition, the symbol's reverberations also stretch to *The Gulf*, to the poem 'Moon' and to the qualities of imagination and creativity which must now separate it from the connotations of the moon's creativity. "[The] lolling Orphic head silently howling, [its] own head [rising] from its surf of cloud . . . a candle mesmerised by its own aura", would now no more represent a source of ambivalence in the context of the poet's resolution in *Another Life*. It is these reverberations, illuminating, extending and linking the range of Walcott's poetry, which confirm my earlier suggestion that the structure of Walcott's poetry in *Another Life* reflects linear time but projects the artistic imagination as simultaneous with all time.

As a pivotal point in *Another Life*, Chapter 7 anticipates other movements in the poem which deal with imaginative rendering, or rather, with the transmission of the Word. After the exposure of the poet's imagination and the direction to which it is striving, the entire poem is an enactment of that fusion of vision and form for which Walcott has been striving. From this point in the poem language and style seem almost entirely free of cliché and abstruseness. Walcott's imagination is less self-consciously playful, less involved with its own dazzle, it becomes totally involved with the reality it creates. Words seem to curl out of the landscape he creates, instead of feeling as if they'd been very 'deliberately' fitted to it by the poet: "I watched the vowels curl from the tongue of the carpenter's plane,/ resinous, fragrant/labials of our forests,/over the plain wood".[20] Here, enacted again, is the kind of poetic language in which the imagination seems twined with the reality it evokes and the poem itself becomes an image of hewed wood from a carpenter's tree; an image which roots it to the landscape and makes artistic creation an honest fusing of imagination and environment. The poet deliberately lengthens his lines to enact the uncurling and birth of the Word and also to demonstrate a new freedom from restrictive forms. In this first line, the rhythm remains in the natural speaking voice of the poet instead of being broken up and frantically matched with other lines. The poet's images undergo a revolution as well. Their ordinariness and easy evocativeness, express those household truths which Walcott's heart had bled for in *The Gulf*:

> those simple, shining lines, in pages stretched
> plain as a bleaching bedsheet under a gutter-
> ing rainspout.[21]

Truths that reveal themselves in

> The smell of our own speech,
> the smell of baking bread
> of drizzled asphalt, this
> odorous cedar.[22]

In *Another Life* such evocations live on every page, enacting the exhilaration of the poet's discovery of identity with landscape and surrounding:

> The sun came through our skins,
> and we beheld, at last,
> the exact, sudden definition
> of our shadow.
> Under our grinding heel
> the island burst to a crushed
> odour of hogplums, acrid, exuding
> a memory stronger than madeleines.[23]

These "simple shining lines", stretched plain in the tones and images of familiar words are far from simplistic and naive, and are capable of evoking and expressing a variety of states and feelings. Their prose-like tone, often mirroring the poet's speaking voice, can be employed in ordinary, straightforward descriptions that evoke the sights, smells and sounds of the island:

The whole sky caught. The thick sea heaved like petrol.
The past hissed in a cinder,
They heard the century breaking in half.[24]

Or, as often happens, the speaking voice can reveal subtleties and ironies behind suggestive household images, as when common words like "laundry" and "hanging washing" sum up the ironic levelling of rigid social divisions in the great fire of Castries:

lives casually tangled like unsorted laundry.
Then, like rifle-fire, the flutes of smoke,
the first, white fangs of washing,
were bravely signalling that some pact
of common desolation had begun.[25]

Sometimes the familiar words glide into a powerful lyricism in the most emotional situations, as when a most simple arrangement of words expresses so potently the overwhelming power of communication between lovers.

We sit by the stone wall

all changes to grey stone,
stone hands, stone air,
stoney eyes, from which

irisless, we stare,
wishing the sea were stone,
motion we could not hear.[26]

Or the exciting delirium of roused passion in the following:

I come out of the cave
like the wind emerging,
like a bride, to her first morning.

I shall make coffee.
The light, like a fiercer dawn,
will singe the downy edges of my hair,
and the heat will plate my forehead till it shines.
Its sweat will share the excitement of my cunning.
Mother I am in love.
Harbour, I am waking.

> I know the pain in your budding, nippled limes,
> I know why your limbs shake, windless, pliant trees.[27]

Here is language with "the force of revelation", but it is its tone, not the dazzling imagery, that ensures its particular authority. The tone emerges from that fusion of conflicting but inter-related presences which the early part of the poem explores so vividly.

History as myth, as elation; language as tone, as the fusion of inter-related presences. This is the vision behind Walcott's use of language in *Another Life*. The explanation of paradox even in the "style past metaphor" is the reconciliation which Walcott seeks between his imaginative urge to heighten, recreate and extend life through metaphor and paradox, and the social need, inspired by a vision of history and man, to be true to landscape and people. The complexities of these tensions are not just limited to the problems of the artist's apprehension and translation of reality; they also involve his conception of time and ultimately his idea of history. The pull between representing reality as it is and recreating it in other reflections is also the pull between arresting the moment, the particular time, and seeing the moment represented in all time.

The tensions of these oppositions represent the drama of Chapter 3 of the poem, 'A Simple Flame', and are the inevitable ramifications of Walcott's commitment in Chapter 7. The dilemma hinges on the 'truth' of the reality represented. If the poet heightens and idealises reality, has he betrayed landscape and people? If he sees the moment repeated and renewed in other moments, in all time, does he negate the connotations of that particular moment? These questions are crucial because they relate to the concept of vision and style which Walcott had arrived at in Chapter 7 and they point to his attempt at confronting not just the ambiguities of imaginative rendering but also the very concept of time, of history.

The poet's presentation of the conflict is dramatised in his relationship with his first love, Anna, the sixteen year old girl who is also an embodiment of his island. Walcott identifies a certain concept of Anna and a particular attitude towards her which is balanced by another conception and attitude:

> when dusk had softened the first bulb
> the colour of the first weak star,
> I asked her, "Choose",
> the amazed dusk held its breath,

> the earth's pulse staggered,
> she nodded, and that nod
> married earth with lightning.[28]

Here, reflected in the images of these lines is the vision of Anna as the embodiment of both the landscape and of the kind of poetry that is a natural twining of environment and language.

Against this vision of Anna is the vision inspired by the poet's need to extend and recreate, and to see several facets embodied in a particular reality. The need, for instance, to present both the calm of the shallop rowing in measured strokes towards Anna's house and the disturbing bay of the "donkey's rusty winch, a herring gull's one creak".

The tensions arising out of these opposites are reflected in the ambivalence of the poet's own attitude: his desire on one hand to arrest the moment, to preserve the uniqueness of Anna, and his tendency on the other, to see her as a reflection of other situations, as an embodiment of all love, of all passion:

> The first flush will pass.
> But there will always be morning,
> and I shall have this fever waken me,
> whoever I lie to, lying close to, sleeping
> like a ribbed boat in the last shallows of night.[29]

The ambivalence of the poet's attitude represents a debate with himself. One part of him rejects this recreation, rejects the reflection of other lights and the transcendence of the moment, seeing it as a negation of the specialness of Anna:

> all that pursuing generality,
> that vengeful conspiracy with nature,
> all that sly informing of objects,
> and behind every line, your laugh
> frozen into a lifeless photograph.[30]

But the poet's other voice counteracts this suggestion in the next stanza, demonstrating that it is possible to see a particular reality or moment renewed and repeated in other situations and at other times:

> In that hair I could walk through the wheatfields of Russia.
> Your arms were downed and ripening pears,
> For you became, in fact, another country,

> You are Anna of the wheatfield and the weir,
> You are Anna of the solid winter rain,
> Anna of the smoky platform and the cold train.[31]

To Anna's accusation that he had made her into a metaphor, represented her as other than she really was ("I became a metaphor, but/ believe me I was unsubtle as salt"), the poet presents another view, explaining the relationship between memory and reality, and pointing to the imagination's capacity to repeat experiences, to recreate them in other moments: "a man lives half of life,/the second half is memory".[32]

In 'A Simple Flame' the ambivalence of these positions is deepened by the poet's realisation that the moment itself could be vulnerable and that, sometimes, preserving it would only mean watching the visionary glare

> tarnish to tin . . .
> [walking] the kelp-piled beach
> and hearing the waves arriving with stale news.[33]

Thus, the poet's desire to be linked to his island even in his absence, his plea to be "doubled by memory", to see his island experience repeated in other ways, at other times, is undercut by reminders of his own past betrayals. When he prays to the Earth-heart:

> uproot me, yet
> let what I have sworn to love not feel betrayed
> when I must go, and, if I must go,
> make of my heart an ark
> let my ribs bear
> all, doubled by
> memory, down to this emerald fly
> marrying this hand, and be
> the image of a young man on a pier
> his heart a ship within a
> ship within a ship, a bottle
> where this wharf, these
> rotting roofs, this sea,
> sail, sealed in glass.[34]

the poem's omniscient voice intrudes, reminding him of past rejections and betrayals that must qualify his new commitment

("How often didn't you hesitate/ between rose-flesh and sepia/ your blood like a serpent whispering/ of a race incapable of subtler shadow,/ of music, architecture and a complex thought").

The poem's final resolution seems to me to rest on these very ambiguities. For the poet points to a depth of feeling and empathy with the people that cut across those ambivalences and which can be repeated and renewed through memory:

> . . . be glad that you were touched
> by some other's sadness, that when your hand trembles
> and the tightening railings sound,
> or the sky, before rain, sounds like a monstrous shell
> where their voices are, be happy
> in every uncertainty. Cherish the stumbling
> that lashes your eyes with branches,
> that, threatened with rain,
> your sorrow is still uncertain.[35]

For Walcott this empathy is a quality that can redeem, and the poet, for all his ambivalence, can free his people by returning them to themselves through the very act of 'naming' them, of capturing their lives, landscape and language:

> I knelt because I was my mother,
> I was the well of the world,
> I wore the stars on my skin,
> I endured no reflections,
> my sign was water,
> tears and the sea.[36]

His description of his vocation in these symbols of redemption remind us of his images on another occasion and indeed complete this encircling vision of the nature and function of the creative imagination.

> People entered his understanding
> like a wayside country church,
> they had built themselves.
> It was they who had smoothed the wall
> of his clay-coloured forehead,
>
> . . .
>
> holding the clear water of their simple troubles,

> he who returned their tribal names
> to the adze, mattock, midden and cookingpot.[37]

From the rootedness of these affirmations the poet can now accept and assert the imagination's power to extend the moment and see it repeated and renewed through the sharing of experience:

> my sign was Janus,
> I saw with twin heads,
> and everything I say is contradicted.
> My clear tongue licked the freshness of the earth,
> and when I leapt from that shelf
> of rock . . . .
> I leapt for the pride of that race
> at Sauteurs![38]

This seems to me to be the poem's reconciliation and triumph in spite of the sense of loss and the mood of despondency generated by the poet's return to the island in the last chapter. The sense of something shrunken, the idea of the repetition of history, creates gloom, but it is a gloom that is deliberately balanced. For the self-defeating image, the moon re-emerging over the untroubled ocean, the moon that will always swing its "lantern", also co-exists with the poet's cherished memory of Gregorias:

> . . . A sun that stands back
> from the fire of itself, not shamed, prizing
> its shadow, watching it blaze![39]

The final triumph then, is the triumph of the imagination and by implication, the poet's ability to preserve or transcend the moment. In Walcott's view the poet achieves this only when he has confronted and extricated himself from the nightmare of linear time; only when he has seen time not as a moment defined and limited by its particularity but as one simultaneous with all time.

This vision of history is not just related to, but is actually the source of Walcott's struggles with language and style in *Another Life*. The "style past metaphor" whose connotations and ambivalences he explores and reconciles, is 'elemental' in the 'Adamic' sense, and for the New World poet, blessed with Adam's task of giving things their names, an appropriate style:

. . . a great poet achieves his level when he reaches what Pound once called "the language beyond metaphor", when he has found his wisdom in clarity, when the naming of things, the simplest things, like buckets, sofas, the sound of rain, are merely, by the act of his naming them, reverberations.[40]

NOTES

1. Patricia Ismond: 'Walcott Versus Brathwaite', *Caribbean Quarterly*, Vol.17 Nos.3–4, Sept-Dec 1971, p.63.
2. As developed, also, in his essays: 'What the Twilight Says: An Overture', *Dream on Monkey Mountain*, New York, 1970, pp.3–40; 'The Muse of History' in Orde Coombs (ed.) *Is Massa Day Dead?*, New York, 1970, p.3–40; 'The Caribbean: Culture or Mimicry?', *Journal of Interamerican Studies*, XVI, February 1974, pp.3–13.
3. 'The Muse of History', p.5.
4. *ibid.*
5. 'What the Twilight Says', p.5.
6. *ibid.*, p.17.
7. *Another Life*, p.41.
8. *ibid.*
9. *ibid.*, p.42.
10. *ibid.*
11. *ibid.*, p.43.
12. *ibid.*
13. *ibid.*, p.44.
14. *ibid.*
15. *ibid.*, p.43.
16. *ibid.*, p.44
17. 'The Almond Trees', *The Castaway*, p.37.
18. *ibid.*
19. *Another Life*, p.9.
20. *ibid.*, p.74.
21. 'Nearing Forty', *The Gulf*, p.67.
22. *Another Life*, p.75.
23. *ibid.*, p.76.
24. *ibid.*, p.83.
25. *ibid.*, p.84.
26. *ibid.*, p.88.
27. *ibid.*, p.92.
28. *ibid.*, p.88
29. *ibid.*, p.92.
30. *ibid.*, pp.95–96.
31. *ibid.*, p.96.
32. *ibid.*, p.101.
33. *ibid.*, p.105.
34. *ibid.*, p.108.

35. *ibid.*, p.109.
36. *ibid.*, p.139.
37. *ibid.*, p.134.
38. *ibid.*, p.139.
39. *ibid.*, p.152.
40. Walcott said this of Boris Pasternak. See V. Questel, 'Walcott's Major Triumph',
     Tapin, 23 December 1973, p.7.

Laurence A. Breiner

Walcott's *Early Drama*

Walcott's *Early Drama*

A charming account of the atmosphere in which Derek Walcott made his debut as a dramatist comes from another West Indian artist who went on to make a name for himself in New York, Geoffrey Holder. The year was 1950. The BBC had been broadcasting Walcott's play, *Henri Christophe*, and in a review of the play Holder describes his experience of the broadcast:

> I was listening at a wayside loudspeaker when the rain began to drizzle and three or four people took shelter. Two men, barefooted, were talking when Christophe momentarily flared up; then his voice grew quieter . . . . The two men stopped talking and even when the rain had ceased, they remained listening to the end of the play. At that late stage they could not have followed the events; they were held by the poetry, striking in its vividness and beauty and spoken with sympathy and sincerity. I thought of the Elizabethans.[1]

However accurately this reports the behaviour of the little crowd, it is a fine portrait of what a sensitive young West Indian thought he saw, or wanted to see, going on around him. In 1950, between the end of World War II and the coming of Independence, many West Indians of talent envisioned their islands as an archipelago of enlightened city-states destined to rival the Aegean of antiquity. The West Indies was to be a world where peasants listened to blank verse, where literature was a shout in the street, and where the material poverty of the theatre was overcome by the profundity of its style and subject. As Walcott wrote, looking back on those days in the essay that introduces his first collection of plays, "Poverty seemed a gift to the imagination, necessity was truly a virtue."[2] These ideals set the tone for the first period of Walcott's career as a dramatist, 1950-70.

In 1950, at the age of 20, Walcott was a local prodigy. His paintings and watercolours had just been shown in an exhibition he shared with

Dunstan St. Omer, and he had already published two books of poetry (*25 Poems* and *Epitaph for the Young*). He was not yet known as a playwright; the half- dozen or so plays he had written in his teens have never been published. *Henri Christophe* at once made his ambitions clear, first of all in the choice of a subject for tragedy that was not Greek, Roman, or British-colonial, or even British West Indian, but pointedly Caribbean. The form too makes claims. This is a kind of revenge tragedy and its verse, diction, and pacing come (like so much of his early poetry) from seventeenth century models – Walcott like many of his comtemporaries inherited the canons of taste established by T.S. Eliot. The play's extravagance was balanced the following year by *Harry Dernier*, a brief, spare play about the last man on earth. Like *An Epitaph for the Young* it drew on Walcott's direct knowledge of Dante, but there are traces also of Eliot's modernist imitations of Dante. These broadcasts by the BBC Caribbean Service made Walcott known to the widest possible audience in the region, and at the same time provided the cachet of metropolitan approval. At twenty-one, he had an international reputation as a dramatist.

By that time too he had left St. Lucia, moving first to Jamaica for a University degree (1950-53), and then to Trinidad. These were formative experiences, but perhaps the most significant stimulus to Walcott's development as a man of the theatre came during two trips to New York, briefly in 1957 and then for several months in 1958 in connection with a Rockefeller Fellowship. The overwhelming artistic life of the city was one factor. There he could see all kinds of plays produced on all kinds of budgets. He himself, in the essay 'Meanings', notes the influence of everything from Brecht to Broadway musicals, and in particular the discovery of classical Chinese and Japanese drama, which he came to not only through Brecht's orientalism but more directly through the Japanese films much in vogue in New York at that time (one of them, *Rashomon*, is the acknowledged model for his play *Malcochon*, 1958). In St. Lucia, plays existed in books, on the radio, and in occasional amateur productions. In New York Walcott was exposed to many different styles of acting and direction, while in addition he became familiar with the concrete realities of the theatre: the details of organization and management, as well as the array of available technical resources.

The plain foreignness of New York was also a factor. Isolation and distance gave Walcott for the first time the perspective from which to formulate a view of what could be distinctive about a West Indian theatrical style. What he found was a vivid physicality inherent in the

West Indian cultural heritage which, among other things, overcame the distinction between speech and action. As he later phrased it, "the strength of the West Indian psyche [is] a fusion of formalism with exuberance, a delight in both the precision and the power of language." What he recognised as the particular gift of West Indian actors, the resource upon which to build a style and a theatre, was "this astounding fusion . . . of classic discipline inherited through the language, with a strength of physical expression that comes from the folk music."[3] He cut short his stay in New York, eager to return to the Caribbean and to set about realizing his vision of a uniquely West Indian theatre company, one that would combine the "visibly, physically self-expressive" character of the West Indian with the "self-annihilating process" of method acting; a theatre of both actors and dancers, "where someone can do Shakespeare or sing Calypso with equal conviction."[4] The result was the Trinidad Theatre Workshop, which he founded in 1959 and left in 1977.

The brief period extending from shortly before his New York experience in 1957 until the founding of the Workshop in 1959 was extraordinarily productive for Walcott. The first versions of nearly all the major plays completed by 1970 date from those years, among them *Ione*, *Ti-Jean and His Brothers*, *Jourmard*, *Malcochon*, *Franklin*, *A Tale of the Islands*, *Drums and Colours* and *Dream on Monkey Mountain*. After 1959 it appears that Walcott was not writing new plays. In the decade of 1960s he concentrated on poetry: four collections were published between 1962 and 1970, and he began work on *Another Life* in 1965. At the same time he was writing hundreds of columns for the *Trinidad Guardian*. His dramatic work was limited (though the word hardly seems appropriate) to the development of the Workshop. Walcott describes the emotional intensity of that project at length in 'What the Twilight Says'. Its first official productions were not mounted until 1966, when the company presented *The Sea at Dauphin* and Albee's *Zoo Story* in a converted bar in the basement of what was then the Bretton Hall Hotel. Later that year there was a four week season of a remarkable repertory: Eric Roach's *Belle Fanto*, Genet's *The Blacks*, and Wole Soyinka's *The Road*. In conjunction with the Workshop's needs Walcott was also revising many plays already drafted. The end of this period is marked by the publication of his first collection, *Dream on Monkey Mountain and Other Plays*.

★ ★ ★

"On the verandah, with his back to the street, he began marathon poems on Greek heroes which ran out of breath, lute songs, heroic tragedies, but these rhythms, the Salvation Army parodies, the Devil's Christmas songs, and the rhythms of the street itself were entering the pulse-beat of the wrist."[5] Thus Walcott depicts his adolescent self, the young poet beset with the disembodied voices of his competing traditions. As that picture suggests, his earliest dramatic efforts were 'plays for voices', but this poet was also a painter, and he took control of the visual possibilities soon enough. All the early plays aspire to a theatre of directness, combining depth with immediate accessibility, and relying as little as possible on conventions that require a trained audience for their effect. This was necessarily a 'poor theatre' in terms of material resources, but it aspired to a kind of prodigality, aiming to include something for every level of audience, to achieve "the right vulgarity."[6]

Walcott's talents as poet and painter gave him at once the means to achieve immediate impact: language, gesture, music, spectacle. From the beginning those are his secure resources, opulently laid on. But if, as even Holder's praise implies, Walcott's early work reliably offered the immediate gratifications of rich language and spectacle, his own object of investigation during this period was the problem of dramatic structure – how, as he puts it, "to transform the theatrical into theatre"[7]; how to construct a unified drama that contains, connects, even generates the great moments of theatrical effect, without diminishing exuberance on the stage or pleasure in the audience.

With this objective, Walcott explored alternatives in the use of both history and Jacobean tragic structure to shape *Henri Christophe*, in the debt to Synge for the tight discipline of *The Sea at Dauphin*, and in the elements of Greek tragedy that shape *Ione* (1957). On the other hand *Drums and Colours*, written as a pageant to celebrate the short-lived West Indian Federation in 1958, takes advantage of the public nature of the occasion to minimize dramatic structure, contriving a sort of Brechtian epic theatre out of brief episodes of dance, mime, and historical vignette.

The Sea at Dauphin (1954) is freely modelled on Synge's *Riders to the Sea*, and its naturalistic elements support an impression of ethnographic intent. The opening conversation, for example, begins in French patois. But this is artful illusion; in the course of the play creole is limited to expletives, songs, and the like, while substantive dialogue is carried on in an English slightly modified to reflect creole vocabulary and constructions.

Similarly the play can seem folkloristic, a stylized representation of the shakily ordered world of a remote fishing village, threatened by rain and sea. But Walcott actually starts with the frugal material of many of his castaway poems: the horizon, the bare beach, and on it bare unaccommodated man – this one, Afa the fisherman, even something of a misanthrope, frankly contemptuous of accommodation; of marriage, loyalty, church. As another character says to him, "you have a hole where man heart should be, you have no God, no dog, no friend, that is why Dauphin fraid you". Through the interrogating figure of Afa, marginal even to that marginal world, the play goes beyond representation to pose a question: what gives shape, gives meaning, to the deceptive picturesqueness of poverty, to the actualities of Caribbean folk life? "It smelled strong and true," writes Walcott in his introduction, "But what was its truth? That in the 'new Aegean' the race, of which these fisherman were the stoics, had grown a fatal adaptability."[8]

Like *Harry Dernier* this play is itself an experiment in adapting to poverty of means, and *Dauphin* is especially notable for its calculated avoidance of depth of reference: there is no myth here but threadbare religion, no culture but habit. 'History' here goes no deeper than the few drowned fishermen that are still remembered by name. Hounakin, the oldest character in the play, remembers a time when the town of Dauphin didn't exist. Though their settings are similar, *Dauphin* is not so grim as Synge's tragedy; it is about the men of the village rather than the women, and (perhaps for that reason) about acceptance of the agon with the world rather than submission to it. The everpresent sea plainly symbolizes the timeless repetition of the cycles of life and death, yet the play gives us the young boy Jules, eager to take on the life of a fisherman. The dominant presence, however, is Afa, raging not only at the world, but also at the vanity of all myths and rituals by which the world is accommodated.

In this explicit resistance to accommodation *Dauphin* is exceptional; most of the other early plays are characterized instead by an active search for 'myth' in nearly the Aristotelian sense: for patterns of character and narrative suitable for, if not actually arising from, Caribbean culture, that can provide forms for drama. Each of the other plays of this period carries on the search in its own way, but the urgency is most patent in *Henri Christophe*, a play which seems to imply an admission that in the region only Haiti readily provided a subject of sufficient magnitude for tragedy. As Walcott later wrote, "Now, one may see such heroes as squalid facists who chained their own people, but they had size, mania, the fire of great heretics . . . Dessalines and Christophe . . . were our only noble ruins."[9]

This 'absence of ruins', the apparent lack of an eventful and dramatic history, seems to frustrate nearly all West Indian writers at the point early in their careeers when they seek a subject large enough for their ambition. Walcott, like the poet Edward Brathwaite and the novelist Wilson Harris, overcame this obstacle by moving up off the beach. The verge of the salt flood is a fine setting for unaccommodated man. But to move inland on an island like St. Lucia is to penetrate the interior, the subconscious, the articulate mystery of dreams. It is the movement dramatized in Brathwaite's *Arrivants* as a passage from the candor (and monotheism) of the desert to the dense mythology demanded by a West African forest, where "leaf eyes shift, twigs / creak, buds flutter, the stick / becomes a snake". The peculiarities of island topography and climate give rise to all sorts of superstitions, visions, terrors – that is, gestures at meaning. So it is out of the mists of the high forest that the forces of myth materialize in such plays as *Malcochon, Ti-Jean and His Brothers*, and above all *Dream On Monkey Mountain*.

★ ★ ★

Walcott has called *Ti-Jean and His Brothers* a West Indian fable, but significantly he wrote it far from home, in only a few days during his first trip to New York in 1957 ("I probably wrote the damned thing because I was afraid to go out"). His brother Roderick produced an early version in St. Lucia at once, though the official opening was in Trinidad in 1958. The revision published in 1970 has been produced frequently throughout the region. For Walcott too the play was a personal success; he saw it as a turning point, "the first real experience I had of writing a stylized West Indian play . . . For the first time I used songs and dances and a narrator in a text . . . Out of that play, I knew what I wanted."[10]

The central story is lucid and archetypal. Each of three brothers confronts the Devil. The strong eldest and the learned middle brother are both defeated; the youngest, "a fool like all heroes", uses his unflappable common sense (and the help of forest creatures he has befriended) to beat the Devil. The victory is not unambiguous: Ti-Jean's mother dies at the same moment, leaving him triumphant but alone, and matters are further complicated by the presence of a figure out of Caribbean folklore, the Bolom: a foetus whose birth has been

frustrated, so that it constantly seeks entry into life. The Bolom, pure
potentiality, functions (like the more familiar Afro-caribbean Eshu)
as an agent of unpredictability confined in but always shaking the
secure form of the play.

As a result of his victory, Ti-Jean has become the man in the moon,
and the fable of the three brothers is framed in the play as a "just-so"
story the creatures of the forest tell one another:

> "God made [Ti-Jean] the clarity of the moon to lighten the doubt of all
> travellers through the shadowy wood of life. And bird, the rain is over,
> the moon is rising through the leaves."

The image of a man in the moon with a bundle of sticks on his back is
not particularly Caribbean; one might recall its appearance in
Shakespeare's *The Tempest.* Yet this story about him is presented as so
chthonic, so indigenous, that the very animals know it. It is a longstanding conviction of Walcott's that even the most deeply rooted
myths to be unearthed in the Caribbean will necessarily turn out to be
creolized at the root, simply as a consequence of the region's history.
The aesthetic equivalent he has formulated as an axiom: "Maturity is
the assimilation of the features of every ancestor."[11] The opening
language of the play subtly insists upon this principle. The action
begins with animal noises. Then the frog sneezes because of the rain,
and so tells the story that will make the moon appear and end the rain.
But in European folklore (and not in the Caribbean as far as I know)
this initial sneeze is an omen that a story is true. And Frog's polite
"Aeschylus me" is not just one of Walcott's overelaborate puns; it also
indicates that the animal noises (written "Greek-croak, Greek-croak"
in the text) involve an allusion to Aristophanes' comic chorus of frogs.
But Walcott has packed further significance into those opening noises:
in "Greek-croak" we are expected to hear "Cric-crac" as well – the
traditional Caribbean formula to signal the beginning of a story. So
the characteristic tone is set: elemental and literary at once.

Throughout his work Walcott resorts to the image of Adam giving
things their names. But in this case the animals do the naming, and the
effect is more Ovidian than Adamic. In naming the moon "Ti-Jean",
this play aims to enrich the natural object with specifically Caribbean
significance. Such an effort goes beyond the appropriation or imitation
of folklore. There is an aspiration to give one's vision the force of myth
and thereby to make it available as a resource to the audience, the
people of these islands: "When one began twenty years ago it was in

the faith that one was creating not merely a play, but a theatre, and not merely a theatre, but its environment."[12] Thus in the plays of this period Walcott is occupied not merely with putting West Indian life on stage, but with making claims, projections about that life, its limitations, its possibilities, its relation to life elsewhere and to representations of life elsewhere.

This is why *Ti-Jean* presents itself not just as an aetiological fable, but as an *effectual* one: the indigenous creatures of the place possess and *use* the story as their own. The telling is an incantation: at the start there is rain and no moon. Frog tells the tale of the origin of the moon, and that invocation makes it appear by recapitulating its creation. Since the fable itself is incidentally a moral guide, the moon, whose presence is both starting point and result of the fable, also stands as perpetual reminder and guarantor of the lesson. Critical interpretations of the play in the West Indies have been extremely varied, spinning out moral, historical, and even (during the 1970's) explicitly political implications. The rather centrifugal allegorical tendency in the responses bears witness that Walcott has achieved his goal: the spontaneous appropriation of the work by the community for its own purposes.

The early plays as a group are about St. Lucia, and in them Walcott is particularly concerned with this dialectic of appropriation: the artist's appropriation of the life of the people for his aesthetic ends, and the justification of that act by the community's (re-)appropriation of the finished work. While these plays carry on Walcott's investigation of form, language, and style, they are also profoundly engaged in working out this author's relation to his material – to his island and to its life, which is not his life. Walcott's passion for St. Lucia is complex, sometimes jealous, finally star- crossed, and he repeatedly identifies its ambivalences as the wellspring of his work, for example when he describes himself as one of "... two pale children staring from their upstairs window, wanting to march with that ragged, barefooted crowd, but who could not because they were not black and poor, until for one of them, watching the shouting, limber congregation, that difference became a sadness, that sadness rage, and that longing to share their lives ambition . . . "[13]

His dilemma was "to enter that life without living it", and the early plays constitute the embodiment, if not the solution, of that dilemma.[14] It is after all a premise of drama that *represented* life can be entered, though not lived. This is true even for audiences, but much more so for actors. It is plausible to suppose that during the long incubation period of the Theatre Workshop Walcott was addressing his personal dilemma in terms of a professional problem: how the actor enters another life.

★ ★ ★

West Indian society, according to V.S Naipaul, "denied itself heroes";[15] Walcott's observation is more specific: "In the West Indies . . . what was missing in the folklore was a single heroic warrior figure."[16] The early plays respond to that deficiency, and so they are especially concerned with one kind of role, that of the protagonist. In Christophe, Afa, Chantal, and other characters Walcott tries out many kinds of heroes. Indeed, *Ti-Jean* could be described as a play about the selection of its own proper protagonist. But as that play demonstrates, Walcott is most interested in the heroic dimension of lowly characters, the extraordinary ordinary people of an island like St. Lucia. Above all it is the castaway, the fisherman, the woodcutter or charcoal-burner who for him represents "the most isolated, most reduced, race-containing symbol", the germ both of drama and of cultural identity.[17] These are the figures he is most attracted to (and presumably most inclined to identify himself with). In his search for the right protagonist, Walcott is seeking a place for himself in the text of his island. That connection is often quite explicit, as in the following passage, a description of his vexed relationship to his island that incidentally illustrates how fully Walcott himself is represented in the irascible Afa:

> "There was more envy than hate towards it, and the love that stubbornly
> emerged showed like weeds through the ruined aisle of an abandoned
> church, and one worked hard for that love, against their love of priest
> and statue, against the pride of their resignation. One worked to have the
> 'feel' of the island, bow, gunwhales and stern as jealously as the
> fisherman knew his boat . . . "[18]

But as he writes the old dilemma immediately asserts itself, with the result that the passage continues into paradox:

> "...and, despite the intimacy of its size to be as free as a canoe out on the
> ocean."

Dream on Monkey Mountain is the culmination of Walcott's style and objectives in the early plays. It was begun in 1959, rewritten for the Workshop's first tour outside Caribbean (to Toronto, 1967), and revised for publication in 1970. The plot is rudimentary: an old charcoal burner known by the name Makak brings his load down from the mountain to sell on market day. Arrested for appearing drunk and disorderly, he spends Saturday night and Sunday morning in jail, then returns to his hut on the mountain. But his behaviour is eventually explained as the result either of a fit brought on by the full moon (according to his friend Moustique), or of his encounter with an apparition, "the moon, the muse, the white Goddess," according to Makak, and the play itself is a moonstruck dream, initiated with evocative music and mime. The body of the play, six scenes framed by a prologue and parallel epilogue, constitutes an enormous, multi-faceted response to a policeman's routine question: "what is your name?" But this is only clear from the perspective of the epilogue, when the moonlit prologue is recapitulated in the prose light of the sun, and Makak at last answers simply with his name, Felix Hobain.

The realm of dream serves Walcott as a compositional wild card, allowing freedom from the responsibilities of form; but in fact the play invokes a redundancy of forms – another feature of real dreams that adds considerable resonance to the action. For example, Makak and his series of "assistants" together constitute a beast fable: mosquito, mouse, tiger, along with the Caribbean macaque. He is variously identified as mimic monkey, remote mountain gorilla, King Kong. But those were the racist epithets of the colonial period; now in the era of independence and black consciousness he is touted as King of Africa, Lion of Judah. The problem of naming raises this central question in the play: on that spectrum from ape to lion, where is the actual man?

Makak's projected journey to Africa is presented as a Jordan crossing to the Promised Land, to a once and future Eden, but it is also quixotic, and in addition to the central relationship between Makak and Moustique several details of the play owe something to Cervantes' *Don Quixote*. Other Biblical elements also help shape the play. The overall pattern of the action (descent from the mountain, Saturday delirium, and Sunday ascent) alludes to the passion and resurrection of Christ, while Tigre and Souris are depicted as the good and bad thieves crucified with Jesus. The historical connection between Easter and Carnival is also exploited: this dream is a brief mardi gras of role-playing, self-dramatization, wish-fulfillment. The white-faced mask of the apparition that Makak carries with him is surely a Carnival mask (and Lestrade's comment that "everybody

round here have one" speaks less to the St. Lucian characters than to
the Trinidadian audience).

By focussing on one of Walcott's "reduced, race-containing"
protagonists and asking, "who is he?", "what should he be called?",
the play investigates West Indian identity. Makak is presented
as a man shaped under pressure. There are the routine oppressions
of a highly stratified society, in which his place is determined by race,
by colour, even by language – his French patois against the English
of authority. There is also the pressure of history with its burden
of slavery and colonialism. Makak's occupation as a charbonnier
provides images that suggest optimism: Moustique for example
describes coal as "one billion, trillion years of pressure bringing
light". The implication is that in the words of Hopkins, familiar
to readers of West Indian literature, "this Jack, joke, poor pots-
herd, patch, match-wood" can become under pressure "immortal
diamond".

In these images, however, Walcott cannot entirely suppress the
implication that black coal improves by becoming white. That
obstinacy in his material points to Walcott's development of another
character, the mulatto corporal Lestrade, who becomes a kind of
second protagonist for the play. Makak seems to be a child of the
century, in his sixties and of the '60s; an African who comes to self-
consciousness in the Caribbean, and must wonder which he should
call home. But it is Lestrade, divided in the vein, who undergoes the
stereotypical *prise de conscience* of that era, moving from "Afro-
Saxon" to "tribe boy" as his own dream progresses. He begins in his
Sunday uniform, defending English law, English language, and
whiteness. In the second half of the play he finds himself naked in the
forest and comes to a moment of self-recognition ("I have become
what I mocked"); but he is also delirious, and black is no more the true
identity of the mulatto than white. Lestrade ends up (within the
dream) dressed in tribal robes as a sort of vizier to an African Makak.
First whiter than his prisoner, now blacker than his master, in both
conditions he manages to tell Makak what to do.

His most crucial command is to kill the apparition, the ambiguous
white woman – angel, demon, or hallucination – who knows Makak's
true name and inspires his new pride in himself. This figure presents
many problems for interpretation and even for production of the play,
but it is clear that she is the source of both his new attachment to the
local soil and his empowering memory of Africa. The apparition thus
stands at the heart of the play's two most troublesome paradoxes.

First, there is the problem that Makak's black consciousness has a white source. Walcott's provocative epigraph from Sartre invites the view that black pride remains less a positive statement than the negation of a negation initiated by Europe; the white world has always called him black, but what he once heard as an insult he now chooses to hear as a compliment. In the racial fanaticism of his own dream, Lestrade takes the opposite position that black pride is quite independent of the white world; in other words that the apparition is not real, only "an image of your longing." But his motivation is compromised; as he sees it, the danger is that "[Makak] will be what I was, neither one thing nor the other." Lestrade insists that he has killed the whiteness in himself, but of course he has not – it is there, patent in his face, even as he speaks.

The other paradox associated with the apparition reflects one of the burning issues of the years around 1970: whether West Indian identity was to be rooted in the Caribbean or in Africa. Makak repeatedly says that the vision had two very different effects on him: it rooted his feet in the earth of the mountain, and it initiated his quest for Africa. The journey to Africa ends in an orgy of executions, and at the conclusion of the play Makak's impulse to return to Africa has been transposed into a return to his own St. Lucian mountain. His upbeat closing speech, complete with music and exit into the new day, fully embraces the mountain as home. In production the end is an apotheosis: Makak becomes a pantheon of one on an unregarded tropical Olympus. In the details of the final speech, however, it is apparent that Makak remains ambivalent about who he is, in relation to this place and its people. He asks to be forgotten, to be "swallowed up in mist again", but at the same time he imagines a future when people will look up to the mountain and say, "Makak lives there. Makak lives where he has always lived, in the dream of his people." This is precisely the ambivalence of Walcott's contemporaneous poems. "Commoner than water I sank to lose my name," he writes in 'Hic Jacet'. But the title quotes the beginning of a memorial inscription; these words, cut into ageless bronze or marble, would be followed by two more: Derek Walcott.

Dream on Monkey Mountain concludes the project of the early drama. After 1970 the playwright's attention turns to a different kind of theatre. He still shapes poetry out of the varied registers of West Indian language, but Trinidad rather than St. Lucia is the usual setting, and the style is more realistic. There is less attention to a single protagonist, less outright mythmaking. Walcott has continued to explore the dialectic of appropriation, but this play marks the end of one phase of that exploration. While the playwright himself certainly stands somewhere behind the troubled mulatto Lestrade, he has figured at least a provisional resolution of his own dilemma in Makak, who kills what he loves, but still lives in the dream of his people.

NOTES

1. Geoffrey A. Holder,'Review of Derek Walcott', *Henri Christophe, Bim 14*, June 1951, p.142.
2. Walcott, 'What the Twilight Says: An Overture', in *Dream on Monkey Mountain and Other Plays*, New York, 1970, p.7.
3. Walcott, 'Meanings', in *Savacou*, No.2, 1970, p.312.
4. *ibid.*, p.306.
5. Walcott, 'What the Twilight Says: An Overture', *op.cit.*, p.22.
6. 'What the Lower House Demands,' *Trinidad Guardian*, 6 July 1966, p.5.
7. Walcott, 'What the Twilight Says: An Overture', *op.cit.*
8. *ibid.*, p.16.
9. *ibid.*, pp.12-13.
10. Walcott, 'Meanings', *op.cit.*, p.304.
11. Walcott, 'The Muse of History', in Orde Coombs (*ed*), *Is Massa Day Done?*, New York, 1974.
12. Walcott, 'What the Twilight Says: An Overture', *op.cit.*, p.6.
13. *ibid.*, pp.21–22.
14. *ibid.*, p.16.
15. V.S. Naipaul, *The Middle Passage*, London, 1962; rpt Harmondsworth, 1969, p.43.
16. Walcott, 'Meanings', *op.cit.*, p.310.
17. *ibid.*, p.308.
18. Walcott, 'What the Twilight Says: An Overture', *op.cit.*, p.15.

Ned Thomas

Obsession and Responsibility

Obsession and Responsibility

In the title-poem with which the volume *Sea Grapes* (1976) opens, a watcher on the shore observes that "a schooner beating up the Caribbean/ for home, could be Odysseus,". The classical hero is then portrayed as a divided man – a father and husband going home, but also an adulterer unable to forget, "hearing Nausicaa's name/ in every gull's outcry". This dual pull is reflected in the varying descriptions of the schooner. Although making for home, it has earlier been described as "tired of islands". Next, the tension is stated in terms of a generalization:

> the ancient war
> between obsession and responsibility
> will never finish and has been the same
> for the sea-wanderer or the one on shore
> now wriggling on his sandals to walk home.

Clearly this is a poem of multiple divisions. The watcher on shore is also divided within himself, watching the schooner with his eye but meeting his ludicrously prosaic responsibilities when he wriggles on his sandals to walk home. And we may wonder, further, whether the poet has not divided himself between the two divided figures.

At this point the poem digresses to consider the relevance of the classics to modern life, and of traditional European poetic forms to the Caribbean. I want to note in particular the movement of the last lines:

> and the blind giant's boulder heaved the trough
> from whose ground swell the great hexameters come
> to the conclusions of exhausted surf.
> The classics can console. But not enough.

The ending emphasises that the consciousness of this poem is, on balance, land-based. The islands are the recipients of the Homeric tide, which comes, exhausted, to rest here.[1] But this movement is offset, the classics partly rejected, in the withdrawing swing of the last phrase – as when, after a wave has broken, it recedes. So we have a literary tension parallel with the more personal tension that has gone before.

These divisions, these contrary movements, this composite tension, can be picked out in a wide range of Walcott's poems which deal with departures and homecomings, guilts and affirmations of allegiance, marriages and erotic obsessions, and the turning of borrowed literary inheritances to new purposes.

It is not difficult, in a general way, to relate these patterns of tension to Walcott's personal life, and, since personal life is always socially shaped and therefore never merely personal, to the conditions of the writer's background in St. Lucia and those of his career as an 'international poet'. But I am not concerned, at least not in the first place, with the general level. I want instead to investigate how these tensions energise the language and imagery of one poem sequence in particular: 'The Schooner *Flight*' in *The Star-apple Kingdom*: and to set that poem in turn against a poem- sequence with a very different emphasis – 'Sainte Lucie' in the volume *Sea Grapes*.

In 'The Schooner *Flight*', the "red nigger" Shabine sets out in the dawn to ship as a seaman on the schooner which will carry him through the islands and scenes of his life on a veritable Odyssey. His departure is a kind of desertion of his woman Maria Concepcion, for whom he has earlier left wife and children, but Maria (like Nausicaa) goes with him as obsession and muse, the power that transforms the scenes of his voyage into metaphor:

> But Maria Concepcion was all my thought
> watching the sea heaving up and down
> as the port side of dories, schooners, and yachts
> was painted afresh by the strokes of the sun
> signing her name with every reflection;
> I knew when dark-haired evening put on
> her bright silk at sunset, and, folding the sea,
> sidled under the sheet with her starry laugh,
> that there'd be no rest, there'd be no forgetting.

What metaphor lies behind the schooner's name? One's first thought in the early stages of the poem is that 'Flight' suggests escape from what Conrad called land-entanglements. By the eleventh and final section, however, two other emphases have been found:

> Though my *Flight* never pass the incoming tide
> of this inland sea beyond the loud reefs
> of the final Bahamas, I am satisfied
> if my hand gave voice to one people's grief.

This must be his poetic *Flight*, as in the phrase "flight of the imagination", for it is the poet's writing hand that gives voice to his people. A little further along we come to the lines:

> The bowsprit, the arrow, the longing, the lunging heart –
> the flight to a target whose aim we'll never know,
> vain search for one island that heals with its harbor
> and a guiltless horizon, where the almond's shadow
> doesn't injure the sand.

Here the Flight is not *from* but *to*; it has a purpose though that purpose is sensed rather than known. The "longing, the lunging heart" is earnest of a strong unfocused need, emotional and sexual but also metaphysical. It has already been stated in that dual form at the end of section 2:

> Where is my rest place, Jesus? Where is my harbor?
> Where is the pillow I will not have to pay for,
> and the window I can look from that frames my life?

The image of the window I find most interesting. It immediately brought to mind Waldo Williams's:

> Hon oedd fy ffenestr, y cynaeafu a'r cneifio.
> Mi welais drefn yn fy mhalas draw.[2]

> [This was my window, the harvesting and the shearing.
> I saw order there in my mansion.]

The reference in Waldo is to the society of his childhood in the rituals of whose brotherly community he found the security through which he might look independently at the world. Behind the image of a window, of course, lies the image of a house, of settlement, a sense of security, possibly even of tradition. Walcott's window, too, suggests a

vantage-point from which reality can be approached in confidence
and security. But in 'The Schooner *Flight*' it represents, of course, a
state of rest imagined while at sea.

'Sea Grapes' concluded by moving the discussion into the literary
area. In 'The Schooner *Flight*' this happens again in a passage at the
end of section one which incidentally offers a kind of reverse
perspective on the schooner in the earlier poem:

> You ever look up from some lonely beach
> and see a far schooner? Well, when I write
> this poem, each phrase go be soaked in salt;
> I go draw and knot every line as tight
> as ropes in this rigging; in simple speech
> my common language go be the wind,
> my pages the sails of the schooner *Flight*.

How are we to read "my common language"? In the first place it must
reflect a commitment to the salted vigour of ordinary speech which
Walcott is attempting to convey by putting the poem in the mouth of
Shabine. However, compared to many West Indian poets, Walcott
achieves that effect by a very few touches drawn mainly from West
Indian syntax and verb-forms, devices that in no way lose Walcott his
international audience. But the adjective "common" is grappled
perplexingly to the possessive pronoun "my". "Our common language" would have proclaimed allegiance to Caribbean English while
at the same time underlining its popular nature, but that, of course, is
not Walcott's position on "nation-language". So "common" must
have a wider reference to the international currency of English, and
"my" must represent the poet's indivdual attempt to wrest it to his
own purpose, an ambitious, individualist undertaking.

Often in Walcott the moment of departure is the moment of
benediction. Shabine, in the first section of this poem, takes a route-
taxi to get to his ship:

> And I look in the rearview and see a man
> exactly like me, and the man was weeping
> for the houses, the streets, for the whole fucking island.

and in the last section this grieving tribute is turned to active
benediction as on board the *Flight* Shabine proclaims:

> and from this bowsprit, I bless every town
> the blue smell of smoke in hills behind them
> and the one small road winding down them like twine
> to the roofs below:

The road like twine recalls an earlier use of the image with a similar structure of feeling, when in the last of 'Tales of the Islands' the young Walcott records leaving his island by plane:

> I watched the island narrowing the fine
> writing of foam around the precipices then
> the roads as small and casual as twine
> thrown on its mountains; I watched till the plane
> turned to the final north and turned above
> the open channel with the grey sea between
> the fishermen's islets until all that I love
> folded in cloud;

Shabine's weeping in the taxi carries us back to the key passage in *Another Life* in which Walcott describes the adolescent experience which gave birth to his poetic gift:

> About the August of my fouteenth year
> I lost myself somewhere above a valley
> owned by a spinster-farmer, my dead father's friend.
> At the hill's edge there was a scarp
> with bushes and boulders stuck at its side.
> Afternoon light ripened the valley,
> rifling smoke climbed from small labourers houses,
> and I dissolved into a trance.
> I was seized with a pity more profound
> than my young body could bear, I climbed
> with the labouring smoke,
> I drowned in labouring breakers of bright cloud,
> then uncontrollably I began to weep,
> inwardly, without tears, with a sense of serene extinction
> of all sense; I felt compelled to kneel,
> I wept for nothing and for everything,
> I wept for the earth of the hill under my knees,
> for the grass, the pebbles, for the cooking smoke
> above the labourers houses' like a cry,
> for unheard avalanches of white cloud,
> but "darker grows the valley, more and more forgetting."

For their lights still shine through the hovels like litmus,
the smoking lamp still slowly says its prayer,
the poor still move behind their tinted scrim,
the taste of water is still shared everywhere,
but in that ship of night, locked in together,
through which, like chains, a little might leak,
something still fastens us forever to the poor.

In this passage we recognize, of course, a characteristic Romantic event, introduced moreover by a Wordsworthian cadence: a walk in nature, and a transaction between the human consciousness and nature that bears all the marks of religious experience, using imagery of religious origin but in an open and non-doctrinal way. But it is also worth looking at the social dimension of the passage. While there is fusion with the landscape, the relationship to the people, the poor, is more complicated, a mixture of estrangement, compassion and connection. The situation of the poet on the hillside, feeling identification with his people while standing at a vantage-point above them and isolated from them, has nice parallels in Anglo-Welsh literature, for example in Alun Lewis's 'The Mountain above Aberdare'. And the tone is not unlike parts of Joyce's *Dubliners*, or the conclusion of Dylan Thomas's story 'One Warm Saturday':

The light of the one weak lamp in a rusty circle fell across the brick-heaps and the broken wood and the dust that had been houses once, where the small and hardly-known and never-to-be forgotten people of the dirty town had lived and loved and died and, always, lost.

That passage too fits Walcott's account in 'What the Twilight Says: an Overture'[3]:

Years ago, watching them, and suffering as you watched, you proffered silently the charity of a language which they could not speak, until your suffering, like the language, felt superior, estranged.

The estrangement is partly, of course, the estrangement of anyone who is putting the world into words. But it is compounded by a gap of class and also (as in Dylan Thomas's case) to some degree by a gap of language, for in St. Lucia the language of the country people is Creole French.

In a colonial society anyone likely to be writing at all will be already isolated from the great majority of people by class and education, but further upward mobility will usually necessitate a shift, geographically or culturally, towards the metropolis and its standards. This produces a conflict of loyalties more acute than those set up by upward mobility in a class-divided metropolitan culture, since a whole place, a whole history, and people perceived as 'a people' must be left behind.

But there is the alternative response, the nationalist reaction, the recognition that "something still fastens us forever to the poor". The place and the people are identified with, are felt to be capable of a social transformation equal to the poet's sense of what they are capable of.

This was Walcott's aim at an earlier stage of his career. The idea of poetic transformation – the dignifying of people's lives through poetry – remains implicit in 'The Schooner *Flight*', but hopes of social transformation have been dashed, at least for the foreseeable future. One of the reasons Shabine is leaving at the beginning of the poem is his disillusionment with the venial politicians of the fragmented West Indies after independence and the collapse of the federal idea:

> If loving these islands must be my load
> out of corruption my soul takes wings.
> But they had started to poison my soul
> with their big house, big car, big-time bohbohl,
> coolie, nigger, Syrian, and French Creole,
> so I leave it for them and their carnival –
> I taking a sea-bath, I gone down the road.

and in section 3:

> I no longer believed in the revolution.
> I was losing faith in the love of my woman
> I had seen that moment Aleksandr Blok
> crystallize in *The Twelve*.

But that moment of potential social transformation was lost, and the only revolution you will now see in his provincial society, Shabine suggests, will be if the projector breaks down during the showing of a spaghetti western.

Political satire, savage as it can only be when written about a society whose hopes and disillusions one has shared, is a main strand in Walcott's work of his middle period, and reaches a peak of intensity in *Sea Grapes* with poems such as 'Party Night at the Hilton', 'The Lost

Federation', 'The Brother', 'The Silent Woman', 'Preparing for Exile' and 'Parades, Parades':

> We wait for the changing of statues
> For the change of parades.
>
> Here he comes now, here he comes!
> Papa! Papa! With his crowd,
> the sleek, waddling seals of his Cabinet,
> trundling up to the dais,
> as the wind puts its tail between
> the cleft of the mountain, and a wave
> coughs once, abruptly.
> Who will name this silence
> respect? Those forced, hoarse hosannas
> awe? That tin-ringing tune
> from the pumping, circling horns
> the New World? Find a name
> for that look on the faces
> of the electorate. Tell me
> how it all happened, and why
> I said nothing.

In the title-poem of the next volume, *The Star-apple Kingdom*, the possibility of a violent revolution is contemplated in a surrealist style suggestive of Spanish-American models, but is then rejected, or rather, transcended at a visionary level. In the volumes that follow, though there is anger and compassion and guilt at his own complicity as the "international poet" who jets between the rich North of the globe and the exploited South, the images are more generalized, the insights more comparative, and the feelings therefore less sharply focused. When Shabine says: "I had no country now but the imagination" it might be the motto (or epitaph) of several international poets using English – Brodsky, Heaney, Walcott. Joyce's "exile and cunning" are their natural weapons. But where is their natural audience? Among those others of us whose contrastive sense is honed by international travel?

This is the place to mention the image of Russia in Walcott's work. Huge, landlocked, a world of its own, it contrasts with the culturally invaded, economically dependent islands of the Caribbean. It is dignified by its own tragedy in the work of its great writers who speak to their own people in their own language. As epigraph to 'The Silent Woman' Walcott quotes Akhmatova:

I was with my people then
there where my people were doomed to be.

Stalin's Russia offered writers the clear alternatives of collaboration or persecution unto death. It was a world of what Heaney calls "the diamond absolutes"; but Walcott, like Heaney, lives in much more ambiguous moral territory, where subject-matter and audience do not have the same coherence (if only because of the language he uses); where necessity is as much a felt internal pressure as an external force; where the moment of betrayal and the moment of integrity are much harder to isolate. Though Walcott's touch is light and the analogies not unduly forced, I cannot help feeling that there is a substantial gap between Walcott's exile and the enforced internal exile of Mandelstam which is evoked twice as a kind of equivalence, in 'Preparing for Exile' (*Sea Grapes*) and again in 'Forest of Europe' (*The Star-apple Kingdom*). That same poem universalises the image of the Gulag archipelago; it directs attention to the violence and misuse of law against the American Indians of the Mid-West and then proceeds to make a comparison with the Caribbean:

The tourist archipelagoes of my South
are prisons too, . . .

Who can resist the argument that suffering is general, that few if any societies bear looking into very far? The trouble is that the suffering is not the very same suffering, the exploitation not the identical exploitation; the poetic statement loses sharpness of focus as it becomes comparative and general. The lines I have just quoted seem over-explicit and tired. This is very different from the magnificent opening out of a generalization from a moment of individual experience in one place, such as we find at the end of 'The Schooner *Flight*':

There are so many islands!
As many islands as the stars at night
on that branched tree from which meteors are shaken
like falling fruit around the schooner Flight.
But things must fall, and so it always was,
on one hand Venus, on the other Mars;
fall, and are one, just as this earth is one
island in archipelagoes of stars.

This has not been an exhaustive analysis of 'The Schooner *Flight*'. Rather I have sought to draw out those elements of division mentioned at the start and to suggest that it is precisely in the holding of the tension between them that the energy of the poem is felt. Another way of describing that tension is to say that the poem is supremely self-aware. This saves it from the self-indulgence which is always a risk when poets embark on extended discussions of the self, and which is felt in some parts of *Another Life*. But in 'The Schooner *Flight*' self-awareness remains closely linked to the original sources of Walcott's feeling, and this endows the poem with an energy that is not matched in Walcott's otherwise very accomplished later work.

Finally I turn to 'Sainte Lucie' (*Sea Grapes*) as evidence of how a great poet can manage an emphasis which is an implicit criticism of much of his other work. This sequence is set on land, in the villages of St. Lucia, and never once does the eye turn out to sea, unless it be in the simile of a homeward-turning boat in the last section:

> After all that,
> Your faith like a canoe at evening coming in,
> Like a relative who is tired of America,
> Like a woman coming back to your house.

The movement is gentle and inward to an implied centre, not outward and obsessive. The person of the poet appears here and there in the sequence, but in passing; the focus is on a place and a people who turn in on their own world. Of the five sections, the third is not Walcott's own at all but what he describes as a "Saint Lucian *conte*, or narrative Creole song, heard on the back of an open truck travelling to Vieuxfort some years ago". It appears, transcribed by Walcott, and with his English rendition on the facing page. This placing of a folk-poem at the centre of the sequence might be seen as the ultimate movement away from the poetry of the self.

The second section has already moved half-way towards French Creole in that a great many Creole words resound within what is still an English poem:

> Pomme arac
> otaheite apple,
> pomme cythere,
> pomme granate,
> moubain,

z'ananas
the pineapple's
Aztec helmet,
pomme,
I have forgotten
what pomme for
the Irish potato,
cerise,
the cherry,
z'aman
sea-almonds
by the crisp sea-bursts,
au bord de la 'ouvière.
Come back to me
my language.

To define fully the sense in which French Creole might be called
Walcott's language would require a sociolinguistic account of the
island which is beyond my powers. But it was clearly one of the
languages of his background, and in his perception here, it is the most
rooted of those languages, the language of the country-people and
fishermen, the language that stresses the Saint Lucian context and the
St Lucian continuity:

generations going,
generations gone,
moi, c'est gens Sainte Lucie.
C'est la moi sorti;
is there that I born.

The fifth and final section is dedicated to the altarpiece of the Roseau
Valley Church, painted by Walcott's friend from school days,
Dunstan St Omer, the Gregorias of *Another Life*. It is a piece of social
art set at the heart of a community:

The chapel as the pivot of this valley
round which whatever is rooted loosely turns –
men, women, ditches, the revolving fields
of bananas, the secondary roads –
draws all to it, to the alter
and the massive altarpiece,

and later:

It is signed with music.
It turns the whole island.
You have to imagine it empty on a Sunday afternoon
between adorations.

T.S. Eliot's *Four Quartets* echoes very strongly in 'Sainte Lucie' both
in terms of ideas and verbally. In St Omer's altarpiece, we are told:

Two earth-brown labourers
dance the botay in it, the drum sounds under
the earth, the heavy foot.

The verbal echoes of section one of 'East Coker' are immediately
heard – the drum, the feet, "under the earth"; but more than that, the
purpose is the same: to emphasise a continuity in a particular place
which, unless it be redeemed from outside, can only be the continuity
of an endless cycle of life and death. Walcott, of course, does not offer
Eliot's doctrinal consolations but the feeling in his church is close to
that in Eliot's 'Little Gidding'. The place exists not only in relation to
other places, but in relation to moments in past time, and to something
outside time:

so that, from time to time, on Sundays

between adorations, one might see,
if one were there, and not there,
looking in at the windows

the real faces of angels.

The similarities of tone are not enough to make of Walcott a
religious poet but they are enough to offer a critique of that other
Walcott, the Romantic poet. He was, we should remember, brought
up in a kind of Christianity very different from the popular
Catholicism evoked in this poem. His mother was the head teacher of
the Methodist Infants School at Castries, and although Methodism is
not often explicitly mentioned in Walcott's work, it is negatively
acknowledged in references to guilt or loss of faith, and it surfaces
constantly in Biblical imagery.

One poem that reflects on his early religion is 'Crusoe's Island' (*The
Castaway*):

I am borne by the bell
Backward to boyhood
To the grey wood
Spire, harvest and marigold,
To those whom a cruel
Just God could gather
To his blue breast, His beard
A folding cloud,
As he gathered my father.
Irresolute and proud,
I can never go back.

It is not difficult to see how such a faith would be in increasing tension with the secular and humanistic riches of literature and art as encountered in Walcott's "sound colonial education" and through his association with the painter Harold Simmons. But in this same relatively early poem Walcott already recognizes the limitations of Romantic art and its transposed religious terminology:

That fabled, occupational
Compassion, supposedly inherited with the gift
Of poetry had fed
With a rat's thrift on faith . . .

'Crusoe's Island' concludes:

And nothing I can learn
From art or loneliness
Can bless them as the bell's
Transfiguring tongue can bless.

The bell resounds through the first section of 'Sainte Lucie'. It seems to stand for some meaning that eludes Walcott but it is also a communal sound that dignifies the collective life in one place. And in his appreciation of St Omer's painted altarpiece Walcott is able to unite his persisting religious sensibility with his well-developed aesthetic sense in a way that Methodism did not allow. Like the altarpiece, Walcott's 'Sainte Lucie' is a work of art dedicated to something beyond self-exploration and self-expression.

NOTES

1.   This reading is more obvious in the other published variants of this poem which are

conveniently collected at the front of *Derek Walcott: a bibliography of published poems 1944–1979* by Irma E. Goldstraw, University of the West Indies, St Augustine, Trindad, 1979.

2.   From Waldo Williams, 'Preseli', in *Dail Pren*, Aberystwyth, 1967. The translation here is my own.

3.   Walcott, 'What the Twilight Says', in *Dream on Monkey Mountain and Other Plays*, New York, 1970.

Mervyn Morris

The Fortunate Traveller

The Fortunate Traveller

Walcott's title alludes to Thomas Nashe's *The Unfortunate Traveller* (1594). Fortunate? Not if condemned to exile, "a colonial upstart at the end of empire,/ a single, circling, homeless satellite."[1] Not "when life has turned into exile,/ and nothing consoles, not books, work, music, or a woman"(14). "There is no sea as restless as my mind"(95). But that may be a positive. There may be others too. Such as – in spite of treacheries, of "broken promises/ that helped make this Republic what it is"(3) – the possibility of "falling in love with America" and trying "to learn her language"(6). The collection is often concerned with the bitter- sweet pleasures of exile, whether literal or metaphoric.

The book is divided into sections: 'North', 'South', 'North'. On the face of it, North represents industrialized, 'first world' countries (such as the United States); South, some poorer places (such as the Caribbean). The North has the power to dominate: "Now, the hot core is Washington,/ where once it was Whitehall"(28). North implies the metropole, distinct from (southern) outposts of the empire. Walcott sets up a North/South dialogue of sorts. But, though the persona will sometimes contrast 'North and South', in important senses he himself is both: "And I, whose ancestors were slave and Roman,/ have seen both sides of the imperial foam"(67). The dialectic is largely internal. Mixed in his racial and cultural heritage, Walcott finds himself both sides of each division. The persona tries the idiom of another country; poems in Caribbean settings turn on European literature, "imperial fiction"(93), classical mythology; Ovid materializes in Trinidad; a calypsonian up from hell – "Hell is a city much like Port of Spain"(57) – integrates local and European satirists; another Caribbean figure invokes and undercuts the myth of the Minotaur, "the old Greek bull"(36). One persona, free from history for a moment, rejoices: "I held air without language in my hands./ My head was scoured of other people's monsters"(36); another, saying he is "tired of words " – and "literature is an old couch stuffed with fleas,/ of culture stuffed in the taxidermist's hides"(13) – has also, at the end of empire, noted the paradox, the enigma of survival: "It's good that everything's gone, except their language,/ which is everything"(11).

Walcott has often been praised for his handling of the English language. There is that early accolade from Robert Graves: "Derek Walcott handles English with a closer understanding of its inner magic than most (if not any) of his English-born contemporaries".[2] There is Seamus Heaney, similarly, reviewing *The Star-apple Kingdom*: "Walcott possesses English more deeply and sonorously than most of the English themselves."[3] Joseph Brodsky, more emphatically, writes: "He is the man by whom the English language lives."[4] Denis Donoghue – reviewing *The Fortunate Traveller* – finds some "gorgeous poems" but he also records his impression that Walcott's standard English style is "dangerously high for nearly every purpose except that of Jacobean tragedy".[5] After reporting this and other responses, James Atlas testifies of an experience I take to be significant:

> The paradox of a colonial identity is that it both liberates and oppresses, offering freedom from a dominating tradition, yet robbing the poet of any natural claim on the language. It is a paradox that has haunted Walcott from the beginning, and that gives his work its quality of artifice, its tension between self-conscious rhetoric and a high style oblivious of the prevailing conviction among poets and readers that eloquence is no longer possible.
>
> Still, to hear him read is to be persuaded that Walcott has managed to forge an authentic voice out of this dilemma. Reciting 'The Star-apple Kingdom' to an attentive audience in a Fifth Avenue apartment, he intoned the long, densely eloquent lines in a melodic vibrato that had nothing theatrical about it. The poem's rhetorical intensity seemed utterly natural, speech harnessed to metre. One could hear the syncopated rhythms of calypso and the sonorous cadences of Walcott's English masters in every line.[6]

It can be useful to have heard the poet's and other Caribbean voices. To know, or to have lived in, some of his socio-cultural contexts may also help. For the voices of the poet express a vision grounded in personal history. Walcott, "the mulatto of style",[7] reminds us often of his dual or multiple heritage. Shabine, in a famous passage (from 'The Schooner *Flight*') identifies himself:

I'm just a red nigger who love the sea,
I had a sound colonial education,
I have Dutch, nigger, and English in me,
and either I'm nobody, or I'm a nation . . . [8]

Walcott often seeks to make us actively aware of the varying cultural elements he pulls together, or of the transfiguring lens of history, literature or myth through which he views the present. In 'Archipelagoes' (from 'Map of the New World') and 'Greece' – which are, I take it, set in the Caribbean – the landscapes are suffused with classical memories. The Greek myth of 'Europa' gets a Caribbean version. There are 'Roman Outposts' in Trinidad. In spite of the Spanish overlay, 'The Liberator' takes place in Trinidad. His Spoiler, who rhymes "scene" with "Caribbean", "suit" with "truth", and "waterproof" with "truth", will quote not only lines that he composed but also lines from Rochester; will allude to Matthew Arnold; will mention Martial, Juvenal, Pope, Dryden, Swift, Byron, as well as Raymond Quevedo, a famous calypsonian, 'Atilla the Hun'.

Walcott frequently echoes other poets. But he has declared himself against what he has called "provincial concepts of imitation and originality. Fear of imitation obsesses minor poets."[9] Some readers, nevertheless, have been bothered by the sounds of other voices. As Helen Vendler puts it: "Hart Crane, Dylan Thomas, Pound, Eliot, and Auden followed Yeats in Walcott's ventriloquism. It seemed that his learnedness might be the death of him, especially since he so prized it." Of *The Fortunate Traveller* she remarks:

> He is still, even as a fully developed writer, peculiarly at the mercy of influence, this time the influence of Robert Lowell, as in the poem 'Old New England' . . . This represents Walcott's new apprenticeship to the American vernacular, as he lyrically describes it:
>
> > I must put the cold small pebbles from the spring
> > upon my tongue to write the language
> > to talk like birch or aspen confidently.
>
> But no one can take on a new idiom overnight, and Walcott's pentameters stubbornly retain their British cadences. It is American words, and not yet American rhythms, that find their way unevenly into these new poems. They ruin some lines and enliven others. Since the only point of using colloquialisms is to have them sound colloquial, Walcott loses momentum when his Americanisms ring ill on the ear.[10]

It is not true, however, that "the only point of using colloquialisms is to have them sound colloquial". The point may be – here, surely, is – to dramatize the fascination with new sounds, while also registering the very different voice of the persona. The 'British' sounds are essential to the poem's meaning. (Walcott has elsewhere hinted American voices through "British cadences"; as in, for example, the word "feral" in 'The Gulf' that also works as one pronunciation of "federal"; of in 'Blues', in which the British Caribbean voice edges towards American talk: "I'm coming on too strong? You figure/ right. They beat his yellow nigger/ black and blue.")[11]

At the end of 'The Man Who Loved Islands', the persona, talking about the need for action in a movie, declares: "things must get rough/ pretty damn fast, or else you lose them, pally . . . "(39). Helen Vendler comments: "The 'pally' for 'pal' is a painful lapse, and one feels no better about it when one sees that it is there to rhyme with 'alley' five lines earlier. No rhyme is worth destroying the illusion of plausible voice".[12] Indeed. (Though "pally" – which also rhymes with "Charlotte Amalie" – seems so egregiously inept it probably enshrines a local joke.) But I do not hear in Vendler's other instances "mismanagement of tone". She writes:

> Here is a monologue by a person planning a movie, impatient of the suggestion that there be any lyric interludes in it, such as shots of the sea:
>
> >   the plot
> > . . . has to get the hero off somewhere
> > else, 'cause there's no kick in contemplation
> > of silvery light . . .
>
> The person who would say "'cause there's no kick in" something or other would not say "contemplation of silvery light"– the voice goes false whether you read backward or forward.[13]

For the plausible voice of the poem is a voice that is mocking another voice. The rather literary voice, of the writer-figure, is sneering at the more colloquial voice it parodies in phrases such as "'cause there's no kick in", "would draw them with", "Coburn looks great with or without a hat", "this/ could be a movie", "I mean things are moving", "that lyric stuff/ goes with the credits", "I can see it, but things must get rough/ pretty damn fast", "or, tell you what". The controlling voice is hankering for "a hint of the Homeric, a little

poetry/ before the whole mess hits the bloody fan"(39). Rather than
"uncertainty in diction" what we have, essentially, is a plausible
monologue presenting the ironic drama of contrasted tones.

Sometimes it is difficult to locate the controlling voice. In 'The
Fortunate Traveller', for example. ("One flies first-class, one is so
fortunate". "I thought, who cares how many million starve?" "I was
rehearsing the ecstacies of starvation/ for what I had to do." ""You are
so fortunate, you get to see the world –'/ Indeed, indeed, sirs, I have
seen the world.") Is there a single "I" in Section 1? What is the
relation between the shifting "I" of Section 1 and the "I" of the other
sections? "A brilliant scary Third World political cartoon of The
Man", writes Calvin Bedient, "the poem perhaps errs in endowing
the speaker – that beetle-like criminal – with the poet's own blazing
conscience: a poetic economy that falsifies".[14] Perhaps. In another
reading, however, the poem centres on the poet's blazing conscience;
but the poet, more publican than pharisee, sees himself as part of the
problem; the oppressors as well as the victims of Section 1 have been
(as the opening lines of Section 2 suggest) "phantoms" of the
imagination: where they most truly live is in the poet's mind.

> Now I have come to where the phantoms live,
> I have no fear of phantoms, but of the real.

The poet-persona stands accused of privileged indifference. "Like
lice, like lice, the hungry of this earth/ swarm to the tree of life." But
"those who starve",

> remain
> compassionate fodder for the travel book,
> its paragraphs like windows from a train,
> for everywhere that earth shows its rib cage
> and the moon goggles with the eyes of children,
> we turn away to read.

By introducing a poet to amplify the charge, the poet-persona hints
his own complicity in artful distancing, and in the dubious priorities
of the literary. Rimbaud, he tells us, "knew that we cared less for one
human face/ than for the scrolls in Alexandria's ashes". In Section 4
the persona talks like a guilty man ("They've found out my
sanctuary"); and the visitors who arrived while he was out sound
menacing. In spite of his satirical vignettes of chicanery and

indifference, the poet-persona takes his place with the materially privileged, threatened at the end in apocalyptic imagery:

> the weevil will make a sahara of Kansas,
> the ant shall eat Russia.
> Their soft teeth shall make, *and not have charity*,
> the harvest's desolation,
> and the brown globe crack like a begging bowl,
> and though you fire oceans of surplus grain,
> *and have not charity*,
>
> still, through thin stalks,
> the smoking stubble, stalks
> grasshopper: third horseman,
> the leather-helmed locust.

Corruption, injustice, hatred, fear, oppression are recurrent concerns in *The Fortunate Traveller*. Victims include American Indians, black people, Jews and Third World people. Conflict and violence seem to be endemic. "The winter branches are mined with buds,/ the fields of March will detonate the crocus".[15] Nature explodes in 'Hurucan', a relentless force tracked carefully through stages: the build-up of lightning, the climactic fury ("You scream like a man whose wife is dead,/ like god who has lost his race,/ you yank the electric wires with wet hands"), the calm survey of damage after the storm. Walcott, as always, shows himself a sensitive poet of landscape; and his rendering of the landscape is often given an historical dimension, as in the USA poems of Section 1; as in such poems as 'Beachhead', 'Roman Outposts', 'The Liberator'; as in the remarkable 'Wales':

> Those white flecks cropping the ridges of Snowdon
> will thicken their fleece and come wintering down
> through the gap between alliterative hills,
> through the caesura that let in the Legions,
> past the dark disfigured mouths of the chapels,
> till a white silence comes to green-throated Wales.

History helps define, and often haunts, the persona in the poems of exile; in 'North and South', for example, the black persona, hearing a Southern accent, reacts "with the paranoid anxiety of the victim" and "child of the Diaspora", partly white, reflects on a possible connection with the Jews. Some of the history is personal: there is the "exile of divorce"(65), there is the thought of death, "an exile farther than any country"(12). 'Early Pompeian', harrowing in its emotional force, confronts a child born dead ("bent in the shape forever/ of a curled seed sailing the earth"), the mother ("On the black wings of your screams I watched vultures rise"), the father, the terrible grief ("Gloria, Perdita, I christen/ you in the shade, on the bench,/ with no hope of the resurrection"). 'Easter', which follows, is an intriguing fable of resurrection; a black dog, shadow of Christ, "crept between the wood/ and the flesh nailed to the wood", then it "slunk away"; then, after three days, having emerged from hiding, "it keeps nosing for His shape/ and it finds it again . . . ", though some of the images – the scarecrow, the yawning man – seem equivocal, less positive than "the white echo of a pigeon/ with its wings extended".

'The Season of Phantasmal Peace' offers, allegorically, a great, if only momentary, vision of universal love. "Then all the nations of birds lifted together/ the huge net of the shadows of this earth/ in multitudinous dialects, twittering tongues,/ stitching and crossing it". The poem celebrates an imagined moment of "Love,/ made seasonless", "one moment" when the privileged show, however briefly, "pity for the wingless ones/ below them who shared dark holes in windows and in houses". Calvin Bedient argues that "this precious fantasy . . . is effectively counter-political, distracting the reader from actual conditions".[15] An oddly literal-minded way to read a lyric poem.

A number of poems touch on or explore the role and situation of artists. 'Piano Practice' – insistently cross-cultural: New York seen looking like Paris, talk of "the old Laforguean ache", Vallejo dying, and "perhaps the *fin de siècle* isn't really finished,/ maybe there's a piano playing it somewhere", – ends with an epiphanic moment, of steel band music in Manhattan:

> Maybe the Seine outshines the East River,
> maybe, but near the Metropolitan
> a steel tenor pan
> dazzlingly practices something from old Vienna,
> the scales skittering like minnows across the sea.

In 'North and South', the persona, defensive, decoding signals of white fear, claims association with the music makers. 'Jean Rhys' describes the contract of a serious artist:

                    one night
        a child stares at the windless candle flame
        from the corner of a lion-footed couch
        at the erect white light,
        her right hand married to *Jane Eyre*,
        foreseeing that her own white wedding dress
        will be white paper.

In 'The Spoiler's Return' the artist, given scant respect, takes off
again, offended: "All you excuse me, Spoiler was in town;/ you pass
him straight, so now he gone back down". In 'The Hotel Normandie
Pool' "corruption, censorship, and arrogance/ make exile seem a
happier thought than home"; and the shade of Ovid discourses on the
benefits: though he missed at first what he had known so long,
eventually he "made reflections that, in many ways,/ were even
stronger than their origin". 'Port of Spain' suggests the tug of the
familiar – "I feed on its dust, its ordinariness" – and the persona
understands "Borges's blind love of Buenos Aires,/ how a man feels
the veins of a city swell in his hand".

There are variations, of course, in style and register. It is not
unusual for Walcott to take us in a single poem from seemingly casual
talk to heightened eloquence. As in 'American Muse': from "No
billboard model/ but a woman, gaunt,/ in a freckled print,/ some bony
aunt/ whose man broke down at the steel mill . . . " to the dreamer –

        who still believes in
        the apparition of wingless angels,
        like that one who stands on the verge
        of the hurtling turnpike
        thumbing a ride from the surge
        of ignorant traffic.

The ambiguity of "like that one" allows both the dreamer's respect
for the wingless angel and the more cynical spectator's placing of a
hitch-hiker. The hitch-hiker on the verge (of the highway, and of the
extraordinary) is set against the movement of the "hurtling" turnpike,
the rush of traffic suggested in the emphatic rhyme word "surge" and
the less insistent but similar vowel sound in "*hurt*ling *turn*pike".

Walcott's knows what he is doing. Listen, for example, to the
opening stanzas of 'A Sea Change' and hear how very differently the
first two stanzas move.

> Islands hissing in rain,
> light rain and governments falling.
> Follow, through cloud, again,
> the bittern's lonely calling.
>
> Can this be the right place?
> These islands of the blest,
> cheap package tours replaced
> by politics, rain, unrest?

The rocking rhythm lulls, though the phrase "and governments falling" warns that all may not be well. With the jolt of the question that opens stanza two, we begin to recognize more menace in the earlier stanza than had perhaps initially been apparent; the descriptive "hissing" and "cloud", for example, also evaluate.

In 'Europa' Walcott takes us through the metamorphic process of imagining. The approach of Zeus (the bull) is made particularly vivid.

> The surf, insatiably promiscuous,
> groans through the walls; I feel my mind
> whiten to moonlight, altering that form
> which daylight unambiguously designed,
> from a tree to a girl's body bent in foam;
> then, treading close, the black hump of a hill,
> its nostrils softly snorting, nearing the
> naked girl splashing her breasts with silver.

The poem is full of wordplay, much of it (appropriately) sexual *double entendre*: a dark cloud "coupling their shapes"; Europa teasing with "those flashes"; "human horniness" that helps us see through "all that moonshine":

> Who ever saw her pale arms hook his horns,
> her thighs clamped tight in their deep-plunging ride,
> watched, in the hiss of the exhausted foam,
> her white flesh constellate to phosphorous
> as in salt darkness beast and woman come?
> Nothing is there . . .

Walcott is fond of wordplay, and is adept at it. Look, for example, in 'Port of Spain', at the throwaway brilliance of the off-rhyme "wolf": "The terror/ is local, at least. Like the magnolia's whorish whiff./ And the dog bark of the revolution crying wolf"(the dog bark of the revolution crying *woof*!). Of course there is plenty of wordplay in 'The Spoiler's Return'. "I decompose, but I composing still". Satan is "that Hot Boy". The most famous pun in the poem has the memorable awfulness of a good calypso joke: "I see these islands and I feel to bawl,/ 'area of darkness' with V.S. Nightfall". Part of the strategy of the poem – which Helen Vendler finds "unconvincing"[16] – is (as in 'The Schooner *Flight*') its modulation between creole and standard English. Listen, for example, to this passage:

> So crown and mitre me Bedbug the First –
> the gift of mockery with which I'm cursed
> is just a insect biting Fame behind,
> a vermin swimming in a glass of wine,
> that, dipped out with a finger, bound to bite
> its saving host, ungrateful parasite,
> whose sting, between the cleft arse and its seat,
> reminds Authority man is just meat,
> a moralist as mordant as the louse
> that the good husband brings from the whorehouse . . . '

The second and the ninth lines here are standard English, and iambic in the English tradition; the sixth line taken by itself, is standard too (and English in tone, with that punning allusion to the sacrament). But they are, I think, absorbed into the overall context, creole. Spoken by a reader who is at home both in creole and standard English, they are a subtle pleasure. By lingering at the end of the fifth line, for example, a performer might hint at what is obvious to the eye, the creole rhythm, "bound to bite".

Nowhere is Walcott's mastery more persuasively displayed than in the poem put at the end of the collection, a poem even Helen Vendler has approved.[17] Profoundly eloquent, it builds on repetition and on the expressive power of silences it contrives to make us hear. Line one, for example, is complete in itself; and the pause at the end of the line makes us feel the weight of the "huge net", two stressed syllables together near the beginning of the second line. There are expressive pauses at the end of the fourth line ("They lifted up . . . "), the seventh ("on a city sill – "), the eighth ("birds' cries", just before the word "soundless"); at the end of line nine there is a weighty pause ("until . . . "); there is a meaningful silence after line eleven ("phantasmal light" establishing itself). In the second stanza there are

significant silences after "could not hear", immediately before "it was
the light" and after it; after "no-one hearing knew", "high concern",
"Love", "wingless ones", "soundless voices"; and of course after
"like the pause", and after "peace" –

> and this season lasted one moment, like the pause
> between dusk and darkness, between fury and peace,
> but, for such as our earth is now, it lasted long.

NOTES

1. Walcott, *The Fortunate Traveller*, London, 1982, p.11. Page references hereafter to *The Fortunate Traveller* appear as numbers in brackets; but when the context makes it clear which poem is quoted, no page reference is given.
2. Quoted on the dust jacket of Walcott, *Selected Poems*, New York, 1964).
3. Seamus Heaney, *The Government of the Tongue*, London, 1988, p.26.
4. *The New York Times Book Review*, 10 November 1983, p.41.
5. *The New York Times Book Review*, 3 January 1982, p.5.
6. *The New York Times Magazine*, 23 May 1982, p.50.
7. Walcott, *Dream on Monkey Mountain and Other Plays*, New York, 1970, p.9.
8. Walcott, *The Star-apple Kingdom*, New York, 1979); London, 1980, p.4.
9. Orde Coombes *ed*, *Is Massa Day Dead?*, New York, 1974, p.25.
10. Vendler review, *The New York Review of Books*, 4 March 1982, p.23.
11. For 'The Gulf' and 'Blues' see Derek Walcott, *The Gulf*, London, 1969 or *The Gulf* New York, 1970, which are different collections.
12. Vendler, *op.cit.*, p.26.
13. *ibid.*, pp.23 - 26.
14. *Parnassus: Poetry in Review*, Fall/ Winter 1981, Vol.9 No.2, p.40.
15. *ibid.*
16. Vendler, *op.cit.*, p.26.
17. *ibid.*, pp.26–27.

Louis James

Midsummer

Midsummer

These poems I heaved aren't linked to any tradition
like a mossed cairn; each goes down like a stone
to the seabed, settling, but let them, with luck, lie
where stones are deep, in the sea's memory.
　　　　Midsummer, L

Midsummer marks a phase of stasis, of reflection in Walcott's poetry. If
Another Life is Walcott's exploration, "a landscape locked in amber",
of childhood experience, this collection of fifty poems, written as
Walcott entered his own fifties, reflects the freedom won by coming to
terms with the burden of his history. It was largely written in the
summer of 1983, while on holiday in Trinidad with his two daughters,
Elizabeth and Anna. The collection is dedicated to them, and
although they appear only briefly, their presence is implicit, as we
shall see, in the sense of cycle and rhythm within the sequence.

　　The collection has within it a stillness, a slow circling of inquiry. In
its form as a reflective diary, it can be compared to Tennyson's *In
Memoriam*. Where Tennyson explored death and afterlife, Walcott
considers nearly four decades struggling to relate life to art, to
reconcile his divided heritage. The first impression may be that of
weariness, a loss of poetic energy. At moments Walcott himself
appears to be confirming this. "The imagination no longer goes as far
as the horizon" (XV). After nearly forty years of struggling with
words, he still faces the irreducible burden of giving expression to his
intuitions: "The lit stage is empty, the set prepared, and I cannot find
the key to let them out" (XIII). Trawling the depths of memory and
imagination, there remains the fear of failure: "What if the lines I cast
bulge into a book/ that has caught nothing?" (XXIV).

　　Yet the poet is expressing not weariness, but the pain of endurance.
"Oh Christ, my craft, and the long time it is taking!" (XIII), "What

work lies ahead of us, what sunlight for generations!" (XVII). A closer reading reveals that within the short poems themselves – approximating to sonnet form without the constriction of exact form – Walcott is moving continually through successive moods and attitudes, from anger to tranquillity, from despair to acceptance. The starting point for this journey is the correlation between subject, object, and poetic form. In his earlier poetry, Walcott had not distinguished between meaning and language, seeing poetry as the flash of lightning that encompasses all in one brilliant stroke. "More skillful now, I'm more dissatisfied" (IX). He now knows the multiplicity of experience, the gap that lies between subjective and objective reality. "They never align, nature and your/ own nature" (IX). It is not impatient striving, but the patience of experience that finds the unexpected inspiration:

> Midsummer bursts
> out of its body, and its poems come unwarranted
> as when, hearing what sounds like rain, we startle a place
> where a waterfall crashes down rocks. Abounding grace!
>   (VIII)

The first section of the book explores the returning to Trinidad from the United States. Returning, even familiar experience draws the poet into a tissue of associations and memories, a complex of subtexts. So, in the second poem, Port of Spain is seen in relation to midsummer in Rome, where each detail is instinctive with the classical past: "That old woman in black . . . her home is Rome, its history is her house". Caesar's life gutters in her candle, and in her stone kitchen, "under the domes of onions,/ she slices a light, as thick as cheese, into epochs". But Port of Spain has a different history, different textures of reality. Walcott faces his reflection in a Port of Spain mirror and tries to recover his childhood experience of the Caribbean, but "I cannot connect these lines with the lines in my face" (III). He remembers associating the Trinidad mornings with Piero della Francesca's 'Resurrection', and the canefields were touched with Traherne's vision of "orient and immortal wheat" (III).

A shift in mood transforms the innocent perspective into a "Spanish port, piratical in diverseness . . . / You can watch it become more African hourly – crusted roofs, hot as skillets/ peppered with cries . . . ", only lacking a paddle-steamer and Mr Kurtz to be Conrad's Congo. But the vision is unstable and contradictory. Across from the wild harbour the plate glass windows of the Holiday Inn incongruously reflect a Western world. "The world had no time to change/ to a doorman's braid from the loincloths of Africa" (IV). His feelings are a shifting weave, too, of associations of dusty summers in New York where hucksters with cardboard luggage "have made the Big Apple a mango" (V), and of the hidden tensions of Borges' Buenos Aires (VI). Walcott contemplates his Caribbean childhood not, as in *Another Life*, through the convex lense of childhood association, but the concave mirror of maturity: "this is the lot of all wanderers . . . however far you have travelled, your/ steps make more holes and the mesh is multiplied" (VII).

Yet Walcott's awareness is undercut by his sense of the limitations of self-conscious reflection. Human nature is active, instinctive, irrational, "To betray philosophy is the gentle treason/ of poets" (XII). He wishes to penetrate the multiplying web to the reality beneath it. "Today I respect structure, the antithesis of conceit,/ the overworked mulch of my paintings, my bad plots!" (XIII). How can he return to the simplicity he knew as a child? "I believe that it is still possible, the happiness/ of truth, and the young poet who stands in the mirror/ smiles with a nod" (XIII).

In the next eleven poems (XIV to XXV) Walcott attempts a contemplative return to his remembered singleness of the artist's vision. With Gregorias he tells us in *Another Life* he was then "drunk" on the painter's vision,

> on Van Gogh's shadow rippling on the cornfield
> on Cesanne's boots grinding the stones of Aix
> to shales of slate, ochre and Vigie blue
> On Gaugin's hand shaking the gin-coloured dew
> from the umbrella yams,
> garrulous, all day, sun-struck.

The older Walcott remembers the unanswerable objectivity of paint, "the lemon-rind light in Vermeer", "the breadfruit's foliage, rust-edged like van Ruysdael" (XVII). Once he brushed a drop of dew from a print of a Flemish still life, believing it to be real. Is this the key to art? A hundred years earlier the Impressionists had created a reality that still outlasts the horrors of "the coiled soldiers piled up on the Somme, and Verdun. And the dead/ less real than a spray burst of chrysanthemums" (XVIII), though an identical carmine paints both life and slaughter.

But experience cannot be easy with the eye of innocence. As Watteau undercuts the picturesque with priapic sexuality, Walcott's knowledge will not let him rest with Gaugin's tropical pastoralism – "I have never pretended that summer was paradise,/ or that these virgins were virginal". He tells "the Evangelists paradise smells of sulphur" (XIX, ii). Rather than objective peace, observation brings the adult's deepening despair at a world torn by war, famine, and the cruelty of man to man. The verse rises to a 'midsummer' of intensity. In religious wars, "children lie torn on rubble for a noun" (XXII); the racial division of empire "is ending/ in the alleys of Brixton, burning like Turner's ships" (XXV). Where did chaos begin? "What broke the green lianas' ropes?" Was it caused by the very civilisation and art in which Walcott seeks to find innocence? "Was evil brought to this place/ with language?" (XXIV).

Or is art the focus for human suffering, and is the artist the sacrificial bearer of the world's pain? "The sun has fired my face to terra-cotta . . . My palms have been sliced by the twine/ of the craft I have pulled at for more than forty years" and "the lines I love have all their knots left in" (XXV). "I wait. Chairs sweat. Paper crumples the floor" (XXV). But after the pain of vision comes a release into calm. The violence of poems XIX to XXV is succeeded by a tranquil sequence as the first section draws to its close. The fevered vision stills to receptivity. He is aware that his experience of the United States has given him a certain stability: "Certain things here are quietly American . . . My own corpuscles/ are changing fast" (XXVII).

Walcott watches his daughters "Lizzie· and Anna/ lie idling on different rafts, their shadows under them". Their presence gives him a sense of stability, of rooting in the moment: "The frame of human happiness is time" (XXVIII). But the return to himself brings self-doubt as to his art. Has his poetry discovered anything? Has "the spool of days that midsummer's reel rewinds" come "bobbling back with its question, its empty hook?" (XXIX).

Part II circles again over his experience, analysing and questioning. If Part I began with arrival in Trinidad, "the jet bores like a silverfish through volumes of cloud" (I), Part II begins with the smells and colour-tones of Boston, "Gold dung and urinous straw from the horse garages/ click-clop of hooves sparking cold cobblestone . . . I return to the city of my exile down Storrow Drive" (XXX). And if in Part I Walcott examines his experience from the viewpoint of his 'Caribbean' self, in the second half he starts from his American consciousness. Almost the same phrase is repeated in both halves:

"summer is the same/ everywhere" (VIII); "I know midsummer is the same thing everywhere" (XXXIV). But both the scenes and the associations through which summer is filtered are different: Eastern America arouses memories of Henry James (XXX), Wales (XXXV), England (XXXVI) and Xenophon (XXXIV). This awareness leads him back to the question raised earlier in XIII: how to relate poetic form to experience. Walcott had turned to the classics, "but palms require translation . . . They didn't know your language . . . There was too much poetry. It was the wrong age" (XXXVIII).

And so Walcott explores the sensibility of the 1980s. Rejecting his insight of poem XXV "that death itself is only another surface/ like the canvas", he sees the contemporary world conditioned by an awareness of two World Wars and the Cold War: "The camps hold their distance – brown, chestnut and grey smoke that coils like barbed wire./ The profit in guilt continues" (XLI). The idyllic pastoral of Nordic children intimates "the chimneys of Dachau, of Auschwitz, of Sachsenhausen" (XLI). Chicago's avenues are "as white as Poland" (XLII). Part I examined the Caribbean experience against the vision of Gaugin and Watteau; here, in the eight poems which make up 'Tropic Zone' (XLIII) he introduces his experiences of Cuba as part of the West Indies changed radically by its contact with Communism, "Imagine, where sand is now, the crawling lava/ of military concrete" (VII). The island is different, the people are different: "The days feel longer, people resemble their cars/ that are as grey as their uniforms" (VII).

Yet the experience of a militarised Cuba paradoxically brings him back to a sense that history here does not change. "Their revolution is that things come in circles./ The socialists do not appreciate that" (V). One colonial tyranny has usurped another. At its centre midsummer heat brings "a sacramental stasis", the sun brings a stillness, a sleep, "as afternoon removes those window bars/ that striped your sleep like a kitten's, or a prisoner's" (VIII).

The concluding sections are dominated by the two themes: language and all it contains in the way of history, memory and culture, and the objective gift of the sun. He cannot escape memory, "I drag, as on a chain behind me, laterite landscapes . . . I pull the voices/ of children behind me that die with the first star . . . " (XLIV). Words lock him into the past and the crises of history. His love of English literature commits him to a cultural perspective, to Shakespeare, to the British troops in Flanders. "No language is neutral" (LII). Whatever his mature knowledge, his education consigns his Syrian neighbour to images of the Old Testament – seventy thousand Assyrians, all of them living next door "muttering a language whose sound/ had winged lions in it, and birds cut into a wall" (LIII).

But the sun is unconditional. It overleaps place, time, even seasons. When it is still February in Columbus Ohio, the sun's heat brings spring: "The law/ that the light has broken winks from windows" (XLVI). Light is more powerful than Prospero to change the injustices of an island world: "Go, light, make weightless the burden of our thought,/ let our misfortune have no need for magic,/ be untranslatable in verse or prose" (XLVIII). The juxtaposition is there in an earlier poem. In 'Crusoe's Island' the poet cries "My skill/ is not enough", and compares his isolation in words to the blessing of the church bell and the sun:

> At dusk, when they return
> For vespers, every dress
> Touched by the sun will burn
> A seraph's, an angel's . . .

Yet there is a difference in *Midsummer*: not anguish but creative acceptance. Walcott sees his daughters, and remembers his father Warwick, who, guiding, lived in Walcott's hand as his children live in his: "Now, when I rewrite a line . . . my daughters' hands move in mine" (L). Words have become linked to love, "Ah, bread of life, that only love can leaven." Butterflies rise from the rotting logs of decay and betrayal, "stuttering 'yes' to the resurrection; 'yes, yes is our answer' " (LIV). To misappropriate lines from 'Ruins of a Great House':

> All in compassion ends
> So differently from what the heart arranged . . .

Edward Baugh

The Arkansas Testament

The Arkansas Testament

In the introduction to his edition of Walcott's *Selected Poetry*, Wayne Brown claims that "the real biography of a writer is to be found in the evolution of his style."[1] Later, Joseph Brodsky, also writing on Walcott, says much the same thing: "A poet's real biography lies in his twists and turns of language, in his metres, rhymes and metaphors."[2] These statements raise questions. For one thing, they seem to claim for the writer a Romantic difference in kind from other men: his true life is his poetry.

They also tease us into conjecture as to what it may be about Walcott that prompts these two distinguished admirers of his work, themselves poets, to buttress their criticism of him by this kind of statement about writers in general. Might it be that they are concerned to protect Walcott from the all-too-easy biographical (in the usual sense) reading which his poetry seems to invite? Brown and Brodsky provide fuel for the ever-burning question of relating the poet's life to his work, and of how best to delineate that relationship.

Whatever may be our responses to these questions, Brown and Brodsky come to mind when we begin to read *The Arkansas Testament* and are struck by the fact that the first seven poems are in quatrains rhyming *abab*. More than half of the poems in the book use quatrains, and almost all of those use the *abab* rhyme scheme. Most, too, exploit the short line, almost always trimetre.

This dominance of the quatrain is all the more noticeable when we come to *The Arkansas Testament* from its predecessor, *Midsummer*, a sequence of what, for want of a better label, one might call 'extended sonnets', with their long lines (variously pentameter and alexandrine for the most part) and irregular rhyming. Immediately preceding *Midsummer*, *The Fortunate Traveller* includes only two poems in quatrains similar to those of *The Arkansas Testament*, the main

movement of which was between long lines and more or less free
verse – a mainstream Walcottian mode associated with a certain richly
textured reflectiveness in the play of metaphorical associations. This is
the mode variously deployed in *The Arkansas Testament* in poems
such as 'The Whelk Gatherers', 'The Light of the World', 'Roman
Peace' and 'A Propertius Quartet'.

And so we could rehearse backwards the story of Walcott's prosodic
journey or adventure, volume by volume, noticing how each has its
distinctive formal/stylistic signature. But the story is not so much one
of evolution or 'progress' as of a continuous acting out of a dialectic of
style and form – plain speaking against oblique and densely textured
utterance, free verse against formal, traditional metrics, informality
against oratorical eloquence.

It is fitting that in *The Arkansas Testament* one of the poems which
exploits the short-line quatrain (in two of its three movements) is the
Audenesque 'Eulogy to W.H. Auden', in which Walcott, addressing
Auden, says:

> but you, who left each feast at nine,
> knew war, like free verse, is a sign
> of awful manners.[3]

Noting immediately that some of Walcott's best poems are in free
verse, one is aware of the dialectic of form in forming these lines. The
patrician colloquialism of 'awful' adds to the tone of relaxed formality
which typifies the manipulation of the quatrain in poems like this – the
low-keyed but well-mannered diction and idiom working against the
strictures and regularity of the stanza-pattern.

Walcott's sustained engagement with the quatrain in *The Arkansas
Testament* is an expression of his insistence on the notion of poetry as
discipline, a craft which one has to learn, and work at, and 'get right'.
He never sees himself as too old to go to school to "the old masters",
and he is ever striving "For more care in the craft of verse".[4]

> If my craft is blest;
> if this hand is as
> accurate, as honest
> as their carpenter's
>
> every frame, intent
> on its angles, would

> echo this settlement
> of unpainted wood.[5]

The poet's stanzas, then, must reflect accurately the simple, "unpainted" lives of the country folk of 'Cul de Sac Valley', and any skilled country carpenter is the emblem of the poet's ideal of craftsmanship.

Walcott handles the quatrain with remarkable flexibility. So, picking up the "manners" of the 'Eulogy to W.H. Auden', the form lends itself easily to the playful, sophisticated ironies of 'French Colonial. "*Vers de Société*"'.

> Maurois, or Mauriac – but not Malraux,
> the morose Marxist, prophet of *Man's Fate* –
> in something I read many years ago
> that stuck, without an accurate memory of the date,
>
> compared the symmetry of a work of art
> to an hourglass. The French are very good at these
> sort of thing; every other frog is a Descartes:
> *Cogito ergo*, that precise *bêtise*.[6]

The grammatically incorrect "these" is no doubt part of the sophisticated play of wit, mimicking a French pronunciation of 'this'.

Again, we may compare the emphatic beat and end-stopping of the following stanza:

> Then, far as that crackling noise
> of a boyhood climbing the wind,
> the kites of breadfruit leaves rise
> from the dry yard of my mind . . . [7]

with the more muted, varied stress pattern and meandering, cumulative effect of the opening sentence of 'Roseau Valley', which runs on over almost four stanzas.

But the craft of quatrain or any other verse form does not exercise itself on nothing. The quality of the poet's techniques must be matched by the quality of his ideas. *The Arkansas Testament* confirms the extent to which Walcott's themes and ideas have become preoccupation, how much he has set his stamp on them, how often he returns to them, usually to re-work them with arresting differences.

The division of *The Arkansas Testament* into two sections, 'Here' and 'Elsewhere', is a case in point. 'Here' denotes St. Lucia, the

Caribbean, home, origins, the heart's anchor. 'Elsewhere' is all the foreign landscapes, physical, literary, cultural and social, which the questioning heart attempts. Crudely expressed, it is a division between poems about the Caribbean and poems about other places. Virtually all of his collections could be so divided. *Sea Grapes*, as one of the clearer examples, moves, broadly speaking, from the Caribbean outwards, mainly to the USA, and back to the Caribbean. There is a similar 'North', 'South', 'North' arrangement of *The Fortunate Traveller*.

To make the division between 'Here' and 'Elsewhere' explicit is a convenient way of helping the reader through *The Arkansas Testament* by imposing a kind of unity and shape on the collection. It has a further function indicating another dialectic which informs Walcott's poetry, that of cultural and social identity, especially where it relates to geography: the dialect of self and other in the context of a sense of place.

In the reality of the poems, the relationship between 'here' and 'elsewhere' is more complex than the simple opposition of the two terms would suggest. Something of this complexity is evident in a serendipitous error in the blurb on the jacket of the U.S. edition of the book, which tells the reader that the collection "is divided into two parts – 'There', verse evoking the poet's native Caribbean, and 'Elsewhere'". In a certain sense, 'here' is always 'there'. The very action of defining it distances it. Besides, with Walcott 'here' has become increasingly a place to which one *returns*, a place one has to re-claim repeatedly in an effort made more and more precarious and compulsive as the gulf of memory widens.

On the other hand, 'elsewhere' always takes its meaning from the point of view of 'here'. In each of the polarities the other is subsumed. Some of the poems could with equal justification have been placed in either section, and in many the active engagement of 'here' with 'elsewhere' is an informing principle. The subject takes his being not only from his locatedness 'here', but also from his necessary involvement with 'elsewhere'.

So, 'Storm Figure' and 'Marina Tsvetaeva' are included in 'Here', the 'voice' of each being located in a Caribbean beach house in hurricane season. However, in both the poet's imagination is fired by literary presences from 'elsewhere' – Thomas Hardy and his fictional heroines in the former, and, in the latter, the Russian poet from whom the poem takes its name. On the other hand, 'Eulogy to W.H. Auden' is understandably placed 'Elsewhere', Walcott speaking on foreign ground in praise of a foreign poetic tradition . But his connection with that tradition, a connection going back to his beginnings on his own home ground, is made explicit:

> Once, past a wooden vestry
> down still colonial streets,
> the hoisted chords of Wesley
> were strong as miners' throats;
>
> in treachery and in union,
> despite your Empire's wrong,
> I made my first communion
> there, with the English tongue.
>
> It was such dispossession
> that made possession joy,
> when, strict as Psalm or Lesson,
> I learnt your poetry.[8]

We may observe, in passing, how at this point the quatrain helps to evoke the Wesleyan hymn-singing. Many a hymn has been written in exactly this metre.

So there is an inter-facing of 'Here' and 'Elsewhere'. They are both necessary states and reference points of the one mind working to locate itself. It is a mind which cherishes its rootedness in a particular small corner of earth, but which at the same time insists upon its free passage through the world. On the one hand, the poet will be happy to identify himself by the street vendor's exclamation that he (revisiting his native land at age 50) "love[s] home harder than youth!"[9] And yet, on the other hand, he will say that:

> To have loved one horizon is insularity,
> it blindfolds vision, it narrows experience.[10]

The imagination *will* travel: "I remember the cities I have never seen / exactly." The true country of the poet is neither 'Here' nor 'There' nor 'Elsewhere', but the imagination, and Shabine, the sailor-poet of 'The Schooner, *Flight*' spoke more truly and less regretfully than one may otherwise have thought, when he said, "I had no nation now but the imagination".[11]

Curiously enough, both 'Here' and 'Elsewhere' are negotiated from the point of view of the transient. In the accounts of both 'countries', we are likely to find the persona *travelling through*, working out of a hotel room (sometimes a beach house) which is at one and the same time an emblem of his precarious, 'floating' condition and a protection or refuge, a mask of anonymity.

In the very first poem, 'The Lighthouse', the poet wanders through Castries at night, reliving "old times" in the painful awareness of how much he has grown away from that past. This anguish is typified by the awkward, hollow joviality of his meeting with a friend from schooldays, a brilliant actor who, never leaving home, was never able to fulfil his promise and is now a ghost of his former self. But the successful poet who grieves for him has, whether he knows it or not, also become a sort of ghost, a revenant. When they "split up on the dark street" (a resonant, widening metaphor), the poet returns "to the black promontory/ of Vigie," presumably to a hotel room, whose "air conditioner's/ freezing", excludes "the heat of home".[12]

A hotel room also claims the poet, symbolising again his sense of alienation, in another poem of return, the richly meditative if somewhat sentimental 'The Light of the World'. Having travelled from Gros-Ilet in a public "sixteen-seater transport",[13] and having fallen secretly "in love" with one of the "common people" who were his fellow passengers, he eventually has to come back down to earth when the transport drops him off at his hotel, whose name becomes ironic in the context of the poem:

> I wanted to be going home with her this evening.
> I wanted her to have the key to our small house
> by the beach at Gros-Ilet . . .
> but I came to my stop outside the Halcyon Hotel.
> The lounge would be full of transients like myself.[14]

Poems like 'The Light of the World' and 'The Lighthouse' extend a line of sadly ironic homecoming poems, beginning with chapter X of the first published version of 'Tales of the Islands', and including 'Return to D'Ennery, Rain', 'Homecoming: Anse La Raye', and the final chapter of *Another Life*[15] – poems which all reinforce the idea that "there are homecomings without home."

In Walcott's poetic view of his native ground there are two main tendencies. A tendency to idealise the poor, their simple peasant virtues, even while depicting the squalor and hardship of their lives, is accompanied by a tendency for his compassion (sometimes expressed as rage) to embalm them in a pathetic stasis. Grieving at his inability to do anything for them, he is unable to perceive in them any capacity to do or speak for themselves beyond what he sees as the escapist "transport" of the Bob Marley song that was "rocking on the transport's stereo".[16] His pity keeps them locked in postures of hopelessness ("Abandonment was something they had grown used to."),[17] sometimes unwittingly so, as with the "thousands of innocents . . . arranged on church steps" for "First Communion" "all across Sainte Lucia."[18]

In the re-enactments of return to home ground, a leading theme is language, which provides another of those dualisms on which Walcott's imagination thrives. So, in eulogising Auden, he will declare again his love of "the English tongue", "despite your Empire's wrong", and will acknowledge as a factor in his poetic beginnings "the hoisted chords of Wesley/ . . . strong as miners' throats".[19] Yet when, in 'Sainte Lucie', he had cried, "Come back to me my language",[20] it was St Lucian patois that he was recalling. From time to time he has made admiring reference in his poems to West Indian Creole dialect/ patois, identifying it with the people's sense of community, their simple strength and capacity for endurance, as when, speaking metaphorically about 'The Almond Trees', he noted "their leaves' broad dialect a coarse,/ enduring sound/ they shared together"[21]. He has also used Creole as his poetic medium on a few occasions, most memorably in 'The Schooner, *Flight*'[22]. *The Arkansas Testament* includes two poems in Creole.

Now, in 'Cul de Sac Valley'[23] and 'A Latin Primer',[24] he is willing to acknowledge that the distance which separates him from the beloved common folk of his 'Here', may be measured in terms of language which for a poet may be the most crucial measurement. Defining himself by identification with the St Lucian people ("moi, c'est gens St Lucie,"[25]), he sees also that his cultivation of "distant literatures"[26] constituted a counter-identity. So, in 'A Latin Primer' he remembers himself as a young assistant master "in tweed jacket and tie",[27] teaching Latin at his old school, and he realises, in hindsight, that:

> The discipline I preached
> made me a hypocrite;
> their lithe black bodies beached,
> would die in dialect . . . [28]

In 'Cul de Sac Valley', as he crafts his dimeter quatrains to "echo [the] settlement/ of unpainted wood", he hears the local trees:

hissing: *What you wish
from us will never be,
your words is English,
is a different tree.*[29]

The self-knowledge and self-assurance with which the trees (the
people) speak here, is underscored by the epiphanic climax of 'A Latin
Primer', when the "frigate bird" with which the poem had begun, an
icon which he had chosen from the "distant literatures" which
nurtured him, becomes its St Lucian patois self,

named with the common sense
of fishermen: sea scissors,
Fregata magnificens,

ciseau-la-mer, the patois
for its cloud-cutting course . . . [30]

The patois name reflects the imaginative power of the people, a power
rooted in their native environment. It sums up their capacity for
metaphor, the sufficiency of their language to name their world.

This capacity of the native language and imagination to fashion a
world, to interpret the world, is further recognised in such poems as
'Gros-Ilet',[31] 'The Whelk Gatherers',[32] 'White Magic'[33] and 'Oceano
Nox'.[34] For instance, the last-named exorcises the ghosts of the
borrowed moon-mythology which had once filled the poet's head.
Now, finding a new meaning in Marlowe's line "Black is the beauty of
the brightest day", he celebrates not the moon but the blackness
which surrounds her. At the end of the poem, as a new day breaks out
of the moon-crazed nightmare of history,

parishes of birds
test a new tongue, because these are their shores,
while the old moon gapes at a loss for words
like any ghost at crockcrow . . . [35]

'White Magic' acknowledges in the folklore and so-called folk
superstitions of St Lucia – such as Walcott had used creatively in *Ti-
Jean and his Brothers*[36] – mythopoeic imagination no different in kind
or quality from that of the mainstream Classical-Christian
mythologies which have dominated Western literature and his own
poetry. As the cynical last line puts it: "Our myths are ignorance,
theirs are literature".[37]

The poet's pain-deep re-connection with native roots, the love of home ground sharpened by a sense of estrangement, finds its fitting obverse in the book's title poem and major piece, itself a hard-won testament of identity. In 24 sections, each of 16 lines (except for the last which has 17) of irregularly rhyming trimeter, the poet wrestles with his feelings for America (the USA). In poems like 'The Light of the World' and 'Oceano Nox' he had celebrated the black beauty of his native people – "the ebony of a high-boned cheek/ . . . each one wrapped in sea cotton, intact from Benin".[38] Now, in 'The Arkansas Testament', he speaks for the black man in general, and particularly for the black man in America:

> this, Sir, is my Office
> my Arkansas Testament
> . . .
> my people's predicament.[39]

The poem is a narrative in which nothing much happens by way of external event. The poet checks into a motel in Fayetteville, Arkansas on a midwinter evening. He wakes before dawn. At first light he walks to a cafe nearby for a cup of coffee. The sun is already up and the city beginning to go about its business when he returns to his motel room. He switches on the TV set to the news on the 'Today' show.

This uneventful and seemingly pointless plot is the occasion for a harrowing mind-journey into the racial nightmare of America. He suffers no racial insult or discrimination during the 12 hours or so that the narrative covers. But there is no need for him to do so. It is telling enough that merely to be in that place, alone, a stranger in a strange land, a black man in a white enclave of the South, brings on an access of fear, suspicion, humiliation, bitterness and hatred – all of which constitute a sort of self-contempt which is the ultimate horror. So the testament is also a confession of these demeaning feelings – "my two cupfuls of Cowardice".[40] It also constitutes an expression of identity; in the bathroom he thinks of "a place for/ disposable shavers as well/ as my own disposable people!".[41]

To use his own words from 'The Bright Field',[42] this poem bears an impressive weight of "mercy for the anonymity/ of every self humbled by massive places". It is also a major addition to the long line of poems by which Walcott has been drawing the map of his varying feelings about America. It is the strongest and most personal expression to date of his identification with the plight of the black American. The poem's imaginative felicity expresses itself in characteristic Walcott manner, in the way in which he turns specific circumstantial images from actual experience to powerful metaphoric use. For instance, "On a ridge over Fayetteville,/ . . . is a white-hot electric cross".[43] This "white-neon crucifix" becomes, ironically, his own cross of race, and the burning cross of the Klu Klux Klan.   *Ku*

In an interview with Walcott, Waldemar Januszcak has said that "The Arkansas Testament was about a choice. He [Walcott] had been thinking of taking American citizenship . . . . But after the heart-searching recorded [in the poem] he opted for a [St Lucian] passport".[44]

> My shadow's scribbled question
> on the margin of the street
> asks, Will I be a citizen
> or an afterthought of the state?[45]

In its discretion, the poem does not report Walcott's decision on the question of whether or not to take US citizenship. To the poet it is the heart-searching that matters, the imaginative re-enactment of the dilemma of feelings. The man had to make a choice, and he might well have had prevailing reasons to opt for citizenship, but such reasons would not have invalidated the heart-searching which the poet has recorded.

The poem ends opening out. When the persona switches on the TV set, the morning news programme is being prefaced by a sequence of 'stills' of the sun rising across America, from "the waves off Narragansett" to "the huge organ pipes of the sequoias,/ [and] the Pacific".[46] These lustrous, heart-uplifting vistas mock the narrow-mindedness, the mean-spiritedness and hatred to which the poem has been reacting. They suggest an America in which it is still possible for the poet to love and to enter imaginatively. Indeed, the whole poem is a feat of that imaginative entry, no less when it is recording those features which contribute to the feeling of alienation.

The Walcott who fears that he may become only "an afterthought of the state", and who can't help thinking of South Africa in the South – "We have shared/ our passbook's open secret/ in the hooded eyes of a cop"[47] – is the Walcott who, in the tradition of poems like 'Preparing for Exile'[48] and 'Forest of Europe',[49] is haunted in imagination by the inhumanity of tyrants and totalitarian systems which crush individuals and whole races. In the poem entitled 'Elsewhere', he writes:

> Somewhere there is a comrade,
> a writer lying with his eyes wide open
> on mattress ticking, who will not read
> this, or write.[50]

The ominous irony of the title is in the fact that the poet's imagination makes the horror so immediate as to cancel the implied distance. That "elsewhere"/"somewhere" might just as well be 'here'. It is the same country of horror that his imagination enters in 'Steam':

> When your own name sounds odd, you're in
> a foreign province. They shouted ours in columns
> on somewhere Strasse under the black rook's reign.
> The drizzle counted our skulls. We became sums.[51]

In other poems in the section 'Elsewhere', Walcott's imagination appropriates other landscapes, contemporary or historical, making them live for him through his experience of 'Here'. For example, in 'Streams':

> Whenever the sunlit rain
> has trawled its trickling meshes
> on the dark hills back of the brain,
> I keep hearing a Wales
> so windswept it refreshes.[52]

He identifies with this Wales because he can recognise in it "the colonial condition", can hear "a language/ built of wet stones and mists/ in each stubborn bilingual sign", and "under slag hills the rage/ of coal-black abolitionists".[53]

In 'Summer Elegies'[54] and 'A Propertius Quartet'[55] he slips easily into the mask of Propertius, urbane, witty, down-to-earth, conversational, poignant; and in 'Menelaus'[56] into that of the fabled old cuckold as he rages in retrospect over the "Ten years. Wasted in quarrel/ for sea-grey eyes. A whore's".

In poems like these the essential landscape is the landscape of the heart, and in one or two of the finest pieces in the book there is no concern with exploring the relationship with either 'Here' or 'Elsewhere'. Walcott's elegiac versatility is nowhere shown with more piercing radiance or finer surprise of conception than in 'For Adrian'.[57] It is an elegy for a child, but its voice is the voice of the child, who, with a childlike directness and simplicity, seeks to reassure his mourners. He speaks out of the wisdom of "the secret that is only a silence", which he shares:

> with the tyrants of the earth, with the man who piles rags
> in a creaking cart, and goes around a corner
> of a square at dusk.

His hushed, unhurried utterance counterpoints the distraction and lack of control of self-control of his mourning relatives, who hardly hear him, deafened as they are by their grief.

'For Adrian' is a good example of Walcott's characteristic negotiation between the natural, speaking voice and the strict discipline of form:

> Look, and you will see that the furniture is fading,
> that a wardrobe is as insubstantial as a sunset,
>
> that I can see through you, the tissue of your leaves,
> the light behind your veins; why do you keep smiling?

And so it goes on, in these unrhymed couplets (though there is the occasional suggestion of a half-rhyme cutting across couplets), with their subdued, irregular stress pattern and long lines, *more-or-less* alexandrines, there are only three lines that have as few as ten syllables. The naturalness and simplicity of the language works with its dignity and with the sense of ceremony attaching to the suggestion of strict form and discipline to deepen the poignancy of the whole.

The pleasure and profit we may derive from the drama of such negotiations would seem akin to a quality which Walcott identifies in the work of Philip Larkin:

> Development, for Larkin, lay not in metrical experiment, or in varieties of stanzaic design, not in Pound's frenzied and very American injunction to "make it new", since Larkin despised the avant-garde . . . . [F]or Larkin the great achievement was not to betray the pulse or the breath of the pentameter by abandoning it or condemning its melody as archaic, but in exploring the possibility of its defiant consistency, until technical mastery became freshness.[58]

If we sense the West Indian context of this statement, we may better catch something of the spirit in which Walcott conducts his own explorations in the possibilities of traditional English verse forms, the spirit in which he too has not sought in any radical sense to "make it new", and the kind of freshness, whether in form or content, which each new collection of his is likely to yield.

NOTES

1. Wayne Brown (*Ed, Derek Walcott; Selected Poetry*, London, Kingston, Port of Spain, 1981, p.xii.
2. Joseph Brodsky, *Less Than One*, New York, 1986, p.164.
3. Walcott, 'Eulogy to W. H. Auden', *The Arkansas Testament*, London, 1987, p.62.
4. Walcott, 'The Lighthouse', *ibid.*, p.6.
5. Walcott, 'Cul de Sac Valley', *ibid.*, p.9.
6. Walcott, 'French Colonial', in 'Vers de Société', *ibid.*, p.75.
7. Walcott, 'The Lighthouse', *ibid.*, p.7.
8. Walcott, 'Eulogy to W. H. Auden', *ibid.*, pp.63–64.
9. Walcott, 'The Lighthouse', *ibid.*, p.8.
10. Walcott, 'Tomorrow, Tomorrow', *ibid.*, p.79.
11. Walcott, *The Star-apple Kingdom*, London, 1980, p.8.
12. Walcott, 'The Lighthouse', *op.cit.*, p.6.
13. Walcott, 'The Light of the World', *ibid.*, p.48.
14. *ibid.*, pp.50–51.
15. In *Bim*, No.26, Jan–June 1958; *In a Green Night* and *The Gulf* respectively.
16. Walcott, 'The Light of the World', *op.cit.*, p.48.
17. *ibid.*, p.50.
18. Walcott, 'Gros-Ilet', *ibid.*, p.35.
19. Walcott, 'Eulogy to W. H. Auden', *ibid.*, p.61.
20. Walcott, *Sea Grapes*, London, 1976, p.44.
21. Walcott, *The Castaway*, London, 1965, p.37.
22. Walcott, *The Gulf*, London, 1970, p.50.
23. Walcott, 'Cul de Sac Valley', *op.cit.*, pp.9–15.
24. Walcott, 'A Latin Primer', *ibid.*, pp.22–24.
25. Walcott, *Sea Grapes*, p.47.
26. Walcott, 'A Latin Primer', *op.cit.*, p.21.
27. *ibid.*, p.22.
28. *ibid.*, p.23.
29. Walcott, 'Cul de Sac Valley', *ibid.*, p.10.
30. Walcott, 'A Latin Primer', *ibid.*, pp.23–24.
31. Walcott, 'Gros-Ilet', *ibid.*, pp.34–35.
32. Walcott, 'The Whelk Gatherers', *ibid.*, pp.36–37.
33. Walcott, 'White Magic', *ibid.*, pp.38–39.
34. Walcott, 'Oceano Nox', *ibid.*, pp.52–55.
35. *ibid.*, p.55.
36. Walcott, *Dream on Monkey Mountain and other plays*, New York, 1970.
37. Walcott, 'White Magic', *op.cit.*, p.38.
38. Walcott, 'Oceano Nox', *ibid.*, p.54.

39. Walcott, 'The Arkensas Testament', *ibid.*, p.116.
40. *ibid.*, p.116.
41. *ibid.*, p.107.
42. Walcott, 'The Bright Field', *Sea Grapes*, p.77.
43. Walcott, 'The Arkansas Testament', *op.cit.*, p.107.
44. Waldemar Januszcak, 'The Longing on St. Lucia', *The Guardian*, 9 July, 1988.
45. Walcott, 'The Arkansas Testament', *op.cit.*, p.114.
46. *ibid.*, p.117.
47. *ibid.*, p.115.
48. Walcott, *Sea Grapes*.
49. Walcott, *The Star-apple Kingdom*.
50. Walcott, 'Elsewhere', *The Arkansas Testament*, p.66.
51. Walcott, 'Steam', *ibid.*, p.68.
52. Walcott, 'Streams', *ibid.*, pp.80–81.
53. *ibid.*
54. Walcott, 'Summer Elegies', *ibid.*, pp.93–97.
55. Walcott, 'A Propertius Quartet', *ibid.*, pp97–100.
56. Walcott, 'Menelaus', *ibid.*, p.101.
57. Walcott, 'For Adrian', *ibid.*, pp.97–88.
58. Walcott, 'The Master of the Ordinary', *New York Review of Books*, 1 June 1989, p.38.

Lowel Fiet

Mapping a New Nile:
Derek Walcott's *Later Plays*

Mapping a New Nile:
Derek Walcott's *Later Plays*

God, I hate actors! They refuse to accept the reality they live in! I pronounce these solemn self-deceivers guilty of doubling the dream that is life.
(*The Joker of Seville*)

That ain't just a bloody poem . . . .
(*Remembrance*)

But if you take this thing seriously, we might commit
Art, which is a kind of crime in this society.
(*Pantomime*)

Give art a rest. This ain't theatre, is Carnival, Mas!
(*The Last Carnival*)

We are not Americans! But give us time . . .
(*Beef, No Chicken*)

Oh, God, a actor is a holy thing. A sacred thing . . . . And it don't matter where it is: here, New York, London . . . . Do your work.
(*A Branch of the Blue Nile*)

In Walcott's 'later' plays, the act of performance itself, the play and/or plays within the play, rehearsals, creative processes, theatre settings, and actor/writer/artist characters become increasingly prominent metaphors in the interpretation of Caribbean culture and society. By 'later' I mean the post-Trinidad Theatre Workshop plays, works written and/or staged after 1976: *Remembrance* (first performed 1977) and *Pantomime* (first performed 1978) were published together in 1980; *Beef, No Chicken* (first performed 1981), *The Last Carnival* (based on the earlier *In a Fine Castle* and first performed 1982), and *A Branch of the Blue Nile* (performed 1983) were published together in 1986. (Plays unpublished or not accessible to the general reader are not included in this discussion.) These are the Trinidad plays – Trinidad-Tobago in the case of *Pantomime*, which takes place on 'Crusoe's island' – and form a thematic and stylistic grouping, especially when contrasted with the rather vaguely labelled 'poetic drama' or St. Lucia plays of the earlier – 1949-1970 – period perhaps best characterized by *Ti-Jean and His Brothers* (performed 1958) and *Dream on Monkey Mountain* (performed 1967).

The earlier work concerns themes and formal considerations voiced in 'A Far Cry From Africa'[1] still probably Walcott's best known poem, and arising from the Afro-Caribbean, French patois and Catholic traditions of the majority population of his native St. Lucia. If *Ti-Jean* is an Aristophanic poetic comedy based on Afro-Caribbean myth, then *Dream on Monkey Mountain* depends on a dream/play-within-a-play structure and becomes Walcott's most fully articulated theatre image illuminating the position of Caliban as the Caribbean issue of Sycorax and colonizer, empire-builder, slaveowner Prospero.

The later plays vary from the early work in their dependence on surface realism. The language remains poetic – and Walcott often writes dialogue in verse – but the mytho-poetic nature of the action changes. These are social plays, plays of commentary and are analytical in form and structure. Ariel's colonial attitude, Crusoe and Friday in a contemporary context, Black Power versus creole aristocracy, modernization, Americanization, government graft, and colonial restraints on creativity assume primary thematic importance. However, a close examination of structural design also reveals the incorporation of dramatic devices that, beneath the surface realism, fragment the action and allow it to double back and comment on itself.

In another sense, these later plays record Walcott's association with foundations, theatre organizations, and universities in the United States, and *Remembrance* and *Pantomime* comply to demands characteristic of U.S. productions: tightly-knit, one-set, small-cast 'realistic' plays that concentrate on conflicts between characters in family, work, and/or social contexts which give them the texture of being more up-to-date, more about real people and possible events.

Between what I'm calling the early St. Lucia plays and the later Trinidad plays two other published works also require mention. They are *The Joker of Seville* (performed 1974), a creolized version of Tirso de Molina's *El burlador de Sevilla*, and *O Babylon!* (performed 1976), a musical evocation of Rastafarianism in Jamaica at the time of Haile Selassie's 1966 visit there, both with original music by Galt MacDermot, and were published together in 1978. (*In a Fine Castle*, performed 1970, *Franklin*, 1973, and *The Charlatan* 1973 as well, none of which has circulated widely, also form part of this transitional period.) *The Joker of Seville* was commissioned by the Royal Shakespeare Company, although not performed by them, whereas *O Babylon!* was one of the last productions of Walcott's years working directly with the Trinidad Theatre Workshop.

With *The Joker of Seville*, Walcott successfully adapted Spanish Golden Age drama to a contemporary idiom. The rhythm of Calypso, the dance of stick fighting, the pageant-like nature of Carnival, and the repartee of Afro- Caribbean oral tradition inform the action. The play begins with "A field, ringed with bleachers, used as a bull ring, a cockpit, or stickfighters' *gayelle*, on a Caribbean estate"[2] as a framing device, and in that setting, Tirso's Don Juan Tenorio comes alive as he probably could not in a standard English translation.

O Babylon! proves less satisfying. The musicalized form captures little of Rasta-based myths and themes that does not find fuller expression in music and lyrics by Marley and the Wailers, Burning Spear, or numerous other Rasta-inspired reggae artists or dub poets, or in Roger Mais' flawed but compelling *Brother Man*. But Walcott's next two plays, *Remembrance* and *Pantomime* represent significant advancements in dramatic form and technique.

I

"*Pre-dawn*" Trinidad, 1977: two men, one old, one young, converse. The older man is a retired schoolteacher, a writer, a known figure in Port of Spain, while the younger, "sitting in the half dark", is the son of a former student and works for *The Belmont Bugle*, a local newspaper edited by the older man's best friend and for which his own son wrote before he was killed seven years before. The younger man holds a tape recorder, it is four o'clock in the morning, and the older, Albert Perez Jordan, is recording "The story of [his] life", "a journey through time",[3] as he calls it.

Jordan's recollections begin with his days as schoolmaster "One Jacket Jordan", "Who taught the wrong things"and continue with "readings" of his two "best-known" stories, one a more recent satire on neo-colonialism, and the other the romance of a failed love affair with an English woman during the Second World War.

At the same time, other characters' versions become intertwined in the events of Jordan's "journey" and provide information not available in the stories.[4] Perhaps most important is Jordan's inability to accept the rebellion and death of his elder son, Albert Junior. He even writes a poem in which he blames his best friend for betraying him and leading his son astray. Later he tries to relive his own past by convincing his artist son, Frederick, to leave Trinidad with the young American he has cast in the role of Esther Trout-Hope, the woman he "lost" 35 years before. At the end, which is really still the beginning, he is left alone with the interviewer to begin, again.

I mistakenly want to call *Remembrance* (first performed 1977) 'Performance', perhaps because it was published with *Pantomime* (also a kind of play within a play), but more I suspect because a 'remembrance' is an already displaced or transformed memory, not so much the memory itself as its staging, its re-enactment. That means that we are all like Brecht's streetcorner actor in the poem 'On Everyday Theatre',[5] giving our versions of facts. But each act of memory, telling, acting, or writing is a displacement, the mediation of a framing device, a means of breaking or segmenting the memory, story, poem, or play from its original context.

Remembrance is memory inside memory, and what is remembered forms an account of 35 years in the life of the writer-character Albert Perez Jordan – a period that corresponds to the modern history of Trinidad and the West Indies: World War II, the fall of empire, emigration, independence, identity crisis, Black Power, and neo-colonialism.

The person who best understands the relation of Jordan's life to his memories and writing is Mabel, his wife. As she prepares to leave him, Mabel asks, "You think I never read 'My War Effort', and realize that if you wasn't such a coward thirty years ago, you would of leave me?".[6] Mabel also seems to understand more about Junior's death, that he was killed by "a frightened policeman in Woodford Square on the day of the riot", and that they both bear some of the responsibility:

> I kill him with hymns and Jesus . . . and maybe he was so ashamed of both of us, all the mockery and the way you talk like a black Englishman, that he had to go out and do something.[7]

When Jordan's friend, Ezra Pilgrim, questions him about the poem 'Remembrance', Jordan squirms and says, "It's just a bloody poem".[8]

But the line "when sons have died and friends betray"[9] implies that Pilgrim turned Junior against his father by allowing him to "read Césaire and Marx and Fanon"[10] and publish articles in *The Bugle* that cast Jordan in the role of an Uncle Tom. Jordan says, "Face the truth, Ezra. It's time. We avoid it . . . . That poem is the truth",[11] no longer "just a bloody poem." For Jordan, Pilgrim betrayed not only friendship – "nearly . . . stealing away my son" – but also the "principles we considered sacred"– "you recanted on all the culture we had known".[12] Falling just short of accusing Pilgrim of being his son's "murderer", he ejects,

> They shot him, Ezra. They put a hole in that boy's body, but they've ripped out a hole in my own heart that nothing, nothing can fill.[13]

Where is Albert Perez Jordan in this recounting of his life? Whether his 'My War Effort (1948)' or 'Barrley and the Roof (1971)' the narrative voice rings of self-aggrandizement, rhetorical posing that moves away from the actual conditions of colonialism and neo-colonialism, the real bases of his stories, into nostalgic romance or sneering, self-justifying satire. From 'My War Effort', Jordan reads,

> . . . I was not English, but I considered myself to be. I was a colonial, but did not consider myself to be so . . . . I adored England and there was nothing more England to me . . . than the adorable Miss Esther Hope.[14]

After he supposedly "went to the men's room for twenty years"[15] – to marry Mabel, to whom he was already engaged, and not his English Esther – the narrator reflects, "Since then I have been a mind without a country".[16] With the loss of England, he feels that he lost himself. That appears to be the "hole in [his] own heart that nothing, nothing can fill."

Esther's lines:

> Albert, I think you're a silly, affected, but lovely man. You've pestered me relentlessly for three months. It's been worse than the Blitz. I've thought very carefully about this, all the possible complications, but if you want me to, I'll marry you.[17]

– the same words Jordan also puts in the mouth of Anna, the "Pavlova from Rhode Island", 35 years later – serve only to puff up the narrator's self-image. Thus, it is not surprising that Frederick, discussing the story with Anna, asks, "You mean, if [Esther] was real?",[18] because the writing seems more like Mabel's description of the young Jordan:

> . . . splattered with duck shit, but he would hold his nose high, and as he throw crumbs to the ducks in that stinking canal, he would say, "We are feeding the swans of Avon."[19]

'Barrley and the Roof' bears the epigraph, drawn from Blake, "A Man's worst enemies are those of his own House and Family", but in fact, the acted story/play demonstrates the opposite: Frederick feels that his father taught him not to sell out, and Mabel understands and cares for him. The story ends as a comic resistance to neo-colonialism, but not without first projecting the narrator's superiority to his environment and situation.

The second act brings the two earlier stories together. Anna Herschel becomes a reincarnated Esther Trout. But Anna's dancing career – "doing the Funky Chicken at ten in the morning with two stars on your tits under the red lights of an empty bar in Jersey" – bottomed out, and she took a plane "South! The farther the better".[20] By accident, she and her baby arrive on Jordan's doorstep.

Jordan tries to force the romantic relationship between Anna and Frederick to correct what he sees as his past mistakes. He tells Frederick to:

> Leave this place. It dried me up and it will dry you up. You're an artist boy. You're one of God's chosen. That's what that blasted poem [Gray's 'Elegy'] is all about. Don't bury yourself out here. Go on that plane.[21]

When Jordan plays out his memory of 'One Jacket Jordan', teaching Thomas Gray's 'Elegy', hearing the jeers of "*Jordan is a honky-donkey white nigger man!*",[22] and beating his own hand, rather than the imagined boy's, with a ruler as he exclaims that in "what is called poetry, and art, color don't matter! Color don't matter!",[23] the importance of teaching to his concept of self becomes apparent. He says, "I was a schoolmaster . . . . Who taught the wrong things",[24] and at play's end – Mabel has left for Brooklyn, Anna returns to the States, Frederick goes to the country – he again sits with the Interviewer, the tape recorder, his memories, and Gray's 'Elegy'. He tells his remembered class,

Your body is the earth in which it springs and dies. And it's the humble
people of this world, you Junes, you Walcott, and you Brown, and you
Fonesca, and you Mango Head, that [Gray] concerned about.[25]

Is there an authentic Albert Perez Jordan behind the posturing, the
borrowed values, the compensating, and the colonial self-
aggrandizement? He "taught with a passion", but not so much the
"wrong things" as only those "things" and not others equally
important as well. Walcott permits Albert Perez Jordan to tell his own
story and by so doing creates the history of a generation of West
Indians who lost themselves when they 'lost' England.

When *Remembrance* works out the position of Ariel in relation to
Caliban after Prospero's departure, its companion piece, *Pantomime*,
re-creates the story of Robinson Crusoe and his man Friday. The
setting is a contemporary Tobago guesthouse run by Harry Trewe, a
retired English actor in his mid-forties, and "his factotum" Jackson
Phillip, a forty-year-old, retired calypsonian from Trinidad. The
central issue is who is to be Crusoe and who Friday in the comedy
sketch Harry has conceived to provide guests who will be arriving in
less than a week's time with the "nightly entertainment" they have
been promised. At first, Jackson refuses to participate, but slowly as
the tension ebbs and flows between the white-English-owner-boss
and the black- Trinidadian-employee and they rehearse their varying
and conflicting social and comic roles, the relationship between them
assumes a new dimension. Race, class, culture, and personal differences become obscured. Jackson kills the "Heinegger, Heinegger"
parrot, Harry admits his own pretending and accuses Jackson of being
"a kind man" who thinks he has "to hide it", and Jackson brings a
photo of Harry's ex-wife, Ellen, and plays her role until Harry chases
him with an ice pick and confesses, "That's the real reason I wanted to
do the panto. To do it better than [Ellen] ever did".[26] Harry was
Friday to Ellen's Crusoe. The ending leaves the men in the same but
different positions: "An angel passes through a house and leaves no
imprint of his shadow on the wall".[27] Harry and Jackson have
changed. They now relate to each other face-to-face, man-to-man,
friend-to-friend.

Pantomime is a compact and searing play. The two characters share
their suspicions, resentments, and scepticism of each other, and the
action becomes a process of bonding through which those socially
generated feelings are at least partially exorcised. The rehearsal is the
play itself, and the characters act out different roles and positions –

now Crusoe, now Friday, now servant, now master – dropping as well as assuming different poses until a new social relation forms.

II

Issues of colonial attitudes, politics, and art characterise *The Last Carnival* (first performed 1982), a rewriting of the earlier *In a Fine Castle*. The play covers the years from the post-war period (1948) to Trinidadian independence (1962) to the Black Power uprising in 1970 and focuses on the aristocratic, French-creole De la Fontaine family, owners of both the Santa Rosa estate and the 'Castle' in Port of Spain. The first act is devoted principally to Victor De la Fontaine, would-be 'Impressionist' painter, and the English governess, Agatha Willet, he hires to educate his children. Victor's wife is dead, and his relation with Agatha assumes romantic and sexual overtones. But where he encases himself in his attempt to re-create and paint the past, Agatha comes from a working-class background and begins to teach the estate's children, white and black, egalitarian principles.

Victor's painting is derivative – unfinished copies of Watteau (he cannot paint Agatha's unaristocratic hands) – and he becomes increasingly a temperamental recluse. By the opening of the second act, during the Black Power uprising at Carnival time in 1970, Victor has committed suicide, and the focus of the action shifts to the conflict between the now more conventional and politically powerful Agatha and Victor's daughter, Clodia. Even though faced by rejection in the country she loves, Clodia sides with Sydney, a former groom on the Santa Rosa estate and one of Agatha's pupils, and the Black Power guerrillas. Miss Jean Beauxchamps, formerly a De la Fontaine family maid but now a government minister, is another of Agatha's ex-pupils. Jean argues for crushing the uprising, whereas the reporter Brown (reduced to a minor as opposed to the major role he plays in *In a Fine Castle*), who comes to write about Victor's paintings, remains in the middle, uncommitted.

At the end of the play, when the rebels burn Santa Rosa and the army kills Sydney, the old servant George, Sydney's uncle, remains stoic when confronted with his nephew's death, Agatha, still a British citizen, is warned of her possible evacuation, and as she sits in customs on the docks waiting to sail to England on the *Antilles*, Clodia retraces for Brown the steps of Agatha's arrival in Trinidad twenty-two years before. In her last speech, Clodia asserts, "I don't want to be like her",[28] and the play leaves a bitter aftertaste, the ambivalent sense that the real tragedy is captured in Brown's question, "All you niggers ain't tired killing your own people?"[29] But the root issue appears better expressed by Walcott in a 1986 *Paris Review* interview:

> The departure of the British required and still requires a great deal of endeavour, of repairing the psychological damage done by their laziness and by their indifference. The desolation of poverty that exists in the Caribbean can be very depressing. The only way that one can look at it and draw anything of value from it is to have a fantastic depth of strength and belief, not in the past but in the immediate future.[30]

The Last Carnival remains problematical: it brings to light the influence still wielded by old wealthy families and makes a striking statement on the economic and political composition of the modern West Indies, but its uneven form makes it less convincing than other later plays.

Beef, No Chicken presents a very different situation. An energetic folk comedy, the play satirizes the neo-colonial Americanization – the McDonaldization – the of Caribbean and the amount of graft, bribery, and swindling the process entails. In that context, progress means fast-food outlets, expressways, shopping malls, credit cards, television commercials, imported consumer goods, and the disappearance of the particular, native character and the products of Caribbean life, economic independence, and political self-reliance.

In *Beef, No Chicken*, Otto Hogan, owner of Otto's Auto Repair and Authentic Roti, and member of the Couva Borough Council, refuses to go along with a highway project that promises to bring profits to fellow Council members. He claims that without his signature the highway is illegal and that he is being harrassed and his business destroyed as a result. But his real reasons for opposing the road seem to be: "Hustle and bribe, run a big racket like the deal between the highway and the Borough Council? My father ain't bring us up so."[31] To retaliate, Otto creates the Mysterious Stranger, a masked woman who haunts the construction area to jinx the highway and publicize his protest.

The tactic brings results: Cedric Hart, American-accented, local television newsman, crashes his car outside the restaurant and begins to recruit the new talent, including Otto's sister, Euphony, courted by schoolmaster Franco but engaged for the past 10 years to the absent boxer and miner Alwyn Davie (alias Cardiff Joe), who returns and threatens to bomb the highway's inaugural ceremony, Calypsonian Limer, Indian *chanteuse* and roti maker Sumintra, a riotous meeting of the corrupt Couva Borough Council, the mysterious appearance ("*A huge shadow crosses the stage*") of "The spirit of the countryside", no longer Otto's creation, and the vagrant Deacon who appears to marry Alwyn and Euphony and functions as a *raisonneur*:

> Pretty soon there'll be no country left. Nowhere to walk, nowhere to sit in the shade, whole place one big concrete suburb. Oh! Yes! It's about McDonaldizing everything, it's Kentucky Frying everything, it's about going modern with a vengeance and televising everything, it's hamming up everything, traffic-jamming up everything.[32]

As it becomes increasingly incorporated into First World, United States dominated, economic spheres, the Caribbean more and more comes to resemble the "mini-Miami" of mogul Mongroo's dream of:

> "Clover-leaf overpass . . . toll booth, rest area . . . .Beefburgers, cheeseburgers . . . no more roast corn by the side of the road, no more . . . shrimp stands, oysters, all those Third World shacks, but just highway humming south . . . [33]

Beef, No Chicken demonstrates sophistication and poetic ease in a genre more often characterized by slapstick farce, dialect buffoonery, and stereo-typed thinking. It effectively captures and satirizes in human terms what neo-colonial economic and political policy is all about: whether it is International Monetary Fund loans, the Caribbean Basin Initiative, or the Grenada Invasion, the West Indies have passed from one pair of colonial hands to another.

The scene is a theatre, the characters are West Indian actors and their English director, they are rehearsing *Antony and Cleopatra*, and the director asks Cleopatra,

> What's all this sexual hesitation, Sheila? You know how sensual his corpse is to her?

But the actress (Sheila) replies that she is not Cleopatra, that she cannot "play" that, to which the director responds that she should act what she "feels" for another cast member, "Chris, not Antony". She replies, "Just leave my personal life out of this please."[34] Suddenly some of the polarities of formal Caribbean theatre materialize on stage: Shakespeare or more profitable 'dialect' comedies? Euro-American methods and attitudes – Stanislavskian acting and Strasberg's 'Method' adaptation of it, for example – or local production standards and expectations? professionalism or amateurism?, and perhaps, Theatre or Carnival, Poetry or Calypso? The difficulties become personalized in Sheila – full-time typist, part-time actress – when she says,

> I'm not a fucking queen, I'm not a celebrity; when you turn my name into mud it stays mud, and no magic in any theatre in the world can turn that mud into gold . . . this foreign Method shit . . . it's bad Method, anyway, and maybe it doesn't travel.[35]

She understands that Port of Spain is not London or New York, that the anonymity enjoyed by metropolitan artists does not necessarily extend to the Caribbean, where cities often remain small towns in every way except size. She is a convert in search of a 'religion' in the theatre, and her "epiphany" while rehearsing Cleopatra – "The soldier's pole is fall'n . . . / . . . / And there is nothing left remarkable/ Beneath the visiting moon." – even though it takes place in the first scene, is perhaps the play's most crucial moment. But when performance demands conflict with her evangelical background, she leaves the theatre group for the revivalist church:

> 'cause the Caroni isn't a branch of the river Nile, and Trinidad isn't Egypt, except at Carnival, so the world sniggers when I speak [Cleopatra's] lines, but not in a concrete church in Barataria.[36]

The other characters cover a range of possibilities: Harvey, the 'professional' director, English background and training, possibly gay and possibly dying of AIDS, his values are metropolitan; Chris, an accountant and successful businessman, the writer of popular 'dialect' plays (one of which is also being rehearsed in the play), married to a white English woman but having an affair with Sheila, and author of the play about the play; Marilyn, pretty, light-skinned, not really talented but willing to let her cleavage help her career – "theatre ain't no religion, it's a whorehouse", she says – and she leaves for New York; and Gavin, the "mercenary" – "a professional sweetheart" – actor, home from battling for parts off- and off-off Broadway to rest up for a while before heading back to New York, where he went "to be an actor and found out that [he] was a nigger . . . ",[37] and at play's end he is teaching acting in Jamaica and considering his options. Thus, the group is really a stepping-stone, a means of making it elsewhere in 'real' theatre, of trying to be, as Marilyn puts it, "another Cicely Tyson, or Meryl Streep, but here . . . Here?"[38] Or, to quote from another context, "They [show] that cursed colonial hunger for the metropolis" ("Twilight" 36).

In 'What the Twilight Says: An Overture', Walcott writes that

> When one began twenty years ago it was in the faith that one was creating not merely a play, but a theatre, and not merely a theatre, but its environment.[39]

That sense of personal history and experience is perhaps more central to *A Branch of the Blue Nile* (first performed 1983) than to any other of Walcott's plays. The action seems to restructure the memory of actual events and constitutes, along with 'What the Twilight Says' (1970), articles in the *Trinidad Guardian* and interviews, a record in play form of the years 1959-1976 when as playwright, director, designer, and critic, Walcott lived in Port of Spain and worked toward the creation of a resident professional company, an ensemble that could equal production standards of non-commercial, regional, state-sponsored and/or subsidized repertory companies and 'art' theatres throughout Europe and the United States.

Set in a theatre, the layered quality of the play of actors rehearsing and performing plays – as well as 'A Branch of the Blue Nile', the play Chris is writing from their experiences – ensures that characters play multiple and overlapping roles. Thus, when theatre should be its most 'realistic', it portrays – or betrays – itself as more seamed, fragmented, and critical than normally assumed.

If Walcott's group portrait does not inspire confidence, it is no doubt because it records a discredited artistic process – a concept outdated even in the First World settings that gave birth to it. Whether in Port of Spain, Trinidad, San Juan, Puerto Rico, Portland, Oregon, Flint, Michigan, Durham, England, or Dijon, France, such semi-professional and community theatres often mistakenly attempt to copy metropolitan production techniques and attempt to make their actors interchangeable with actors in New York, Hollywood, London, or Paris, where 'real' acting happens. The critical tone in *A Branch of the Blue Nile* is harsh, and the play reveals bitterness and loss; perhaps the sense that "In these new nations art is a luxury, and the theatre the most superfluous of amenities" ('Twilight' 7), and that a different kind of theatre and artist is necessary. The mad, ex-singer Phil describes the difficulties –

'Tain't rain they 'fraid, nuh, sister, 'cause if it ain't rain, the sun too hot. People always have a excuse, is natural. Like if it don't rain in London or New York! Rain don't stop white people, snow, tornado, what they have to do they does do. Here, if a butterfly fart, they jump. They would dance in the rain Carnival time, though. They would roll in the mud self. But all you doin' something serious, you see. I was in that scene. Is to go 'way, that is all. Leave them home sheltering, and head for greener pastures. Give up early, or they kill you self in this place, yes. Slow death. Something in them out kill you, dead or alive.[40]

– but also supplies the insight that art can happen:

Even in this country. Even here . . . And it don't matter where it is: here, New York, London . . . Continue. Do your work.[41]

III

To speak of Walcott's later plays is premature. At least three other, as yet unpublished works have been performed: *The Isle Full of Noises* (1982), *Haitian Earth* (1984), and *To Die For Grenada* (1986) – perhaps there are more, for Walcott's productivity shows no signs of faltering. The early, St. Lucia plays such as *Ti-Jean and His Brothers* and *Dream on Monkey Mountain* established Walcott's reputation as a poetic, West Indian playwright and, no doubt due to the colonial history of his native St. Lucia, resemble the drama of francophone writers – Aimé Césaire, Edouard Glissant, Daniel Boukman, Ina Césaire, and Simone Schwarz-Bart – more than plays by fellow English-language Caribbean dramatists. (And perhaps only Césaire begins to equal Walcott's overall accomplishment as playwright and poet.) Other West Indians – Dennis Scott and Trevor Rhone (Jamaica) and Errol John, Errol Hill, and Earl Lovelace (Trinidad), to mention only a few – share many of Walcott's concerns but none matches his creativity and critical stature.

The most notable of his post-1970, Trinidad plays – *Remembrance, Pantomime, Beef, No Chicken,* and *A Branch of the Blue Nile* – demonstrate Walcott's versatility and secure his position as a playwright whose works compare favourably to those of international contemporaries such as Dario Fo, Harold Pinter, Wole Soyinka,

Heiner Müller, Athol Fugard, Slawomir Mrozek, and Sam Shepard and as well as to major modern figures such as Shaw, O'Neill, Brecht, and Beckett.

The first major dramatist from the anglophone Caribbean, Walcott and his plays hold central positions in the development of the idea of a Caribbean theatre. His work futher distinguishes itself through his practical theatre experience and the effort to establish a professional, regional company. Thus, along with other notable groups such as Cuba's Teatro Escambray, Martinique's Théâtre de la soif nouvelle, and Jamaica's Sistren, the Trinidad Theatre Workshop has contributed to the formation of a genuine and unique theatre aesthetic. If the Trinidad or later plays form a chapter in Walcott's career as playwright, then perhaps the yet-to-be-published works of the 1980's promise another that broadens the focus to reinterpret *The Tempest* for the entire Caribbean region.

NOTES

1. Walcott, *In a Green Night*, 1962, *Collected Poems*, 1986, p.17.
2. Walcott, *The Joker of Seville* and *O Babylon*, London, 1979, p.7.
3. Walcott, *Remembrance* and *Pantomime*, New York, 1980, pp.6–7.
4. Robert D. Hamner, *Derek Walcott*, Boston, 1981, p.128.
5. Bertolt Brecht, 'On Everyday Theatre', in John Willett and Ralph Mannhein *Eds*, *Bertolt Brecht: Poems, 1913–1956*, New York, 1976, pp.176–79.
6. Walcott, *Remembrance* and *Pantomime*, *op.cit.*, p.72.
7. *ibid.*, p.31.
8. *ibid.*, p.51.
9. *ibid.*, p.50.
10. *ibid.*, p.51.
11. *ibid.*, p.52.
12. *ibid.*, p.53.
13. *ibid.*, p.54.
14. *ibid.*, p.36.
15. *ibid.*, p.45.
16. *ibid.*, p.46.
17. *ibid.*, p.45.
18. *ibid.*, p.76.
19. *ibid.*, pp.19–20.
20. *ibid.*, pp.61–62.
21. *ibid.*, p.80.
22. *ibid.*, p.8.
23. *ibid.*, p.9.
24. *ibid.*, p.7.
25. *ibid.*, pp.86–87.

26. *ibid.*, p.164.

27. *ibid.*, p.169.

28. Walcott, *The Last Carnival*, *Three Plays*, New York, 1978, p.101.

29. *ibid.*

30. Walcott, 'The Art of Poetry, XXXVII', in interview with Edward Hirsch, *Paris Review*, 101, Winter 1986, p.213.

31. Walcott, *Beef, No Chicken, Three Plays*, *op.cit.*, p.128.

32. *ibid.*, p.204.

33. *ibid.*, p.168.

34. *ibid.*, p.213.

35. *ibid.*, p.218.

36. *ibid.*, p.285.

37. *ibid.*, p.249.

38. *ibid.*, p.258.

39. Walcott, 'What the Twilight Says: An Overture', *Dream on Monkey Mountain and Other Plays*, New York, 1970, p.6.

40. Walcott, *A Branch of the Blue Nile*, *Three Plays*, p.297.

41. *ibid.*, p.312.

Fred D'Aguiar

Ambiguity without a Crisis?
Twin Traditions, the Individual and
Community in
Derek Walcott's Essays

Ambiguity without a Crisis?
Twin Traditions, the Individual and Community in Derek Walcott's Essays

Central to Derek Walcott's thinking in his major essays is the self avowed split between two traditions and the tension generated by this dichotomy as the artist moves towards their reconciliation and synthesis in his art:

> I am a kind of split writer; I have one tradition inside me going in one way, and another tradition going another. The mimetic, the narrative, and dance element is strong on one side, and the literary, the classical tradition is strong on the other.[1]

A number of factors are commandeered by these two opposing traditions, opposed but with the inbuilt contradiction of being attracted to each other, at least for the unifying artistic imagination scrutinising them. The two traditions are divided mainly along African and European lines, with a communal orientation in the former and a more individual base for the latter.

This distinction between the outer world of the community and the inner, contemplative world of the individual artist has implications for the ways Walcott conceptualises his art. His imagination is shot through with both traditions but on the inner/outer front imagination is on the side of the artist, whereas memory, a close relative of imagination, belongs to the community. History is a community commodity, while the artist lays a claim on myth. But these are not compartments exclusive of each other – aspects of memory and history inevitably impact on the artistic imagination – and the relationship between the two traditions is more organic.

In 'What the Twilight Says, an Overture', the preface to Walcott's first published collection of plays *Dream on Monkey Mountain*, this individual/communal divide which characterises the split between the two traditions is most marked. To read it is to experience something of the process by which Walcott came, in Wilson Harris's phrase, to "consume his biases", to recognise, as Walcott himself puts it, that: "maturity is the assimilation of the features of every ancestor".[2]

If division is there, so too is reconciliation and synthesis, but in the early stages of his career this felt tension between the two traditions predominates. Walcott as a playwright appears to occupy a blank space with few indigenous precursors to act as guiding lights. He is in a community hostile to his brand of a 'moulded' theatre, holding its own ideas about theatre's inseparableness from communal life. To portion off that life from the community generating it and call it art was bound therefore to bring the artist into conflict with those who could not see a palpable difference between art and the community. But equally, merely to transcribe community life onto the stage would have proved insufficient to an artist like Walcott, as preoccupied with his art form as with the material he would use. Ultimately, the material and the form it took would be testimony to an organic whole. But in these early stages with the notion of a theatre in its infancy there was clearly a distinction to be made between the two perceptions of the 'dramatic'.

In 'The Figure of Crusoe', a talk Walcott gave at the University of the West Indies in Trinidad in 1965, the figure of the isolated artist – alienated and alienating himself from his society – transmutes into a psychological condition, necessary at that juncture in the growth of the poet if he was to arrive at certain key premises. If the artist was not really alienated from his community by any will on the latter's part then he, the artist, was going to invent his own alienation – or dramatise it as a condition – in order to highlight his status as an artist. Already, in this early talk, using a poem from *The Castaway* (1965) in which the Crusoe 'condition' is explored as a metaphor for the Caribbean artist – indeed any artist engaged in the aesthetics of artistic practice – Walcott presents both conflict and the drive towards a resolution of conflict as intrinsic elements in his organic conception of the piece;

> I am trying to make a heretical reconciliation between the outer world
> and the world of the hermit, between . . . the poet and the objects
> surrounding him that are called society.[3]

Here the hermit figure stands in for the creative artist; the hermit's
solitary contemplation of a fire built from materials around him
reconciles the distinction between outer and inner, between the
individual and the community:

> Fire mesmerizes us. We dissolve in burning. The man sits before the
> fire, its glow warming his face, watching it leap, gesticulate and lessen,
> and he keeps throwing twigs, dead thoughts, fragments of memory, all
> the used parts of his life to keep his contemplation pure and bright.
> When he is tired and returns into himself, then he has performed some
> kind of sacrifice, some ritual.[4]

The hermit consumes the world and aspects of his self, in order to
perceive both differently. The isolated artist has to jettison parts of the
world he knows in order to come into possession of previously
unknown sides of it.

While, in that early essay, Walcott directs our attention to the
division in his make up, what is most apparent in Walcott's essays
overall is a striving towards a coalition between the artist and his
community, a unification of the two traditions he embodies. The
divisions are both imaginary and real. Their union is seen when both
conditions are galvanised to facilitate the creative moment. The
relationship generates a creative tension which has ramifications not
only for the artist's assessment of history, religion and language but
for his very being. The separation between interior and exterior
worlds is symptomatic of a primary divide in Walcott's consciousness,
rather than a clinical divide that might lead to dissociation of self *from*
the world, as is the case with a full blown psychosis. Walcott's sense of
dissociation generates a creative tension that feeds into his poetry.
The two traditions inform his ambiguous consciousness so that he can
never settle for a single solution to a posed problem. If something is
one thing, then it is equally another, or as a bare minimum, it suggests
its opposite.

Walcott's art of duality is partly explained by his childhood
experience:

> In that simple schizophrenic boyhood one could lead two lives: the
> interior life of poetry, the outward life of action and dialect.[5]

In 'A Far Cry from Africa', an early poem included in *In A Green Night*, he is equally dualistic, declaring himself "divided to the vein". Already there is the ambivalence which hints at synthesis at the heart of the proclaimed division, a wish to artificially expose long buried oppositions between ancestries in need of reconciliation if the artist – and his community – are to grow. A legitimate task of the creative artist in such circumstances, Walcott argues, is to try and resolve this conflict by dramatising the relationship between those ancestral cultures in an imaginative return to an earlier phase in the history of their relationship. He does this by examining his own past. Walcott sees his generation as typifying this quest for self-definition and by extension the definition of a community:

> My generation had looked at life with black skins and blue eyes, but only our own painful, strenuous looking, the learning of looking, could find meaning in the life around us, only our own strenuous hearing, the hearing of our hearing, could make sense of the sounds we made.[6]

Where the Caribbean is an Adamic new world the artist has a blank canvas and the chance of a first response to it – "if there was nothing, there was everything to be made".[7] But Walcott's is an Adam who retains the memory of a previous failure and determines, now, to get things right. In other words a pre-lapsarian world is inhabited by a post-lapsarian consciousness, that Walcott refers to in 'What the Twilight Says . . .' as "the faith of using the old names anew". 'The Muse of History' sees Walcott making his peace with both of his "inwardly forgiven grandfathers". To them he gives

> strange and bitter and yet ennobling thanks for the monumental groaning and soldering of two great worlds, like the two halves of a fruit seamed by its own bitter juice, that exiled from your own Edens you have placed me in the wonder of another.[8]

That the response is not 'simple' is a condition of the artist's understanding of his situation. If there is an ambiguity in the creative response there is a matching ambiguous result,

> darkness still preserves the awe of self-enactment as the sect gathers for its self-extinguishing, self-discovering rites.[9]

The toll on the artist is a partial death of sensibility, in exact measure for the insights gained. Such trade-offs between the artist and the world that is his obsession promote the idea of a contract, unwritten and unspoken but intuitively agreed, between the artist and his community.

In Walcott's poetry this covenant with community – what he calls his "ancestral debt"[10] – registers on a number of diverse levels; from the emotionally benign – "this shelving sense of home"[11] – through the empathetic – "these shacks that made me"[12] – to an intellectual insistence on some distance and detachment:

> These poems I heaved aren't linked to any tradition like a mossed cairn . . . [13]

Here Walcott suggests an inevitable symbiosis between the shapes that define a space and place and the forms and shapes of the poems that come out of it,

> A panel of sunrise
> on a hillside shop
> gave these stanzas
> their stilted shape.[14]

The quatrain stanza is itself a panel added to the overall building of the poem. Its stilted shape reflects the literal house on stilts and counters any charge of stiff, unnatural formality by pointing to the natural origins of the stanza. Those hillside shacks and shops seem somehow to have grown out of the landscape, seem outcrops of the elemental world. By locating the tightness of the quatrain form firmly in the 'natural' world Walcott is partly absolved from the criticism of literariness, of devices imported to contain and organise material that would otherwise take on looser, less formal shapes. He does this by claiming that in this example it is nature which dictates what form the poem takes and not the poem which gives shape and form to nature. This is an important indicator of the types of solution Walcott seeks in his prose; the yoking together of apparently unreconcilable opposites to show resemblances and likenesses where none was previously perceived. A metaphysical preoccupation, to an extent, but one customised by Walcott to reconcile two distinct traditions in himself through a process of self-exploration – teasing out instances of coalition and synthesis between them.

Walcott's relationship to 'home', though verifiable and complementary to his art, remains an uneasy one. There is both contradiction and ambiguity in his attitude towards the place, alongside his unabashed acknowledgement of an indebtedness to it which no amount of creativity can settle. The essays tackle this notion of a covenant with place and its people. Whereas in the poems Walcott is keen to demarcate home from elsewhere, (see the format of *The Arkansas Testament* and *The Fortunate Traveller*) he also presents other places as vying for his loyalty or at least his engagement with them. This has given rise to Walcott's stance being defined as 'internationalist', a status of homelessness he himself accredits in *The Fortunate Traveller* by the term "homeless satellite". Certainly in the range of his subject matter Walcott is not confined to one geographical location. But all these excursions into other places are surely mediated by his rootedness in a Caribbean landscape. The covenant with place must be seen as integral to Walcott's sense of owing divided-but-dual loyalty to the two distinct cultural traditions played out historically in the one landscape. At the level of language, Walcott traces these traditions back to their separate origins in order to come to terms with some primal and original hurts in himself. He attempts to confront and heal those hurts in order to arrive at a better understanding of himself:

> mongrel as I am, something prickles in me when I see the word Ashanti as with the word Warwickshire, both separately intimating my grandfathers' roots, both baptising this neither proud nor ashamed bastard, this hybrid, this West Indian.[15]

This self definition is also a definition of community. By an unflinching scrutiny of his 'self' Walcott also – paradoxically – achieves some understanding of the communal psyche branded West Indian. It is an understanding that draws on:

> a memory of imagination . . . which has nothing to do with actual experience.[16]

Through the "living element"[17] that is language Walcott finds that it is possible to dramatise splits which are otherwise too convoluted – as organic processes – to unravel:

> Our bodies think in one language and move in another . . . the language of exegesis is English.[18]

Perhaps the distinction is too sharp (contemplating in English, moving in dialect), failing to account for the fact that a long tract in dialect is as pure a thought or meditation as one in standard English. And presumably someone who is unaware of all the rigours of standard English grammar will think in the nearest equivalent made up of dialect words and grammar as well as English ones. Certainly, in the Caribbean context, if a person is thinking, using all the language resources at his or her disposal, s/he would be foolish to ditch some tools from the kit just to conform to a notion of the 'superiority' of one kind of language over another.

Dramatising these splits can seem artifical given their organic basis. How can it be meaningful to speak of a purely African or a purely English thought in the West Indian mind? According to Walcott,

> the West Indian poet is faced with a language which he hears but cannot write because there are no symbols for such a language and because the closer he brings hand and word to the precise inflections of the inner language and to the subtlest accuracies of his ear the more chaotic his symbols will appear on the page . . . his function remains the old one of being filter and purifier, never losing the tone and strength of the common speech as he uses the hieroglyphs, symbols or alphabet of the official one.[19]

The synthesis Walcott ascribes to the poetic imagination faced with two opposing languages exemplifies the problem; the problem in the case of English is that the words symbolise objects and concepts which do not belong in the landscape, while the dialect – although it confirms the symbols – lacks the magnitude necessary to account for the poetic psyche. Walcott's solution is to couple English forms – the alphabet or symbols – with the fluidities of the dialect – its tone, pace, and inflection. This synthesis serves both to broaden the strictures of the former and to 'purify' the latter.

> What would deliver him from servitude was the forging of a language that went beyond mimicry, a dialect which had the force of revelation as it invented names for things, one which finally settled on its own mode of inflection, and which began to create an oral culture of chants, jokes, folk-songs and fables; this, not merely the debt of history was his proper claim to the New World.[20]

Walcott refuses to simplify the issues around the West Indian poet's choice of language to a straightforward choice between 'dialect' and

'English'. What emerges in both the poems and the essays is a subtle shifting of emphases according to the dominant artistic needs and practices taxing Walcott at any given moment. He rejects outright the two 'extremes' open to the West Indian writer – on the one hand a championing of dialect – "however gross and incomprehensible" – and on the other English at the expense of dialect. Rather he opts for a third option, envisaging a writer "dedicated to purifying the language of the tribe . . . He is the mulatto of style."[21]

This adaptation of the language is akin to a possession of it. Where language "is the empire"[22] the subjects of the empire can strike back by making that language their own:

> the speeches of Caliban are equal in their elemental power to those of his tutor. The language of the torturer mastered by the victim.[23]

Walcott makes a case for the power of the imitative. In the Caribbean context, where the people have been enslaved and colonised into a different language and culture, imitation is seen to be as legitimate as any self-conscious originality. It becomes a measure of the flexibility of the slave that s/he is able to master the language and religion of 'the Master' and so gain mastery over his/her own psyche. Walcott argues that by internalising the ruler's culture and re-invigorating it to suit the new surroundings, colonised people defied the very foundations of enslavement, effectively achieving their own self-emancipation. Aspects of the slave culture had to be shed if that adaptation to a new place – under sufferance – was to succeed. Mimicry therefore becomes "an act of imagination"[24] rather than the mindless 'aping' of a hollow people that V.S. Naipaul sees. Walcott turns Naipaul's infamous curse –

> "nothing has ever been created in the West Indies and nothing will ever be created"[25]

– into the mechanism for originality and inspiration:

> Nothing will always be created in the West Indies . . . because what will come out of there is like nothing one has ever seen before.[26]

If, during slavery, mimicry was a mechanism for survival and usurpation of the slavers' language and religion – "he adapted his master's religion, he also adapted his language"[27] – the creativity is seen in the way that language and religion are changed under the new proprietorship of the slaves:

> the tribe in bondage learned to fortify itself by cunning assimilation of the religion of the Old World. What seemed to be surrender was redemption. What seemed the loss of tradition was its renewal.[28]

By taking and 'turning' that language to their own inflections, Walcott argues, it was the slaves who guaranteed its survival in the New World – "their own God was being taken away from merchant and missionary by a submerged force that rose at ritual gatherings."[29] The language inherited by the poet, then, was the bequest of slaves. It is in this knowledge that Walcott derides simplistic attempts to reclaim an idea of Africa that the West Indian can no longer possess:

> Ogun was an exotic for us, not a force. We could pretend to enter his power but he would never possess us, for our invocations were not prayer but devices.[30]

In the essays he consistently attacks the glorification of ignorance which he sees in arguments that promote dialect as 'African' and abjure English or which see the poor as somehow exalted in their culturally 'pure' condition. Read against the background of the rise of the Black Power movement in the Caribbean and the re-Africanisation of popular consciousness, what is remarkable about these essays is their passionate, sceptical refusal to be swayed by the fashionable ideas of the time.

History, as process, Walcott argues, is nullified in this New World setting. History cannot be relied upon in a place where there isn't a past accessible to historical enquiry. History is jettisoned for myth and a view of time as ever-present – "the timeless yet habitable moment". According to Walcott's argument all that has happened in the past of the Old World is made actual or simultaneous by what takes place in the New World. An original act in the present is at once a re-enactment of the past. Subsequently the bias in the idea of an unknowable past or a grand past belonging to another world is neutralised.

> These writers reject the idea of history as time for its original concept as myth, the partial recall of the race. For them history is fiction, subject to a fitful muse, memory. Their philosophy, based on contempt for historic

time, is revolutionary, for what they repeat to the New World is its simultaneity with the Old. Their vision of man is elemental, a being inhabited by presences, not a creature chained to his past.[31]

If the writer is to grow s/he must go beyond the "confrontation of history".[32] The writer who has cultivated this awareness, Walcott insists, is not prone to nostalgia, nor to despair at the weight of this "absence or ruins", since the most ordinary of acts is synonymous with large historical ones:

> Violence is felt with the simultaneity of history. So the death of a gaucho does not merely repeat, but is, the death of Caesar. Fact evaporates into myth.[33]

This releases the poet from the burden of the past – "it is not the pressure of the past which torments great poets but the weight of the present"[34] – freeing his/her imagination.

Walcott deploys biographical details extensively in his essays as if to argue that any account of the artist and his community must be corroborated by the life and personal history of the artist. For example the fact that Walcott's upbringing is middle class, Methodist and half-white in a St. Lucia dominated by Catholicism and poor blacks might bear some relation to his sense of a lack of involvement in the life and – what he perceived in boyhood as – the vitality of the island. This 'distance' becomes useful and necessary for the telescoping of that island's life into sharp focus in his art. In his early years though, Walcott agonised over that separation and wanted dearly to be a Catholic peasant. The 'theatre of the poor' is there in the street festivities and the night life of the island, but in order to create dramas of his own making the young Walcott had to turn his back on that 'other life', while yet always keeping an ear tuned to its 'frequency'

> On the verandah, with his back to the street, he began marathon poems on Greek heroes which ran out of breath, lute songs, heroic tragedies, but these rhythms, the Salvation Army parodies, the Devil's Christmas songs, and the rhythms of the street itself were entering the pulse-beat of the wrist.[35]

In his essays Walcott stops short of an assertion that duality and the binary opposition of these twin-traditions cannot be an end in itself but rather marks the beginning of real thinking on the Caribbean condition. He does not go on to show the complexity inherent in dualities when they compound themselves into plurality. In this stopping short of a plural vision he is not alone among his generation of writers. He has bettered many of his contemporaries in at least introducing the idea of an 'other' as a counter to the main progenitor, thereby setting into motion a dynamic whose impetus complicates into plurality. Only Wilson Harris, in the form and ideas in his novels and essays, comes to grips with this complex reality made up not of composite pairs but a kaleidoscopic whole. Wholeness, according to Harris, can only ever be partially grasped by the writer. This is in keeping with the limits of linear thought and comprehension. It therefore becomes necessary for the writer to make repeated, unending, explorations of the same terrritory since each journey will throw up new truths. Harris calls these thought-expeditions 're-hearsals' which, in their repetition, yield a cumulative understanding. Walcott touches on a similar complexity in his understanding of the sophisticated language situation in his native St. Lucia with its French and English based creoles co-mingling with their standard equivalents as well as cross-pollinating between themselves. His essays are blueprints which any attempt at an understanding of the condition of artists in his generation cannot ignore, charting as they do, the making of the Caribbean artistic mind.

NOTES

1. Walcott, 'Meanings', *Savacou*, No.2, 1970.
2. Walcott, 'The Muse of History', in Orde Coombs (ed), *Is Massa Day Done?*, New York, 1974, p.1.
3. Walcott, 'The Figure of Crusoe', unpublished lecture, University of West Indies Library, Trinidad and Tobago, 1965, p.3.
4. *ibid.*, p.1.
5. Walcott, 'What the Twilight Says, an Overture', *Dream on Monkey Mountain and Other Plays*, New York, 1970, p.4.
6. *ibid.*, p.8.
7. *ibid.*, p.4.
8. Walcott, 'The Muse of History', *op.cit.*, p.27.
9. Walcott, 'What the Twilight Says: An Overture', *op.cit,*, p.5.
10. *ibid.*, p.38.
11. Walcott, *Midsummer*, London, 1982, p.11.
12. *ibid.*, 'LIV'.
13. Walcott, 'L', *Midsummer*, p.70.
14. Walcott, 'Cul de Sac Valley', *The Arkansas Testament*, London, 1987, p.9.
15. Walcott, 'What the Twilight Says, an Overture', p.10.
16. Walcott, 'The Muse of History', p.25.

17. *ibid.*, p.25.
18. Walcott, 'What the Twilight Says, an Overture', p.31.
19. Walcott, 'The Muse of History', p.13.
20. Walcott, 'What the Twilight Says: an Overture', p.17.
21. *ibid.*, p.3
22. Walcott, 'The Muse of History', p.15.
23. *ibid.*, p.4.
24. Walcott, 'The Caribbean: Culture or Mimicry?', *Journal of Interamerican Studies and World Affairs*, Vol.16, No.1, February 1974, pp3-13.
25. V.S. Naipaul, *The Overcrowded Barracoon*, p.8.
26. Walcott, 'The Caribbean: Culture or Mimicry?', *op.cit.*, p.9.
27. *ibid.*, p.13.
28. Walcott, 'The Muse of History', p.7.
29. *ibid.*, p.12.
30. Walcott, 'What the Twilight Says, an Overture', p.8.
31. Walcott, 'The Muse of History'.
32. *ibid.*, p.2.
33. *ibid.*, p.7.
34. *ibid.*
35. Walcott, 'What the Twilight Says, an Overture', p.22.

Clara Rosa de Lima

Walcott, Painting and the Shadow of Van Gogh

Walcott, Painting and the Shadow of Van Gogh

in our ears
sang Baudelaire's exhortation to stay drunk,
sang Gauguin's style, awarded Vincent's ear.[1]

An uncollected poem by Walcott, published in the journal *Caribbean Quarterly* in 1980, is entitled 'Self Portrait':

The loneliness of Van Gogh.
The humbleness of Van Gogh.
The terror of Van Gogh.

He looks into a mirror,
and begins to paint himself.

He discovers nobody there
but Vincent Van Gogh.
This is not enough.

He cuts off an ear.
He looks into a mirror;
there is Vincent Van Gogh
with a bandaged ear.

It resembles his portrait,
he is attempting to remain,
first, he must disappear,

he will arrive by reductions
beyond any more terror
by a lonely process.

When the mirror will proffer
neither fame nor pain,
neither no nor yes

Or maybe, or once, or
no. Nobody there,
Not Vincent Van Gogh,

humble, frightened and lonely,
only,
a fiction. An essence.[2]

Although this is obviously a portrait *of* Van Gogh *by* Walcott looking *at* Van Gogh's self portrait (either 'Self Portrait with Mutilated Ear' or 'Self Portrait with Pipe and Bandaged Ear', both painted in Arles in January/February, 1889), its ambiguously neutral title suggests that the "essence" the portrait is finally seen to capture is one shared, or at least embraced, by the poet. Such an assertion might not seem to be justified by that one instance, but in fact this identification with Van Gogh is one of many that appear throughout Walcott's work. In this essay the significance of that identification is examined, both in terms of Walcott's attitude to the roles and 'duties' of the artist – poet or painter – and in relation to his own practice as a painter which has re-asserted its importance as a facet of his creative output in recent years.

Although he gave up painting 'seriously' – in the sense of wanting to make a career as an artist – in his early twenties, painting has always been a passion of Walcott's. His father, Warwick, who died in his thirties when Derek and his twin brother Roderick were a little over a year old, had aspired to be a painter. In his essay 'Leaving School' Walcott remembered the force of his father's presence in the house through the years of his childhood:

On the walls of the drawing room were a copy of Millet's 'The Gleaners', a romantic original of sea-birds and pluming breakers, he called 'Riders of the Storm', a minature oil painting of mother, a self portrait in water colour and an avenue of pale coconut palms . . . . These objects had established my vocation and made it as inevitable as that of any craftsman's son, for I felt that my father's work, however minor, was unfinished. Rummaging through stuffed dark cupboards, I sometimes came across finely copied verses, evidence of a polite gracile talent, and once on a sketch book of excellent pencil studies. I treasured the books he used; two small blue covered volumes on *The Topographical*

Draughtsman and on *Albrecht Durer*, and thick ridged, classical albums
of John McCormack, and, I think, Galli Curci. It was this veneration
that drew his friends to me.[3]

Most important of those friends was Harry Simmonds, a painter
who became Walcott's teacher and spiritual mentor, instilling in the
young man and his comrade Dunstan St. Omer both a passion for art
and an understanding of the commitment that a particular perception
of the artistic life demands. Harry Simmonds had converted an old
army morgue on Barnard's Hill into a studio, and it was there that the
young men and their 'teacher' would meet and work. Walcott writes
of the subtle ways Simmonds encouraged the young men to feel more
professional about their work.

> Harry would let me have the use of his studio on Saturdays and
> during vacations. This meant permission to play his classical records
> on the grey- metal red-buttoned radiogram as loudly as I wanted, the
> use of his neat battered Royal typewriter, his library and his liquor
> cabinet.[4]

But Simmonds would also 'correct' his pupils' work; the opening
section of *Another Life* ends with the image of the adolescent Walcott
carrying the drawing of the harbour, that he had struggled with all
afternoon, over to Simmonds's desk, where "with slow strokes the
master changed the sketch."[5]

It is in *Another Life* Walcott begins the comparison of the
relationship between Van Gogh and Gauguin with that between
Dunstan St Omer (Gregorias) and himself. The two young artists
believed themselves blessed with a mission: to paint "every neglected
self-pitying inlet"[6] of their landscape and so to found a Caribbean
Renaissance. To that end they tramped the island's "roads limp from
sunstroke"[7] often contriving to be "drunk// as Van Gogh's shadow
rippling on a cornfield".[8] They were:

> orphans of the nineteenth century,
> sedulous to the morals of a style
> we lived by another light . . . [9]

That "style" is the style of Van Gogh and Gauguin, the "other light",
both the distinctive light of the Caribbean and their vision of what art
should be.

Looking back on the same period of his life in poems XVII and
XVIII of *Midsummer* Walcott's description of himself as "the painter

with easel rifled to his shoulder" who took "the road to paint in my eighteenth year"[10] inevitably calls to mind Van Gogh's picture of 'The Painter on his Way to Work' – an image which shimmers behind several of the references to himself and St. Omer at that time. In those years writing poetry and painting were part of the same obsession for Walcott, but because he gradually came to accept that his talent as a painter was not adequate to his ambition, that his painting could not "capture thought", could not accommodate that "crystal of ambiguities" that seemed the only adequate response to his situation, Walcott's energy was diverted into poetry. Van Gogh's life and work remain, though, as the measure of Walcott's primal, 'Adamic' response to experience, it exemplifies the power of true art to reach to the core of being:

> I have been comparing the sea almond's shape to the suffering
> in Van Gogh's orchards. And that, too, is primal . . . [11]

And he continued to paint, too, though for years only as an adjunct to his playwriting activities, designing sets, costumes and 'painting' characters as he worked out their parts. For a revised version of the early play *Henri Christophe*, re-titled *The Haitian Earth*, for example, performed in St Lucia in 1984, Walcott produced an extensive collection of sketches with written specifications of how the scenes should be directed together, with a few formal paintings. He made very detailed sketches of the particular actors he had in mind for particular parts. These 'working drawings' had an 'independent' existence in the sense that they were all displayed in the main window of one of the island's stores as part of the advertising for the production and some were subsequently exhibited elsewhere.

Although Van Gogh is not always named, the basis for the assertion that he functions as a model of Walcott's *true* artist is suggested in many places throughout the poetry where aspects of his life, character or work are echoed or invoked. Walcott has several times referred to his own Dutch ancestry as a key to his interest in Flemish art, and there is even the suggestion of a physical resemblance – Van Gogh was of "reddish fair complexion"[12] – which Walcott, being keen on such 'omens', arguably picks up on with his Shabine persona in 'The Schooner *Flight*'.

That comparison is stretching the allusion somewhat but the 'presence' of Van Gogh is felt in all sorts of ways throughout Walcott's work. Most importantly it offers a model for the synthesis of the conflicting strands of allegiance that his determination to be both the Romantic artist – the unique individual talent – *and* the outspoken, committed poet of the West Indian people, created in his mind.

In many ways Van Gogh seems a remote and unlikely master for an aspiring young Caribbean artist but Walcott's understanding of the Dutch painter's relevance to his own situation was one of the things he learnt from Harry Simmonds. Indeed, in his portrait of Simmonds' final breakdown in *Another Life*, Walcott invokes Van Gogh (and Gauguin) as the elder man's "saints", his mentors in both passion and despair. Their fate anticipates Simmonds' own end, hence the importance of "his yellowing *Letters to Theo* and *Noa Noa*".[13]

Van Gogh's absolute commitment to art and the obsessional manner of his pursuit of that commitment was a fundamental tenet of Simmonds' teaching for his two students. That the lesson was absorbed is apparent in the other references throughout Walcott's work to the necessity of such a commitment. In *Another Life* Walcott draws this portrait of the young poet at work:

> Sunset and dawn like manacles chafed his wrist
> no day broke without chains,
> bent like a carpenter over the new wood
> a galley-slave over his scarred desk,
> hours breaking over his head in paper.[14]

The compulsion that drives such an artist is a kind of natural violence, Walcott argues, an uncontrollable "Force" comparable to the "brutal exchange between breaker and rock".[15] Shabine, in 'The Schooner *Flight*', who at one point resorts to bloody violence in defence of his art, declares that he "has no nation but the imagination";[16] he is the classic image of the 'Van Goghic' artist who values everything – love of country and love of family – less than his commitment to his art.

To hold passionately to values, beliefs or methods of working which the society one would serve by that work regards as irrelevant, dangerous or downright retrograde is to court a kind of madness. Mandelstam's "divine fever" ('Forest of Europe'), Ovid's indifference to the literary fashions of his period ('The Hotel Normandie Pool') and Van Gogh's obsessive quest to catch the essence of the life light in his painting (which society regarded as garish, ugly and crude) are classic expressions of that madness. Walcott has always been interested in artists and poets who were regarded as exhibiting such madness because he has always equated the urgent force of his own creative imagination with that kind of obsessive commitment. In 'Poetry – An Enormously Complicated Art', an article he wrote in 1962, he explained that

> I am not mystifying the process of composition, which is often downright hard work, as magic, but I believe that poetry originates in magic in the sense that one accepts the possibility of God. What is true is that the good poet is the proprietor of the experience of the race, that he is and has always been the vessel, vates, rainmaker, the conscience of the king and the embodiment of the society, even when society is unable to contain him.[17]

The last phrase is the crucial one really, "even when society is unable to contain him". For Walcott the true poet or artist must, as he has said in another interview,[18] trust his instinct, his "inner ear" to the exclusion of all else, for, the logic goes, if he is a true poet he will express the essence of the time regardless of the opinions of his peers.

Several poems chart the course of Walcott's own creative madness; most strikingly in *Another Life* the section recalling Walcott's attempt to become a painter establishes the link between the early image of Van Gogh "mad at Arles"[19] and Walcott's own understanding of creative madness. In Chapter 9 the account of the young man's growing frustration over his felt inability to render in paint the *essence* of the landscape he so loved, is prefaced by this talisman "remember Vincent, saint/ of all sunstroke".[20]

The passage that follows is made up of a collage of images from some of Van Gogh's most famous paintings (such as 'Irises', 'Crows Over A Cornfield', 'Sunflowers') and a line from Van Gogh's letters to his brother, in which he chronicles the course of his obsession:

> The sun explodes into irises
> the shadows are crossing like crows,
> they settle, clawing the hair,
> yellow is screaming.
>
> Dear Theo I shall go mad.[21]

The remainder of the section attempts to evoke the symptoms of that madness; an intensified perception magnifying all the elements of his situation, a sense of being somehow threatened by the natural world around him, and the tantalising certainty that the mystical essence is close by but always just out of reach, that he is actually being mocked by the very landscape he would capture:

Is that where it lies,
in the light of that leaf, the glint
of some gully, in a day
glinting with mica, in that rock
that shatters in slate
in that flashing buckle of ocean?
The skull is sucked dry as a seed,
the landscape is finished.
The ants blacken it, signing.
Round the roar of an oven, the gnats
hiss their finical contradiction.
Nature is a fire,
through the door of this landscape
I have entered a furnace.

I rise, ringing with sunstroke![22]

In his earlier work Walcott had often made the identification with artists who, like Van Gogh, were driven by their "divine fever" to the point of suicide. In 'Elegies' in *25 Poems*, for example, the young poet considers the achievement of poets like Chatterton and Keyes, and acknowledges that their poems acquire a special authority as a consequence of their early deaths. It is in 'Hart Crane' in *Poems*, however, that Walcott identifies most plainly with the suicide's mentality. In that poem Walcott *celebrates* the American poet's suicide as the culmination of the true artist's "natural despair". By the time he took his life, the poem suggests, Crane was so deranged:

The sea was only ritual, he had
already seen complexity go mad
in the asylum metaphor.[23]

Walcott identifies himself with Crane in the final stanza when he describes Crane's leap:

From Brooklyn, on the brink
Of being, a straw doll blown
From Manhattan to Mexico to sink
Into that sea where vast deliriums drown.[24]

"That sea" includes, of course, the Caribbean. Although in these early poems the concern with suicide reads rather like a pose that the young poet strikes as part of his determination to become a 'true' artist, the sense of the despair that led those other artists to suicide, isolation, exile, betrayal, somehow feeding inspiration continues throughout his work. Walcott developed his interest in Crane in a visual form in the series of illustrations he created for a documentary made by the New York Centre for Visual History in 1986.

The link between suffering and a particular kind of vision which Hart Crane's life and work exemplifies is another aspect of the Van Gogh metaphor that Walcott's work has always embraced. Although he condemns Caribbean society for its neglect of its artists, one feels that no matter what provisions any society made, Walcott's *true* artists would be, by definition, destined to be outsiders, to be "saints of self torture".[25] Part of that self torture is the tension between a felt duty to *speak for* the "theatre of the poor", and yet also to speak against the mediocrity of spirit which characterises bourgeois life.

Van Gogh's commitment to the poor was an aspect of his religious vocation to minister to the spiritual needs of his people. He was not a success as a minister, being, people said, too intense and uncompromising about the meaning of Christian belief in relation to the condition in which much of the Dutch peasantry lived. His simple socialism inevitably made him unpopular among the more affluent members of his congregation and, at the same time, alienated the peasants he aspired to help, for he was not *of* them in terms of his class and background and didn't seem to comprehend the complexity of their situation. The echo of Walcott's controversial 'humanism' rings in that account. And just as Van Gogh's religious vocation gave way to his vocation as a painter, so Walcott's passionate religiosity as a boy was undermined by a growing commitment to the role of the artist.

The conversion from a religious to an artistic vocation was traumatic for Walcott too. But if art replaced religion as the structuring ethos of Walcott's life the commitment to 'the people' which was fundamental to his faith and which, indeed, put him at odds with the Church, was carried over into his artistic function, just as Van Gogh's had been. Walcott's assertion that "before the people became popular / he loved them"[26] and his portraits of island life in poems like 'Testament of Poverty', 'Tales of the Islands', the alphabet of St Lucian characters in 'Another Life', 'Homecoming, Anse la Raye', and even 'Laventille' equate with Van Gogh's drawings of farm labourers and peasants, eloquent statements of both outrage and compassion. Walcott aspired, as he says in 'Another Life', "to make out of these foresters and fishermen/ heraldic men!" That this was an aspect of Van Gogh's practice that Walcott admired is made plain in 'Another Life' when Harry Simmonds is inserted among the pantheon of the great painters:

> the stars
> of Raphael, Saint Greco, and later
> not stars but the people's medals,
> with Siqueros, Gauguin, Orozco,
> Saint Vincent and Saint Paul.[27]

If Van Gogh is one of "the people's medals" alongside the mural painters of the Mexican revolution, Siqueros and Orozco, then it follows that his own ambition – and that of his St Lucian disciples – might also be read as 'revolutionary'. Walcott has been outspoken in his criticism of the shallow, philistine attitude of the neo-colonial black bourgeoisie who have, as far as he is concerned, perverted the promise of a new order which the end of colonial rule promised. He argued his case position in both his poetry and the many articles he wrote as arts critic for the *Trinidad Guardian*. His 'rage' against the shallow, hedonistic ethos of West Indian society is evident as early as 'Epitaph for the Young', however,

> Who talks of culture without civilisation?
> Where is your civilisation?
> A civilisation of tennis and country club,
> Hovels, and men who pulled themselves up by the braces
> [where] The arts flourish on irregular Thursdays.[28]

and in 'Montego Bay – Travelogue 11' from *Poems* he laments a society dedicated to the amusement of tourists, those "assassins of culture".[29] The ambition of the society's young artists is perverted into a flamboyant exoticism to conform to the tourist's stereotypes; so just as Van Gogh's vision of the south turned sour so the Caribbean becomes a "cracked playground", "just another climate for despair".[30]

That despair is made specific in the bitterness of the last line of 'Castilane' which records the young poet's loss of a lover to a "gold toothed" "merchant".

> A merchant claims the daughter
> A man who hawks and profits in this heat
> Jeering at poets with a gold toothed curse.

> Girl you were wise, whoever lived by verse?
> The future is in cheap enamel wares.[31]

In the angry condemnation of Harry Simmonds' fate as a symbol of the society's valuation of its artists in 'Another Life', Walcott laments a talent "wasted" "among a people with no moral centre".[32] Lacking this centre the society can have no respect for the achievements of its artists, hence the corrupt minister in 'The Schooner, *Flight*' gets "somebody to kick/ my crutch out his office" not "like a dog" but "like I was some artist."[33]

In his essays Walcott consistently campaigned for better treatment for artists within West Indian society. In his first year as arts critic for the *Trinidad Guardian* (1960) Walcott was declaring in essays like 'Artists Need Some Assistance' that since the Trinidad and Tobago government had a Ministry of Culture the state should make some tangible contribution to the housing and finances of the arts.[34] In an interview in 1975 he complained that Caribbean governments ignored their artists except as a means of impressing foreign dignitaries "then as fools we all go together, jump up and down three times and go home . . . to nothing."[35]

The state's indifference to the arts except as a means of gaining revenue from those "assassins of culture" and Walcott's feeling that the potential power of the arts had been subverted by such apathy and corruption was finally the cause of his abandoning the Theatre Workshop in Trinidad and choosing to live abroad for much of each year. In 1979 he complained:

> My generation has gone through a pioneering phase but it's all still to be done. There's no support. The Caribbean is a wearing out place.[36]

Although there was always an element of self-interest in his demands that, at the very least, a theatre and arts training school should be built in Trinidad, his concern was genuinely for the development of both the quality of life in the society and of the individual talents that were being squandered by the lack of experience of different possibilities when he had been appointed official playwright to the West Indian Federation in the late fifties, and commissioned to write *Drums and Colours* for the grand celebration of the Federation's inauguration. He has spoken of the fillip such recognition and support was to a then virtually unknown young playwright.[37]

But if Walcott was worn out and disillusioned by the philistine nature of West Indian society he was also critical – as Van Gogh had been in his time – of the artists and poets who preferred, rather than to try and change that society, to accept it and make an art that reinforced its prejudices. He has been consistently critical of the region's poets:

> . . . the bulk of West Indian verse is bad, only bearable if one forgives its origins and sympathises self-insultingly with its efforts. It has lagged far behind the novel, its structure is either sprawlingly *modern* or embarrassingly imitative. It is weakened into mere rhetoric by such themes as national pride and racial peevishness.[38]

As Victor Questel remarked, it sometimes seemed, reading Walcott's criticisms of West Indian literature, that he felt himself "the only serious artist in the society".[39] But there was more than just ego-massage in this critique, it was an aspect of his vision of the kind of alternative 'militancy' that the artists should be involved in.

Such outspoken criticism of one's political rulers, the philistine middle classes and one's fellow poets is not likely to make many friends, and we have already seen that Walcott felt himself alienated by his education, language and religious disillusion from the life of the West Indian peasantry. So it was perhaps inevitable, given his absolute conviction of a vocation to be *the* West Indian poet, that so much of his early poetry should revolve around the image of the outcast artist, the castaway soul.

Walcott's vision of the artist as revolutionary, in the sense of one who changes people's perceptions, who might *enlighten* the world, may be seen to derive from several aspects of Van Gogh's practice, though as I shall argue later it perhaps roots further back in art history to the idea of the Renaissance artists, who were more self-consciously determined to open the eyes of the world. When Walcott says in 'What the Twilight Says, an Overture' that "the future of West Indian militancy lies in art"[40] it would seem that that was what he meant. He puts it more plainly in an interview given in 1980,

> The possible realisation in the West Indies is art. I see no possibility of the country becoming unified and having its own strengths except in its arts. Because there is no economic power there is no political power. Art is lasting. It will outlast these things.[41]

Defined in those terms, Walcott's (and Van Gogh's) artist is a revolutionary, the dissenting voice that refuses to be cowed by conventional wisdom or the fashionable view, insisting on the importance of the individual talent while acknowledging the power and dignity of the un-politicised peasant and the "theatre of the poor".

But although the beach boys of Anse la Raye and the stoic peasants of Tobago may form part of his heartland's constituency, the community that Walcott's poems really speak to is indicated by the quality of his language and the range of his references. His use of European paintings, for example, has been seen both as evidence of his cultured, all embracing humanism and as a sign of his alienation from the world inhabited by the mass of his West Indian compatriots, part of his residual *colonised* vision. But although European painting might seem to have no tangible connection with the experience of the Caribbean, in an historical sense the changes in European society which those paintings record and reflect[42] bore directly on the facts of life in the Caribbean. Some of the images, too, so often reproduced on great house, school room and middle class household walls, infiltrated the imagination of a certain stratum of West Indian society, as images of Europe if nothing else.

Walcott's references to particular paintings have been thoroughly catalogued – at least in all the collections before *The Star-apple Kingdom* – in two excellent articles: Edward Baugh's meticulous 'Painters and Paintings in *Another Life*'[43] and Marian Stewart's imaginative 'Walcott and Painting'.[44] Victor Questel also devotes considerable space in his mammoth thesis to a head count of the painters Walcott alludes to.[45] The list of artists named or unmistakably evoked is almost as long as the list of writers felt to be an influence on Walcott's style in his apprenticeship – from Botticelli,[46] Brueghel[47] and Bellini[48] through Caravaggio,[49] Giotto,[50] Hobbema,[51] Leonardo,[52] and Raphael,[53] to Turner,[54] and Whistler[55]. Walcott uses these references in a similar way to his literary allusions – to give authority to an image, to point a way of seeing, to claim that culture as legitimately his own.

The most direct purpose of Walcott's references to painting emerges in the many evocations of the Renaissance in the early poetry. These repeated references seem to invite comparisons, if not in terms of achievement at least as far as intention was concerned, between the three artists in Simmonds' studio and the artists of the Italian Renaissance. Working at a time of intense local and geopolitical upheaval, breaking with a bankrupt tradition and "making it new" with a determination to catch "another light" adequate to the New

World they were discovering, Simmonds' *school* were inspired by the image of themselves as Renaissance men. As Baugh remarks, Walcott found in the Renaissance the "supreme example of a great age defined by its art, so to speak, the idea that it is art that brings the age to fullest self awareness, that *signs* the epoch."[56]

This is the root of the ambition to make an art that will 'change the world', not just appease fashionable conventions. So St. Omer is repeatedly dubbed the Caribbean's Giotto or Masaccio, the founding spirits of the Renaissance; artists emerging, as it were, from the primitive darkness of the Middle Ages and establishing a new tradition. The Renaissance comparison is made several times in 'Another Life', but it was implied earlier in 'The Cracked Playground', and in 'Allegre' in *In A Green Night*, which begins with an evocation of light:

> Some mornings are as full of elation
> As these pigeons crossing the hill slopes,
> Silver as they veer in sunlight and white
> On the warm blue shadows of the range.
>
> And the sunward sides of the shacks
> Gilded, as though this was Italy.

and goes on to suggest that the light of a new age may be dawning "like young Italy",

> No temples, yet the fruits of intelligence,
> No roots, yet the flowers of identity,
> No cities, but white seas in sunlight,
> Laughter and doves, like young Italy.[57]

If the idea of the Renaissance fired Walcott's imagination, images of the art of many periods became touchstones of a *life* against which the world was measured. Walcott acknowledges this in his use of the quotation from Malraux's *Psychology of Art* as an epigraph to Book One of *Another Life*,

> What makes the artist is the circumstance that in his youth he was more deeply moved by the sight of works of art than by that of the things which they portray.[58]

Many times in Walcott's work events and ideas are presented *against* images from art; Edward Baugh comments on the way Walcott

infiltrates images from painting into his description of local scenes in
'Another Life', for example the St Lucian hills are seen,

> stippled with violet
> as if they had seen Pissarro.[59]

Similarly in 'Roots' the landscape is viewed "As if it were Poussin or a
fragment from Bellini",[60] and in 'Brise Marine', recalling a lovers'
meeting:

> Sunday. The grass peeps through the breaking pier.
> Tables in the trees, like entering Renoir.[61]

More recent examples of this same manner of seeing occur in 'Spring
Street 58' from *Sea Grapes*. Here Walcott recalls that as an
impressionable young poet in New York

> . . . I could look at Mimi washing her feet
> as life imitating Lautrec.[62]

And in 'Piano Practice' from *The Fortunate Traveller*, the district
around the Metropolitan Museum of Art in New York is seen,
appropriately, through an extended metaphor of life being constructed to imitate art, "down avenues hazy as Impressionist
clichés".[63]

The whole stanza in which that line occurs is itself constructed in an
impressionist manner, detail piled on detail so that one must stand
back to see what is being said. That technique is an example of what is
perhaps the most original influence of that early training as a painter,
the sense we have of Walcott painting, so to speak, with words,
employing painterly techniques and devices in the creation of an
image or a scene. Walcott has always been painterly precise in his
exact descriptions of colour ("flesh the gamboge of lightning" in
'Hurrucan'[64]), but his painterly technique involves much more. At its
most straightforward it means composing a scene, as in *Midsummer*,
II, where Brodsky is posed as if in an Old Master painting:

> you are crouched in some ancient pensione
> where the only new thing is paper, like young St Jerome
> with his rock vault. Tonsured, you're muttering a line
> that your exiled country will soon learn by heart,

to a flaking, sunlit ledge where a pigeon gurgles.
Midsummer's furnace casts everything in bronze.[65]

Similarly, an earlier poem like 'Sunday Lemons' is a still life, an evocation of the appearance of lemons in a basket with the shadowy figure of a woman behind them. The subject is composed in just the way a painter arranges his objects for a still life, and they are related in terms of light and shade, mass and space. It is an intensely visual poem in the sense that nothing happens, but the image is so tangibly and powerfully drawn that it has the mysterious quality of the best still-life paintings which play with the conventions of the genre and draw the viewer beyond contemplations of the surface to question the presence of the articles, the story behind them, who, in this case, is the woman who is, one feels, the real subject of the poem, how is she defined by this sumptuous but melancholy evocation?

> hexagonal cities where bees
> die purely for sweetness
> your lamps be the last to go
>
> on this polished table
> this Sunday, which demands
> more than the faith of candles
>
> than helmeted conquistadors
> dying like bees, multiplying
> memories in her golden head;
>
> an afternoon vagues
> into indigo, let your lamps
> hold in this darkening earth
>
> bowl, still life, but a life
> beyond tears . . . [66]

Van Gogh painted lemons in a basket, of course, but this poem does not suggest Van Gogh's style. Stewart reads Van Gogh's manner in some passages of 'Another Life' however, particularly the section describing the journey of the coaster *Jewel*. In terms of colour, at least, one can see what she means in descriptive passages like:

> Her course sheared perilously close to the ochre rocks
> and bushy outcrops of the leeward coast,

sometimes so closely that it seemed to us
"that all the shoreline's leaves were magnified
deliberately, with the frightening detail."

Yet the yellow coast uncoiling past her prow
like new rope from a bollard never lost intent,
especially when the coiled beach lay
between black coves blinding
half moon of sand[67]

That "yellow coast" one can see "screaming" in Van Gogh's impasto. In one of his *Trinidad Guardian* essays Walcott remarked that "Van Gogh would have plastered thick sunlight onto his Provence canvasses instead of pure paint, if he could".[68] It is in 'Another Life' that we also find the most extended application of this technique. Baugh tells us that Chapter 9 was entitled 'The Act of Painting' in an early draft of the poem[69] and it is, as he says, a unique attempt to render the experience of painting in words. Walcott intertwines technical, emotional and art historical languages and references in an attempt to suggest the poised, seemingly illogical or surreal mental and physical process of making a painting:

Blue on the tip of the tongue,
and this cloud can go no further.
Over your shoulder the landscape
frowns at its image. A rigour
of zinc white seizes the wall,
April ignites the immortelle,
the leaf of a kneeling sapling
is the yellow flame of Lippi's Annunciation.
Like the scrape of a struck match, cadmium orange,
evened to the wick of a lantern.
Like a crowd, surrounding the frame
the muttering variegations of green.[70]

Certainly that is an ambitious and audacious way of writing, and insofar as it is possible, one that seems to have caught the *madness* that was Van Gogh's and, for Walcott, every true artist's obsessional pursuit.

But, as we have seen, Walcott's obsession took another route, and after his self-perceived 'failure' with paint in his teens he seemed to have abandoned 'serious' painting.[71] But he retained his passionate

interest in art and continually sketched and painted for sets, character developments, costumes, programmes and posters for his plays. His graphic work ranges from the bold and dramatic poster for *O Babylon!* (see illustration) through to the subtle line and wash illustrations he makes continually in the process of thinking about his plays (see illustration of the design for *The Joker of Seville*). But in the last few years Walcott has held two one-man exhibitions of his paintings, at the Art Creators Gallery in Port of Spain in 1986, and at the Artsibit Gallery in St Lucia in 1988. Returning, perhaps, to that idea of his father's work as unfinished, Walcott's paintings are mostly water-colours, with a few oils, and almost all were painted during his annual period of 'repose' in the Caribbean. In 1982 he painted a series of views from his hotel in Port of Spain, looking down on the Savannah with its race course and paddock. The fascination with the early morning light and with shadow and movement are plain to see, but there is still a stiffness about the way the paint is handled – one senses the 'caution' of which he wrote in *Another Life* crabbing his style. In a recent television interview he spoke modestly of his talent:

> There's a very big difference between someone who can paint pretty well and somebody who's a painter . . . it's how the paint is moved along recklessly, you know, without any kind of caution. And although I can paint pretty competent water-colours I just don't have that bursting confidence of someone, you know, sloshing the paint around. . . . I just don't slosh, I pull . . . It's all very Methodist.[72]

Walcott paints now as part of his process of focussing on a theme or idea. The Savannah paintings were done at the time Walcott was writing the Trinidad Hotel poems in *The Fortunate Traveller*. Later paintings in this new resurgence are much more successful. 'The Death of Gauguin' is a magnificently vivid water-colour (see cover) painted in 1985 and envisaged as part of a series he intended on the lives of the Impressionists. He attempted a version in oils but gave that up. The painting is a companion to the poem 'Gauguin' in *Midsummer* (XIX). It was painted at the same time and is part of that process of getting 'inside' the character which the Van Gogh poem quoted at the beginning of this essay epitomised. For Van Gogh and those who work in his shadow, painting – and painting in words – is "a lonely process" that makes things real. Is it Gauguin or Walcott who says, in the poem,

> I have baked the gold of their bodies in that alloy;
> tell the Evangelists paradise smells of sulphur,

that I have felt the beads in my blood erupt
as my brush stroked their backs.[73]

NOTES

1. Walcott, *Midsummer*, London, 1982, XVII, p.27.
2. Walcott, 'Self-Portrait', *Caribbean Quarterly*, vol.26, nos 1/2, p.94.
3. Walcott, 'Leaving School', *London Magazine*, vol.5, no. 6, Sept. 1965, pp.4–14.
4. *ibid.*
5. Walcott, *Another Life*, London, 1972, p.5.
6. *ibid.*, p.52.
7. *ibid.*, p.53.
8. *ibid.*, p.51.
9. *ibid.*, p.77.
10. Walcott, *Midsummer*, XVII, p.27.
11. *ibid.*, p.39.
12. Robert Wallace, *The World of Van Gogh*, Netherlands, 1969, p.23.
13. Walcott, *Another Life*, pp.119–20.
14. *ibid.*, p.75.
15. Walcott, *Sea Grapes*, London, 1976, p.84.
16. Walcott, *The Star-apple Kingdom*, London, 1979, p.8.
17. Walcott, *The Trinidad Guardian*, 18 June 1962, p.5.
18. Walcott, 'Any Revolution Based on Race is Suicidal', interview with Raoul Pantin, *Caribbean Contact*, July 1973, Vol.1, No.7, p.14.
19. Walcott, *Epitaph for the Young: A Poem in XII Cantoes*, Bridgtown, Barbados, 1949, p.29.
20. Walcott, *Another Life*, p.56.
21. *ibid.*, p.57.
22. *ibid.*.
23. Walcott, *Poems*, Kingston, 1951, p.14.
24. *ibid.*.
25. Walcott, *Another Life*, p.128.
26. Walcott, 'Hic Jacet', *The Gulf*, London, 1970, p.70.
27. Walcott, *Another Life*, p.75.
28. Walcott, *Epitaph for the Young*.
29. Walcott, *Poems*, p.6.
30. Walcott, 'The Cracked Playground', *Poems*, p.17.
31. Walcott, *In a Green Night*, London, 1962, p.46.
32. Walcott, *Another Life*, p.123.
33. Walcott, *The Star-apple Kingdom*, p.7.
34. Walcott, 'Artists Need Some Assistance', *The Sunday Guardian*, 3 March 1960, p.7.
35. Ric Mentus, 'Interview with Derek Walcott' in *The Jamaica Daily News*, cited by Rex Nettleford in *Caribbean Cultural Identity*, p.154.
36. David Pryce-Jones, 'Island Fling' in *The Radio Times*, 25 January 1979, p.4.
37. See Umberto Bonsignori, unpublished PhD thesis, *Derek Walcott: Contemporary West Indian Poet and Playwright*, University of California, Los Angeles, 1972, pp.6–7.
38. Walcott, 'Anthologies', in *Trinidad Sunday Guardian*, 12 April 1964, p.15.

39. Victor Questel, 'Blues in Caribbean Poetry' in *Kairi*, Port of Spain, 1978, pp.51–54.
40. Walcott, *Dream on Monkey Mountain and other plays*, New York, 1970, p.18.
41. Edward Hirsch, 'An Interview with Derek Walcott' in *Contemporary Literature*, vol.20 no.3, 1980, p.284.
42. In terms, for example, of the portraits of an emergent merchant class, images of events in nineteenth century European history, even simply in the portrayal of clothes, manners and architecture, all of which bore directly on colonial life and values.
43. Edward Baugh, 'Painters and Paintings in *Another Life*' in *Caribbean Quarterly*, vol.26, nos.1/2, 1980, pp.83–93.
44. Marian Stewart, 'Walcott and Painting' in *Jamaica Journal*, no 45, 1981, pp.56–68.
45. See Victor Questel's unpublished PhD thesis *Paradox, Inconsistency, Ambivalence and their Resolution in Derek Walcott's Writings, 1946–1976*, University of West Indies, Trinidad, 1979. For example, pp.131–33.
46. See 'Choc Bay'.
47. See 'Epitaph for the Young' and 'Schloss Erla'.
48. See 'Roots'.
49. See 'Che'.
50. See 'Another Life', p.61 and 'Sainte Lucie'.
51. See 'Another Life', p.6.
52. See 'Another Life', p.65.
53. See 'The Cracked Playground' and 'Another Life', p.44.
54. See 'A City's Death by Fire'.
55. See 'The Bridge'.
56. Edward Baugh, *op. cit.*, p.84.
57. Walcott, *In A Green Night*, pp.58–59.
58. Walcott, *Another Life*, p.1.
59. *ibid.*, p.74.
60. *In A Green Night*, p.60.
61. *ibid.*, p.59.
62. Walcott, *Sea Grapes*, p.58.
63. Walcott, *The Fortunate Traveller*, London, 1982, p.9.
64. *ibid.*, p.40.
65. Walcott, *Midsummer*, p.12.
66. Walcott, *Sea Grapes*, p.58.
67. *Another Life*, p.32–33
68. 'Patterns of Existence' in *The Trinidad Guardian*, 24 March 1966, p.5.
69. Edward Baugh, *Memory as Vision: Derek Walcott: 'Another Life'*, London, 1978, pp.39–40.
70. Walcott, *Another Life*, Chapter 9, p.55.
71. Notwithstanding a brief flirtation with the idea of making a career as a professional artist after he completed his university studies at the UWI in Jamaica. See 72, below.
72. Walcott in interview with Melvyn Bragg, *The South Bank Show*, 1988.
73. Walcott, *Midsummer*, XIX ii, p.30.

John Figueroa

Omeros

Omeros

Introduction

Sunt lacrymae rerum . . .

These are days not only of fast food but also of immediate literary comment and judgement. Even before *Omeros* was out one was given an advance copy – and six weeks to write a chapter on the book for the then forthcoming *The Art of Derek Walcott*. I have been acquainted with parts of the work for some time. But the complicated concerned music of the poem I met just six weeks ago. So I realise that although I must say what I have to say clearly and without hedging my bets, there will be much that I have missed, and more that I will see in a different light after prolonged re-reading.

Of one thing I am quite sure: this 325 page poem is an outstanding achievement, by a gifted and hardworking poet whose multifaceted Caribbean upbringing and experience was a necessary but not sufficient condition for the production of this masterpiece. While not lacking in any way lyrical fire, it makes meaning, and displays deep human concern, through a sort of novelistic structure of a mosaic kind.

I intend to examine this remarkable poem through well tried, or if you prefer old fashioned, categories: Historical, Metaphorical, Moral and Anagogical.

Historical

> We helped ourselves
> to these green islands likes olives from a saucer,
>
> munched on the pith, then spat their sucked stones on a plate.[1]

Like all history this poem tells a story, a complicated story, which in modern times we tend to associate with a novel rather than a poem. But in another sense it is, of course, fiction. It is fashioned, it is made up – the better to make sense of human actions, which of necessity happen in time, and along a continuum of time.

Its chief characters are taken from the island of St Lucia which was once struggled for, in the old empire days, by the then powerful forces of France and England. In fact it changed hands fourteen times between these two powers aiming to split the green calabash of the world between them. When at the Battle of the Saints De Grasse was defeated, if not outwitted, by the new tactics of Rodney, Britain was certain of its predominant position, not only in the Caribbean but also in Canada and India.

It is his preoccupation with this battle that prompts the character Plunkett's research, and brings him to the distinguished historical work of Breen:

Now he could roar out Breen's encomium by rote

. . . He taught Maud to say it by heart:
"*When we consider the weighty interest involved in the iss-*

ue . . . " (there was always a spray of spittle with this part,
as the sibilants reared with an adder's warning hiss),
"*Whereby the mighty projects of the coalesced powers*

were annihilated and Britain's dominion on the seas
secured . . . " Maud recited it to the yellow allamandas
as if they were fleurs-de-lys, as her clicking secateurs

beheaded them into a basket and up the stone stairs.[2]

St Lucia – much fought for – which played its part in this battle, is one of the main characters in the history that is this poem; it is also the home or operating focus for other main characters: Hector, Helen, Achille, Philoctete, Seven Seas, Ma Kilman, Dennis and Maud Plunkett, the Narrator and his father and mother, the barber, the tall standing black women who like ants carry their hundred weight loads of coal.

But the poem is historical in the wider sense of bringing in not only the French and the English and the Dutch in their so self-confident attitude of pillage and ownership: the Indians of the Plains are seen also as they are expected, by the citizens of the newly formed, revolutionary, democratic United States of America, to disappear like their smoke signals, meaningless and no longer visible as night falls over the Dakotas. The devastation of chattel slavery upon parts of Africa is also spelt out; and the dilemma faced by the modern 'development' of a place like St Lucia is brought clearly before our eyes.

But it must be stressed that the lyric intensity of the poem remains throughout what is of necessity outlining in a rather abstract and summary way:

> Art is History's nostalgia, it prefers a thatched
>
> roof to a concrete factory, and the huge church
> above a bleached village. The gap between the driver
> and me increased when he said:
> > "The place changing, eh?"
>
> where an old rumshop had gone, but not that river
> with its clogged shadows. *That* would make me a stranger.
> "All to the good," he said. I said, "All to the good,"
>
> then, "whoever they are," to myself. I caught his eyes
> in the mirror. We were climbing out of Micoud.
> Hadn't I made their poverty my paradise?[3]

Another main character who moves in and out of the poem, and plays a significant part, is Omeros, Homer himself, in the guise of the old blind poet, the seer without eyes, the beggar full of riches, the master of that long resounding line beating upon the conscious and unconscious ear like the ever breaking waves in the Peloponnesus or the Caribbean – *poluphlois boio thalasses. Toujours recomencée la mer!*

The structure of this history or fiction is, as in so much of Walcott, with his Horatian background, mosaic. We do not start with the Wrath of Achilles nor end with the funeral rites of Hector the tamer of horses. We do not have a straight line development, but rather like Penelope's weaving, under pressure from suitors, or Maud Plunkett's knitting of birds – those animals of wonder to the Greeks, and of shame to those moderns who long to be *rooted* somewhere or in some Nowhere – we have complicated patterns, and some puzzling juxtapositions, made less, rather than more, clear by the author's direct interventions in the style of old time novelists. Sometimes it is but the intervention of the *narrator*, but sometimes it appears to be the author, and in one place, at least, the *I* becomes a kind of general consciousness, or the locution of one of the characters, as if in the author's voice. A prime and rather confusing example of this takes place in the incident between the young Plunketts on the hillside during the war, as the camouflaged ships steam under the cliffs, and Dennis decides not to take the physical possession of Maud which she in her generosity is offering.

> . . . with gulls buzzing the cliff
>
> and screeching above us when she parted both lips
> and searched for his soul with her tongue, her wild grey eyes
> as flecked with light as the sea, then she was urging
>
> me to go in, port of entry, with my fingers
> and I could not.[4]

This particular intrusion of *I*, whether it be the voice of Plunkett or of the authorial voice is not, of course, new in Walcott. It appears in *Another Life*[5], but also long before that in 'Tales of the Islands'.[6] At times it is not clear enough just what is happening, or rather who is intended to be speaking.

To return to the Historical aspect, the historical theme is not so much, as had been asserted, *exile*. It is rather *where is home?* And, of course, man's inhumanity to man. The historical movement of people is often forgotten now, even in places like the Caribbean, which has been one of the greatest recipients and results of this movement, whether voluntary or forced. It cannot be by accident that the poem opens with what is to the local fishermen their main means of movement:

> "This is how, one sunrise, we cut down them canoes".
> Philoctete smiles for the tourists, who try taking
> his soul with their cameras . . . [7]

And notice too that the tourists are also involved in this process of the movement of people.

Much later in the poem we hear of Plunkett that his wanderings are over:

> Despite that morning's near accident, the old Rover
> sailed under the surf of threshing palms and his heart
> hummed like its old engine, his wanderings over,
>
> like the freighter rusting on its capstans.[8]

And the poem ends with the beach and "the sea was still going on."[9]

In the beginning and the end, Achille has travelled back to Africa, the Indian (sub continental) diaspora has taken place, the Indians of the Plains have been moved very nearly into extinction; we have been to Holland, where the young midshipman, also called Plunkett, has been spying for Rodney. We have been in the desert with Plunkett's fighting colleagues, we have been in Istanbul, and seen Athens and Atlanta, Georgia. We have, as they say in Nigeria, 'travelled'. And although the pivot and focal point is St Lucia, and Maud and Hector, and the father of the narrator, end their lives there, and Omeros appears there to show the narrator the way, there appears to be a secular version of the Augustinian conclusion somewhere in the background – "our hearts are restless until they rest in Thee". Or as we hear in connection with Seven Seas, who is the islander who has travelled most, and has lived among the "Red Indians":

> Seven Seas sighed. What was the original fault?
> "Plunkett promise me a pig next Christmas. He'll heal
> in time, too."
>   "We shall all heal."
>   The incurable
>
> wound of time pierced them down the long, sharp-shadowed street.[10]

But that is perhaps to anticipate the last aspect of our probing and analysis.

The historical aspects of this remarkable poem, then, are wide ranging. It is not only Helen of St Lucia who is portrayed and explored, but St Lucia herself – one of her names was Helen – and the displacement of people as an aspect of their human condition. The poem, much more a novel than an epic, while never losing its lyrical fire, is complicated in structure, gaining some of its meanings by the juxtaposition of episodes. For instance, an outburst on the part of the author:

> There was no difference
> between me and Philoctete . . . [11]

comes in between Ma Kilman's search for the proper native,
traditional herbs which will cure Philoctete of his longstanding
wound which stinks, and which isolates him, as it does his namesake in
the Iliad, from human comradeship. And the cure that works on him,
the prayerful use of the traditional, of the *native*, which is downgraded
by the modern, whether secular or religious, that cure works, in a
different way, on the narrator for his heart wound, the wound of living,
and perhaps loving not wisely but too well. So the fictional and poetic
power of the poem, and the poet, seem to suggest to us. But I have to
say that on this occasion, when recollected in tranquillity, the sleight
of hand does not seem quite to work.

It is now time to say something about the appearance of Homer in
this poem, as well as the appearance of the Homeric characters, or
more accurately names, already mentioned. For despite its title, and
despite the loving appearance of the blind bard himself – in St Lucia
and on the steps of St Martins-in-the- Fields – this poem is in no way
written, as it were, over the template of the Iliad or the Odyssey.
Helen (of St Lucia) appears, and Hector and Achille. And there is a
fight over her mysterious beauty. But these St Lucians also bear these
names because of the tradition started in slavery of giving slaves such
heroic names. Walcott somewhere calls the result of this custom "the
shadow of names". Perhaps as a poet he has always exaggerated the
power and importance of names, the giving of which he has more than
once reminded us was Adam's role and privilege.

The Homeric aspect, and context of meaning, in this poem is more
in the sea and the struggles with it, in what men fight for in Homer and
elsewhere, in the displacement and dislocation of people; the Wrath of
Achilles, in the Iliad, sent the souls of many noblemen to Hades,
leaving their bodies as carrion for the dogs and passing birds.

But the real heroes in this poem are not nobles, or "Kings of Men"
as they are in Homer; they are noble people, but most without rank.
There are a few with rank, such as Comte de Grasse and Rodney,
rivals at the Battle of the Saints. But they are few and unimportant.
The real heroes are Hector and Achille and Helen and Philoctete and
Seven Seas, some of them fishermen finding it difficult to make a living
in the days of trawling fishnets almost as big as St Lucia:

> banks robbed by thirty-mile seines,
> their refrigerated scales packed tightly as coins,

and no more lobsters on the seabed. All the signs
of a hidden devastation under the cones
of volcanic gorges. Every dawn made his trade

difficult and empty . . . [12]

Aristotle's dictum about the hero needing to be a prince or a leader of men is turned around. This is in fact one of the achievements of *Omeros*. And not only in the respect of the fishermen: Ma Kilman, who cures Philoctete, is a shop-keeper and a sybil/obeah woman; Helen is a maid and waitress; Maud Plunkett, one of the book's most sympathetic characters, is a gardener from Ireland in St Lucia because her husband is there looking for a son and for a connection with History. They are indeed noble people, but not people of the nobility. They belong to another stage and type of History.

Metaphorical

"This is how, one sunrise, we cut down them canoes".[13]

This is how Philoctete is made to start this long poem. Here we have the language of metaphor at work: that move beyond, but at the same time with, the purely ostensible signification of the words at hand. It is the way language is often used in every day converse, although there the cliché, and the hidden metaphor, often hide from us what is really going on. It is often forgotten that language as metaphor belongs not only to poetry, but also to other forms of fiction such as novels and short stories.

But, of course, poetry uses more intensely, and in a more structured way, this quite common kind of language. Philoctete continues:

"Once wind bring the news

to the *laurier-cannelles*, their leaves start shaking
the minute the axe of sunlight hit the cedars,
because they could see the axes in our own eyes.[14]

Notice the use of "shaking" in which, as so often happens in poetry, the ostensible and the metaphorical use are equally evident; whereas in "the axes in our own eyes" the metaphorical has taken over, in a rather sinister way. For the trees and the waterfalls and the mountains and the ground-doves' mating call – as they are used here as the poem becomes air-borne – continue to play on our feelings in a certain way because they have been made to become not only sentient but personal communicating beings, realising what the work of the axe means to the *laurier-cannelles*. Whereas to the fishermen, as to the warriors of the Iliad, the felling and hollowing by fire of the proud trees are but necessary steps in their vocations.

Note also that because of the dramatic and novelistic nature of this poem, these words are put into the mouth of Philoctete, who uses a slightly bantering tone: he is showing off just a little to the tourists. After all, he is going to get to the very important matter of 'raising' some money from them by showing them the scar on his leg: "It have some things" – he smiles – "worth more than a dollar".[15]

No doubt there is no need to labour the importance of being constantly aware of how the poet is using metaphor to have us react in a certain way, not only to make the meanings he desires, but also to have us feel and respond in a certain way. The poem is, in the sense discussed, History, it is a story. But it is pre-eminently metaphor. Not only in its words and images, but in a larger sense, in its structure, story, the characters it delineates and the way it relates its various parts to the whole which it slowly becomes as we develop our relationship with it. We need a careful knowledge of the poem in order to enjoy and appreciate it, but it is as much a knowledge of acquaintanceship as of learning.

I shall draw attention to a few more ways in which metaphor works in this poem, as much to keep us sensitive to one of the main poetic uses of poetry in general as to acquaint us with Walcott's way with language. Just as single words or images – the *shaking* of the leaves above, for instance – take on meanings beyond their first or 'literal' significance, so episodes or persons can metaphorically signify some thing beyond themselves, and so involve us in seeing, and learning to see, further significance:

> She was selling herself like the island, without
> any pain . . . .[16]

This is said of the St Lucian Helen, whose preparation for the Friday night festivities has made Achille *nauseous with jealousy*. So much so that Achille, like his namesake Achilles, sulked "in his tent" and refused to join in the fête. He has watched her taking her careful bath in the outside shower. "Is the music,/ the people I like" she says. But

he sat in the frame of the back door to the yard
watching her head, in the shower he'd built for her
from brand-new galvanize, streaming from the white foam

with expensive shampoo, and, when it disappeared,
came back, the mouth parted, the eyes squeezed with delight.[17]

She makes her full preparation; she tries to persuade him to join in,
but he goes off to the canoes on the beach from which point he can
watch

her high head moving through the tourists,
through flying stars from the coalpots, the painted mouth
still eagerly parted. Murder throbbed in his wrists

to the loudspeaker's pelvic thud, her floating move.
She was selling herself like the island, without
any pain, and the village did not seem to care

that it was dying in its change, the way it whored
away a simple life that would soon disappear
while the children withered on the sidewalks to the sounds[18]

By metaphorically linking the island with Helen in the aspects of
the new, the vibrating, the flying stars, as well as the pelvic 'self
selling', the author intensifies our involvement in the history and the
fiction which have their value in being images of the real world.
Whether it is easier to understand, and to sympathise with, Helen or
with the neonatal St Lucia is difficult to say. But both are images of
each other; both cast light on the other's predicament. Whether when
we realise this we are any nearer an insight into what might be the
solution to this 'developmental' problem, we shall discuss when we
look at the moral aspects of this poem.

In another part of the world, in another aspect of the human
condition, the author deepens our insight by a different use of
metaphor. We are with the sad experience of the Native Americans,
more commonly called the Amerindians. Immediately after the
moving interlude which starts "House of umbrage, house of fear",[19]
and which refers to the breakdown of his third marriage, our author
turns to the fate of the Crow horsemen among the Dakotas. There is
no doubt a metaphorical significance in this structual juxtaposition:
"Our contracts// were torn like the clouds, like treaties with the

Indians,/ but with mutual treachery."[20] And a new woman, Catherine Weldon, comes onstage. Walcott's woman has left; but Weldon is present to the Indians, even though her hopes for them are to be betrayed:

> The nausea stirring her loins
> was not from war, but from the treachery that came after
>
> war, the white piece of paper so ornately signed
> that perhaps that sound was really the loon's laughter
> at treaties changing like clouds, their ink faded like wind.
>
> . . .
>
> She had believed in the redemptions of History,
> that the papers the Sioux had folded to their hearts
>
> would be kept like God's word, that each signatory,
> after all that suffering, had blotted out their hates,
> and that peace would break out as widely as the moon.[21]

The original image of "nausea stirring in her loins" is, in this context, made even more powerful, and throws more light on the plight of the Indians, because it does not here anticipate birth, but rather contemplates treachery and murder. Similarly the soon to be used metaphor of 'flour' for 'snow' gains an intensity by obliterating, while still bringing to mind, all the gentle associations we have with flour. And to baste a corpse with dry, cold flour is as "contrary to nature" an activity as one can imagine.

Note how these passages reinforce each other by the image of changing clouds and torn tatters of paper. The white piece of paper also echoes the white snow which the author tends to make something frightening, choking like dry flour:

> The snow blew in their wincing faces like papers
> from another treaty which a blind shaman tears
> to bits in the wind . . .
>
> . . .
>
> The flour basting their corpses on the white fields.[22]

In fact throughout the Indian pieces one is reminded of the frightening nature of whiteness and the white snow as portrayed in Walcott's early poem 'God rest ye merry gentlemen':

> What had I heard,
> wheezing behind me with whitening breath? . . . .
> The night was white. There was nowhere to hide.

One feels in fact that Walcott's reference in *Omeros* to Melville about the supremacy of the white is somehow mistaken. I find it hard to think of any embodiment through metaphor of what can be so uncomfortable about 'whiteness' than the book *Moby Dick*. This we find not only in the main character, the cruel whale, but also in the slightly sick-making enormous squid, in the monomania of Ahab, and in all the other matters brought up in the chapter on whiteness! It quite puts into the shade the references in Shakespeare to "lily livered" and "death's pale flag".

But whatever Melville thought of whiteness, Walcott manages here by using that image, to cast a sickening veil, created by others out of perversity, callousness and disdain, over the being and experience and absence of the native Americans:

> As the salmon grows tired of the ladder of stone,
> so have we of fighting the claws of the White Bear,
> dripping red beads on the snow. Whiteness is everywhere.[23]

The Metaphor of Homer

I have stated already that Walcott's poem is not an imitation of either the Iliad or the Odyssey. Even though some of the characters in a sense match some of the Homeric personnae: Helen, Hector, Achille, Philoctete. The author even speaks of himself as Telemachus to Plunkett's, and his father's, Odysseus. But the point of the use of Homer lies elsewhere. Certainly Homer is honoured as the great creator, especially of the long hexameter line which he uses so skillfully to delineate, among other things, the combers of the sea: "the breakers slow-dolphining over more breakers".

Walcott has always admired this clean Homeric line, especially when it spoke of the sea, the roaring sea, and likened to it the rushing back of the army from their boats and tents to their meeting place:

> exe ws ote kuma poluphloisboio thalases
> aigialw megalw bremetai, smargei de te pontos.[24]

In fact the author tells Omeros

> I have always heard
> your voice in that sea, master, it was the same song
> of the desert shaman, and when I was a boy
>
> your name was as wide as a bay, as I walked along
> the curled brow of the surf; the word 'Homer' meant joy,
> joy in battle, in work, in death,[25]

But Homer is honoured also as the Blind Seer. Two of the many traditions which attach to him are quite contrary: one is that of a sort of court poet singing what are essentially praise songs, epics that give a failing aristocracy a kind of legitimacy by associating them with the heroic deeds of the past; the other is more that of the wanderer, the beggar poet who was not treated too well. It is the latter figure which Walcott really uses; that plus the always fascinating all-seeing blind person, like Tirisias. (Blind people play an important role in this poem: Seven Seas, Homer and St Lucia herself.) Omeros also acts as a guide to the Narrator in the manner that Virgil guided Dante through Hell.

In discussion of what his works have meant to our author, Homer tells him to "Forget the gods".[26] He is referring to the way in which, in his epics, the struggles among the gods and godesses influence the story and the fates of its characters. Walcott has followed this advice; he ranges all over the world, enabling us to look at suffering and the human condition in many places, but this suffering and displacement are not brought about by the almost childish games of Grecian gods.

Omeros comes to guide our author through his own St Lucia. Before that Homer has been the blind beggar and wanderer met in London as well as in the ruins of the Amerindian tents. In these places he is the witness to suffering and stupidity, and the means of our gaining insight. On the banks of the Thames, in the guise of an old sailor, or a sort of Wandering Jew, with his manuscript tucked underneath his arm, he watches the river go by like a barge drawn along by Time.

One may wonder whether he would have been treated as badly as is portrayed in this poem, on the steps of St Martins in the Fields! But as he sits "curled up on a bench underneath the Embankment wall"[27] he watches empires pass:

> And the sunflower sets after all, retracting its irises
> with the bargeman's own, then buds on black, iron trees
> as a gliding fog hides the empires: London, Rome, Greece.[28]

The appearance of Homer in London, and the treatment he receives (on which he comments later) leads to a remarkable passage. It is as though the long-lasting blind bard, who has seen so much, stirs up the universal conscience to ask a series of questions about our destiny, questions which seem to be answered (by our author?) with no little bitterness. The questions include: "Who decrees a great epoch?", "Where, in the stones of the Abbey, are incised our names?", "Who screams out our price?", "Who will teach us a history of which we too are capable?", "Where is the light of the world?", "Where is our sublunar peace?"[29]

The answers to these questions are deep and depressing: one wonders whether we should go on living, or rather go on dying.

> Where is the light of the world? . . .
> . . . In the City that can buy and sell us
> the packets of tea stirred with our crystals of sweat.[30]

This section, juxtaposed to, and in some ways stirred up by, the presence of Homer and the treatment he receives ends, as it must, in the shadows: "dark future down darker street."

But when next the metaphor of Homer emerges – of Omeros – the colours are lighter, "One sunrise I walked out onto the balcony/ of my white hotel".[31] The marble head of Omeros arises on the shores of St Lucia, metamorphoses into human form, and the author sets off with his guide, Omeros, to a deeper knowledge of his own St Lucia, whose patron saint was herself blind but seeing all, blind to preserve her honour:

> but I saw no shadow underline my being:
> I could see through my own palm with every crease
> and every line transparent since I was seeing
>
> the light of St Lucia at last through her own eyes,
> her blindness, her inward vision as revealing
> as his, because a closing darkness brightens love,
>
> and I felt every wound pass. I saw the healing
> thorns of dry cactus drop to the dirt, and the grove
> where the sybil swayed. I thought of all my travelling.[32]

It is Omeros and Seven Seas who bring him to a point of peace and reconciliation, and it is Omeros who saves him from the pit of hell in which certain poets are stewing in their pride and envy.

Finally, Homer, Omeros, as metaphor, allows the narrator of this poem once again to raise a question which concerns West Indian critics, and some West Indian politicians and nationalists, not a little: the role of the foreign in West Indian culture, especially of the non-African foreign:

> All that Greek manure under the green bananas.
>
> . . .
>
> when would I not hear the Trojan War
> in two fishermen cursing in Ma Kilman's shop?[33]

Notice the pointed ambiguity of "manure". The answer of our author to this question about "foreign" influence, as to all those about "the angst of influence", is quite simple: "But is was mine to make what I wanted of it".[34] It is the "making of something" out of it that matters; and the making of this magnificent poem from the Greek and other influences clearly shows that the question is not so much what influences are at play, and whether some are more relevant and more acceptable to the culture customs officers than others. The test will always have to be the quality of what is made – and that is the most likely point at which relevance and heritage will more or less automatically play their part.

Our consideration of the metaphor of Homer in *Omeros* must stop at this point. Space does not allow further consideration of this matter or of much more that should be considered under the heading of Metaphor, whether the role of images, of structure or of other personae. Under 'structure' we would have to investigate the further meanings added to the historical or story elements by the way in which episodes are juxtaposed in what is a complex mosaic treatment. Of the metaphorical use of other personae one need only mention the role played in this remarkable poem by such 'historical' inhabitants of St Lucia as the Father and Mother of the narrator, and of such characters as the Plunketts and Ma Kilman, and Achille in his journey back to Africa, to mention only a few.

Aspects of Moral and Anagogical Interpretation

This poem is too important, too well constructed, and too *concerned*, not to note its implication for human living and its echoes, at least, of what Dante called 'eternal matters'. It quite often depicts, not without at least implied comment, the suffering inflicted on whole groups of people: Plains Indians, enslaved Africans, Poles who left their country for North America. It speaks in moving terms of the over-fishing of the Caribbean, the changes caused by tourism and the doubtful decisions made by local politicians, whose existence has hardly "made any difference" to Philoctetes's life.

But in the end it seems to project some sort of satisfied acceptance on the part of the Narrator, even to a sort of celebration. To what extent does this seem, to the reader, on quiet re-examination, justified:

> "but the right journey
> is motionless; as the sea moves round an island
>
> that appears to be moving, love moves round the heart
> with encircling salt, and the slowly travelling hand
> knows it returns to the port from which it must start.
>
> Therefore, this is what this island has meant to you,
> why my bust spoke, why the sea-swift was sent to you:
> to circle yourself and your island with this art."[35]

True these words are spoken in a dream by Seven Seas/Omeros. But some such resolution connected with love and care and art does seem in the end to be suggested as in the final gesture when with Hector dead, Maud Plunkett dead, and Philoctete cured, and the special canoe, 'In God We Trust', back in place, "Achille put the wedge of dolphin/ that he'd saved for Helen in Hector's rusty tin".[36]

Does this resolution ring true? It is a question which must be asked because this superbly crafted poem is not the work of some clever dandy showing us how well he can handle and vary *terza rime*, although he can certainly do that as any careful reading will show. Moreover in the poem itself moral questions are raised such as the ineptitude and dishonesty of local politicians, in connection with tourism, for instance, making other people's children waiters while their own read law.

The Narrator also shows clearly how human beings displace others at will, noting of the Revolutionary Citizens of America "all colonies inherit their empire's sin,/ and these, who broke free of the net, enmeshed a race."[37] This question of the moral and anagogical implications is a topic that one would have desired much more space to ruminate upon, let alone discuss, and I would not be surprised to be found wrong by those who come after. But the topic is too important to dodge.

To what extent is a certain sort of fatalism and quietism implied in this poem? Is that really the way of human history: what will be, will be? How deeply has the *Salve Regina* sent its roots? *Exules filii Hevae?* To ask these questions simply underlines the respect and pleasure with which one reads and re-reads this poem.

The question about fatalism and quietism can be phrased differently: does the *denouement* seem contrived? Not perhaps in the heat of reading, such is the intensity of the lyrical quality of the poem and its rhythmic sweep. But in quiet contemplation of the poem as a whole one wonders if one has not too easily acquiesced in the image of the "motionless journey"

> "...as the sea moves round an island
> that appears to be moving, love moves round the heart".[38]

Of course the full meaning even at the moral level, and at the level of "eternal verities", must rest in the tension built up between the parts. It is a question of whether the displacement parts – what one might call the 'whiteness is everywhere' parts – do not totally outweigh the integrative parts, represented by Achille, for instance, and by the guidance of Omeros himself. It is not a matter easy to settle at this early stage of the public existence of this remarkable poem. But it would be cowardly and trivialising not to raise it.

It is connected with what one might call the '*Salve Regina*' aspect. This needs some explanation. Towards the end of the poem we read:

> Behind lace Christmas bush, the season's red sorrel,
> what seemed a sunstruck stasis concealed a ferment
> of lives behind tin fences, an endless quarrel . . . [39]

then Seven Seas, in his penetrating blindness, contemplating the whole situation,

> . . . at his window heard their faint anthem:

> '*Salve Regina*' in the pews of a stone ship,
> which the black priest steered from his pulpit like a helm,
> making the swift's sign from brow to muttering lip.[40]

In whatever way the "swift's sign" might alter the basic message of the '*Salve Regina*' (and it might in fact underline it) it is worth looking at the '*Salve's*' words which are usually sung to one of the most haunting of Gregorian plain chants; it is, of course, addressed to that Star of the Ocean, Star of the Sea, Mary the mother of Jesus:

> *Salve Regina, Mater misericordiae, vita, dulcedo et spes nostra, salve. Ad te clamamus, exules filii Hevae. Ad te suspiramus, gementes et flentes in hac lacrimarum valle.*

It is the *clamamus, exules filii Hevae* which particularly interests us: "We cry to thee; we are exiles, children of Eve, groaning and weeping in this valley of tears." And it ends "after this exile show unto us the blessed fruit of thy womb, Jesus".

Notice the notion of exile, and of *Another Life* in which the blessed fruit will be experienced, and notice also the popular hymn connection between Mary and the sea and the wanderer, Star of the Ocean, Star of the Sea "Pray for the wanderer, pray thou for me". And of course Homer's Odysseus is one of the great wanderers, a fit icon for modern humans, driven from the islands, dragged from Africa, beaten across the snow-floured plains of North America, hastening from Poland and Nazi Germany, consoled only from time to time by birds that are free to leave, to return either every night, or annually like the cattle bird of Couva.

This displacement of human persons Walcott brilliantly delineates. But he goes out of his way to say that he has lost his faith in myths and religion; and Omeros seems to persuade him to the view "to love your own above all else". How does the loss of faith square with his real heroes, who are consoled by the *Salve*, cross themselves before most activities, seek cures in the old tradition, sympathetic medicine? They groan for the coming of justice but, for good or ill, they are consoled by something that is to happen *after this exile*.

And is not one of the main reasons for the disappearance of the Amerindians – like their smoke signals in the evening – precisely that the pale-faced loved their own? And Plunkett not only learnt to accept Maud's death but his real relationship to St Lucia; he had no longer found "his own" all that lovable.

There are other echoes of the eternal in human experience which are worth mentioning as they go well beyond the usual uses of metaphor. Unfortunately we have not time to explore them now, but the reader will easily see their implications for matters that are of more than passing interest. We will mention a few.

When Achille goes back to Africa in his vision he, who was originally called Afolabe and was renamed Achille by his master as a kind of honour, enjoys an interesting encounter with his father. One of the things his father has to say to him is cruelly moving, and relates to human experience at a deep level indeed:

> Why did I never miss you until you returned?
> Why haven't I missed you, my son, until you were lost?
> Are you the smoke from a fire that never burned?[41]

What lives, what loves, what faith we do not miss until they are lost? And what sons and daughters did Africa not miss until they returned?
   Another echo occurs in the lines

> This was the shout on which each odyssey pivots,
> the silent cry for a reef, or familiar bird,
> not the outcry of battle or the tangled plots
>
> of a fishnet but when a wave rhymes with one's grave,
> a canoe with a coffin, once that parallel
> is crossed, and cancels the line of master and slave.[42]

This certainly pertains "to eternal matters". "Death lays his icy hands on kings". But is death only the leveller? Is death in any sense the reliever? What of paradise?
   Finally, I believe this epigram from the Interlude contains pithily one of the antinomies in this poem so concerned with displacement and the location of home:

> House where I look down the scorched street
> but feel its ice ascend my feet
>
> *I do not live in you, I bear*
> *my house inside me, everywhere*[43]

[my emphasis]

How does this view of bearing my house inside everywhere – with which I certainly sympathise – fit in with the special place St Lucia is to have, and with the notion of being displaced when not being in one's original home?
   One stresses again the realization that in a poem like this one is dealing with a tension and structure of images and ideas, but there can

be a point at which parts seem to be hauling away from the overall design. Do we have examples of this in the three cases cited above as being concerned with "everlasting verities"?

"Where is our home? Is there ever any everlasting rest?" might well be questions which cannot be answered in entirely terrestial terms, any more than the fate of the Native Americans should have been decided entirely by where it suited the railroad companies to drive in the iron spike that linked the East to the West of the United States by rail.

L'Envoi

And so we come to a closure, if not a conclusion.

> Why waste lines on Achille, a shade on the sea floor?
> Because strong as self-healing coral, a quiet culture
> is branching from the white ribs of each ancestor,
>
> deeper than it seems on the surface; slowly but sure,
> it will change us with the fluent sculpture of Time.[44]

There is much in the poem I have not been able to cover, especially its touches of humour, and its connection with Homer and his great epics, and the role of the sea and the sound of the sea in *Omeros* and in the hexameters of Homer.

Omeros is not an epic, and it hardly touches on the gods. It has characters such as Helen and Hector and Achille. Of the St Lucian Helen one has to note that she is brought much closer to the reader than thy Homeric lady whose face "launched a thousand ships". Homer was very sparing in his description of her, leaving it to the old men chirping on the wall as she passed by pointing out her country's fighting men doing battle to regain her, leaving it to these worn-out fellows merely to say "No wonder there is a war, for her face is like that of an immortal."

But what is much more important than forced likenesses with the Iliad and the Odyssey is the not widely known fact that at the time of slavery in the Caribbean the masters had the custom (an obscure custom worthy of examination) of giving slaves grand names: Pompey, Phoebe, Cloe and Caesar. In Jamaica in 1760 during Tacky's rebellion Thomas Thistlewood, in reporting on run-aways, tells us that Achilles was at liberty until 6 December when "about 3 p.m. our Achilles (alias Hercules) and Paradise Achilles came home together, of their own accord." And a Plato and Abraham also came back from liberty, to the bilboes, alas, despite the grand names. But it is possible that some of these names were given in recognition of feats performed not least of all in the European wars which then took place in the Caribbean.

In *Omeros* the grand names are given to simple folk some of whom had the kind of problems the noble heroes had in Homer's poems. With these problems they struggled, as with the "loud sounding sea", with no less dignity and humanity than all the heroes in the bloody wars that sprung from wrath, and saw so many become the spoils for carrion crows and wandering dogs. But what is common to Homer and *Omeros* is not only struggle and coming to terms with death and violence and separation from home, but the sea, the loud sounding *poluphloisboio thalassesie*. and its moods and sounds.

The armies gathered in Homer with the sound of rushing waves; in *Omeros*, in the end Achille

> scraped dry scales off his hands. He liked the odours
>
> of the sea in him. Night was fanning its coalpot.
>
>   . . .
>
> A full moon shone like a slice of raw onion.
> When he left the beach the sea was still going on.[45]

The sea is still going on.

NOTES

1. Walcott, *Omeros*, London, 1990, Book 1 Chapter V, p.25.
2. *ibid.*, Book 2 Chapter XIX, pp.99–100.
3. *ibid.*, Book 6 Chapter XLV, p.228.
4. *ibid.*, Book 7 Chapter LXI, pp. 304–05.
5. Walcott, *Another Life*, London, 1972.
6. 'Tales of the Islands', *In a Green Night*.
7. Walcott, *Omeros*, Book 1 Chapter I, p.3.
8. *ibid.*, Book 6 Chapter LI, p.259.
9. *ibid.*, Book 7 Chapter LXIV, p.325.
10. *ibid.*, Book 7 Chapter LXIII, p.319.
11. *ibid.*, Book 6 Chapter XLVII, p.245.

12. *ibid.*, Book 7 Chapter LX, p.300.
13. *ibid.*, Book 1 Chapter I, p.3.
14. *ibid.*
15. *ibid.*, p.4.
16. *ibid.*, Book 2 Chapter XXI, p.111.
17. *ibid.*, p.110.
18. *ibid.*, p.111.
19. *ibid.*, Book 4 Chapter XXXIII, p.173.
20. *ibid.*, Book 4 Chapter XXXIV, p.175.
21. *ibid.*, Book 4 Chapter XXXV, p.180.
22. *ibid.*, Book 5 Chapter XLII, p.214.
23. *ibid.*, Book 5 Chapter XLIII, p.217.
24. Homer, *Iliad B*, lines 209–10.
25. Walcott, *Omeros*, Book 7 Chapter LVI, p.283.
26. *ibid.*
27. *ibid.*, Book 5 Chapter XXXVIII, p.195
28. *ibid.*, p.196.
29. *ibid.*, pp.196–97.
30. *ibid.*, p.197.
31. *ibid.*, Book 7 Chapter LVI, p.279
32. *ibid.*, p.282.
33. *ibid.*, Book 6 Chapter LIV, p.271.
34. *ibid.*, p.272.
35. *ibid.*, Book 7 Chapter LVIV, p.291.
36. *ibid.*, Book 7 Chapter LXIV, p.325.
37. *ibid.*, Book 5 Chapter XLI, p.208.
38. *ibid.*, Book 7 Chapter LVIII, p.291.
39. *ibid.*, Book 7 Chapter LXII, p.310.
40. *ibid.*
41. *ibid.*, Book 3 Chapter XXV, p.139.
42. *ibid.*, Book 3 Chapter XXX, p.159.
43. *ibid.*, Book 4 Chapter XXXIII, p.174.
44. *ibid.*, Book 7 Chapter LIX, p.296
45. *ibid.*, Book 7 Chapter LXIV, p.325.

SELECT BIBLIOGRAPHY

Works by Derek Walcott

Collections of Poetry

(Where both British and American editions of Walcott's collections were published I have cited only the British editions as page references in the text are to those editions.)

25 Poems, Port of Spain; Guardian Commercial Printery, 1948.

Epitaph for the Young: a Poem in XII Cantos, Bridgtown, Barbados, Advocate Co., 1949.
Poems, Kingston; Kingston City Printery, 1951.
In a Green Night, London, Cape, 1962.
Selected Poems, New York, Farrar, Strauss & Co., 1964.
The Castaway and Other Poems, London, Cape, 1965.
The Gulf, London, Cape, 1970.
Another Life, London, Cape, 1972.
Sea Grapes, London, Cape, 1976.
The Star-apple Kingdom, London, Cape, 1979.
The Fortunate Traveller, London; Faber & Faber, 1982.
Midsummer, London; Faber & Faber, 1982.
Collected Poems 1948-1984, London; Faber & Faber, 1986.
The Arkansas Testament, London; Faber & Faber, 1987.
Omeros, London; Faber & Faber, 1990.

Collections of Plays

Dream on Monkey Mountain and Other Plays, New York; Farrar, Strauss & Giroux, 1970.
'Remembrance' and 'Pantomime', New York; Farrar, Strauss & Giroux, 1980.
'The Joker of Seville' and 'O Babylon', London, Cape, 1979.
Three Plays, New York; Farrar, Strauss & Giroux, 1986.

Interviews

'Walcott on Walcott', interview with Dennis Scott, *Caribbean Quarterly*, Vol.14, no.162, 1968, pp.77–82.

'Man of the Theatre, an interview', *The New Yorker*, June 26th, 1971, p.30.

'We are still being betrayed', interview with Raoul Pantin, *Caribbean Contact*, July 1973, Vol.1, No.7, pp.14–16.

'Any Revolution Based on Race is Suicidal', interview with Raoul Pantin in *Caribbean Contact*, Vol.1, No.8, August 1973, pp.14–16.

'Conversation', (with Robert Hamner) *World Literature Written in English*, Vol.16, No.2, November 1977, pp.409–420.

'Reflections Before and After Carnival', an interview with Sharon Ciccarelli, in Harper and Stepto (Eds.), *Chants of Saints*, Chicago, University of Illinois Press, 1978, pp.296–309.

'An interview, conducted by Edward Hirsch', *Contemporary Literature*, Vol.20, No.3, 1980, pp.279–292.

'An interview with Ned Thomas', *Kunapipi*, Vol.III, No.2, 1981, pp.42-47.

'An interview with Nancy Schoenberger', *Threepenny Review*, Fall, 1983, pp.16–17.

'The Art of Poetry, XXXVII: an interview by Edward Hirsch', *The Paris Review*, No.101, Winter 1986, pp.196–230.

'An Interview with Derek Walcott', by Charles H. Rowell, *Callaloo*, Winter 1988, No.34, pp.80–89.

'Thinking Poetry: An Interview with Derek Walcott' by Robert Brown and Cheryl Johnson, *The Cream City Review*, Vol.14, No.2, Winter 1990, pp.209–33.

Major Essays

'Leaving School', *London Magazine*, Vol.5, No.6, September 1965, pp.4–14.

'The Figure of Crusoe', unpublished lecture, given at the University of West Indies, St. Augustine, Trinidad and Tobago, 1965, (Text held in library there.)

'Meanings', Savacou, No.2, 1970, pp. 45–51.

'What the Twilight Says; an Overture' in *Dream on Monkey Mountain and Other Plays*, op.cit.

'The Muse of History', Orde Coombs (Ed.) *Is Massa Day Done?*, Anchor/Doubleday, New York, 1974, pp.1–27.

'The Caribbean: Culture or Mimicry?', *Journal of Interamerican Studies and World Affairs*, Vol.16, No.1, February 1974, pp.3–13.

'On choosing Port of Spain', David Frost (Ed.), *David Frost Introduces Trinidad and Tobago*, 1975, pp.14–23.

'Caligula's Horse', in Stephen Slemon and Helen Tiffin (Eds.), *After Europe*, Coventry, Dangaroo Press, 1989, pp.138–142.

'A Colonial's Eye-View of the Empire', *Triquarterly 65*, Winter 1986, pp.73–84.

'Derek Walcott Talks About *The Joker of Seville*', *Carib*, 1986, No.4, pp.1–15.

'The Poet in the Theatre', *poetry Review*, Vol.80, No.4, Winter 1990-91, pp.4–8.

Books or Essays on Walcott or Substantially Referring to His Work

Adekoya, Olusegun; 'Between Beasthood and Godhead: An Inquiry into the Definition of Man', *Literary Half-Yearly*, Jan. 1987, Vol.28, No.1, pp.53–60.

Aiyejina, Funso: 'Derek Walcott and the West Indian Dream and Veneration of Africa', *Literary Half-Yearly*, Vol.XXXVI, No.1, January 1985 pp.180–193.

—'Derek Walcott: The Poet as a Federated Consciousness', *World Literature Written in English*, Spring 1987, Vol.27, No.1, pp.67–80.

Alcock, Peter:' " . . . Some deep, amnesiac blow"; Amnesia in the Poetic Development of Derek Walcott', *Span* (Canterbury New Zealand), No.21, October 1985.

Alleyne, Keith: 'Epitaph for the Young: A poem in XII cantoes by Derek Walcott', *Bim*, Vol.3, No.11, 1949, pp.267–272.

Asein, Samuel O.: 'Derek Walcott: The Man and his ideas', *The Literary Half-Yearly*, Vol.XVII, No.2, 1976, pp.59–79.

—'Walcott's Jamaica Years', in *The Literary Half-Yearly*, Vol.XXI, No.2, July 1980, pp.23–41.

—'Derek Walcott and the Great Tradition', *The Literary Criterion*, (Mysore, India), Vol.16, No.2, 1981, pp.18–30.

—'Drama, The Church and The Nation in the Caribbean', *The Literary Half-Yearly*, Vol.XXVI, No.1, January 1985, pp.149–162.

Atlas, James: 'Derek Walcott: Poet of Two Worlds', *New York Times Magazine*, 23rd May 1982, pp.32–51.

Bagchee, Shyamal: 'Derek Walcott and the "Power of Provincialism" ', *World Literature Written in English*, Spring 1987, Vol. 27, No. 1, pp.80–86.

Barker, Thomas & Dameron, Charles: 'The Twighlight And The God; Two Long Poems of Walcott and Soyinka', *ACLALS Bulletin*, 5th series, No.3, December 1980, pp.51–61.

Baugh, Edward: 'Metaphor and Plainess in the Poetry of Derek Walcott', *Literary Half-Yearly*, Vol.11, No.2, 1970, pp.47–58.

—*West Indian Poetry 1900-70*, Savacou Pubs. Kingston, Jamaica, 1970.

—'Ripening with Walcott', *Caribbean Quarterly*, June–September 1977, Vol.23, No.2 & 3, pp.84–90.

—*Memory as Vision: Derek Walcott: Another Life*, Harlow, Longman, 1978.

—'The poem as autobiographical novel; Derek Walcott's 'Another Life' in relation to Wordsworth's 'Prelude' and Joyce's 'Portrait of the Artist', *Awakened Conscience*, ed. C.D. Narasimhaiah, 1978, pp.226–235.

—'Painters and Paintings in Another Life', *Caribbean Quarterly*, Vol.26, No.1–2, 1980, pp.83–93.

Bedient, Calvin: 'Derek Walcott, Contemporary: The Fortunate Traveller', *Parnassus: Poetry in Review*, Vol.9, No.2, Fall/Winter 1981, pp.31–44.

Benson, Robert: 'The New World Poetry of Derek Walcott', *Concerning Poetry*, Fall 1983, Vol.16, No.2, pp.23–37.

—'The Painter as a Poet: Derek Walcott's *Midsummer*', *The Literary Review: An International Journal of Contemporary Writing*, Spring 1986, Vol.29, No. 3, pp.259–268.

Birkits, Sven: 'Heir Apparent: Midsummer by Derek Walcott', *The New Republic*, January 23rd 1984, pp.31–33.

Brathwaite, Edward: 'Edward Brathwaite looks at Walcott's *In A Green Night*', *The Voice of St. Lucia*, April 13th 1963, p.4.

—'The Castaway; Derek Walcott', *Bim*, Vol.11, No.42, 1966, pp.139–141.

Breiner, Laurence: 'Tradition, Society, the Figure of the Poet', *Caribbean Quarterly*, Vol.26, No.1/2, 1980, pp.1–12.

—'Lyric and Autobiography in West Indian Literature', *Journal of West Indian Literature*, Vol.3, No.1, January 1983, pp.3–15.

Breslaw, Stephen P.: 'Trinidadian Heteroglossia: A Bakhtinian Nile', *World Literature Written Today: A Literary Quarterly of the University of Oklahoma*, Winter 1989, Vol. 63, No. 1, pp.36–39.

Breslin, Paul: "I Met History Once, but He Ain't Recognise Me': The Poetry of Derek Walcott', *Triquarterly*, Winter 1987, Vol. 68, pp.168–183.

Brodsky, Joseph: 'On Derek Walcott', *New York Review of Books*, 10th November 1983, pp.39–42.

Bromwell, Nicholas: 'Having to Ask: The Loss of Self in Contemporary Culture', (Review of *The Fortunate Traveller*), *Boston Review*, Vol.VII, No.2, April 1982, pp.9–13.

Brown, Lloyd: 'Caribbean Castaway New World Odyssey: Derek Walcott's Poetry', *The Journal of Commonwealth Literature*, Vol.II, No.2, 1976, pp.149–159.

—'The Isolated Self in West Indian Literature', *Caribbean Quarterly*, Vol.23, Nos.2 & 3, pp.54–65.

—*West Indian Poetry*, Boston, Twayne Publishers, 1978.

Brown, Stewart: 'Walcott's Fortunate Traveller: A Patriot in Exile', *Carib*, (Kingston, Jamaica), No.5, Winter 1989/90, pp.1–18.

—'Spoiler: Walcott's People's Patriot', in *Wasafiri*, No.9, Winter 1988, pp.10–15.

—'Derek Walcott: The Poems' in *A Handbook for the Teaching of Caribbean Literature*, ed. David Dabydeen, Heinemann, London, 1988. pp.96–103.

Brown, Wayne (ed.): *Derek Walcott: Selected Poetry*, London, Heinemann Educational Books, 1981.

Burton, R.D.E.: 'Derek Walcott & the Medusa of History', *Caliban*, Vol.III, No.2, Fall/Winter 1980, pp.3–48.

Collier, Gordon: 'Artistic Autonomy and Cultural Allegiance: Aspects of the Walcott–Brathwaite Debate Re-examined', *The Literary Half Yearly*, January 1979, Vol. 20, No. 1, pp.93–105.

Collymore, F.A.: 'An Introduction to the Poetry of Derek Walcott', *Bim*, Vol.3, No.10, 1949, pp.125-132.

—'Poems: Derek Walcott', *Bim*, Vol.4, No.15, 1951, pp.224–226.

Colson, Theodore: 'Derek Walcott's Plays; Outrage and Compassion,' *World Literature Written in English*, Vol.12, No.1, pp.80–96.

Cooper, Carolyn: 'A Language Beyond Mimicry: Language as Metaphor and Meaning in Derek Walcott's Oeuvre', *The Literary Half-Yearly*, Vol.XXVI, No.1, January 1985, pp.23–41.

D'Aguiar, Fred: 'Lines With Their Knots Left In, Third World Poems by Edward Kamau Brathwaite and Midsummer by Derek Walcott', *Wasafiri*, Vol.1, No.2, Spring 1985, pp.37–38.

Donoghue, Denis: 'Waiting for the End', *New York Review of Books*, No.16, May 6th 1971, pp.27–31.

—'The Two Sides of Derek Walcott', (review of *The Fortunate Traveller*), *New York Times Book Review*, January 3rd 1982, Vol.LXXXVII, No.1, p.5.

Dove, Rita: 'Either I'm nobody or I'm a nation', *Parnassus: Poetry in Review*, 1987, Vol. 14, No. 1, pp. 49–76.

Eagleton, Terry: 'New Poetry', *Stand*, Vol.24, No.3, June 1983, pp.77–80.

—'Plenty of Life', (review of *Midsummer*), *Times Literary Supplement*, November 9th 1984, p.1290.

Fabre, Michael: 'Adam's Task of Giving Things Their Names', *New Letters*, Vol.41, No.1, 1974, pp.91–107.

—'The Poetical Journey of Derek Walcott', *Commonwealth Literature and the Modern World*, Hena Maes Jelinek (Ed.), Brussels, Didier, 1975, pp.61-67.

Fido, Elaine: 'Walcott and Sexual Politics: Macho Conventions Shape the Moon', *Literary Half-Yearly*, Vol.XXVI, No.1, January 1985, pp.43–60.

—'Value Judgements on Art and the Question of Macho Attitudes: The Case of Derek Walcott', *The Journal of Commonwealth Literarture*, 1986, Vol. 21, No. 2, pp. 109–119.

Figueroa, John: 'Our Complex Language Situation', *Caribbean Voices*, 1971, pp.225–228.

—'A Note on Derek Walcott's Concern with Nothing', *Revista Interamericana Review*, Vol.IV, No.3, Fall 1974, pp.422–428.

—'Review of *Another Life*', *Bim*, Vol.15, No.58, June 1975, pp.160–170.

—'Some Subtleties of the Isle', *World Literature Written in English*, Vol.15, No.1, April 1976, pp.190–224.

—'Derek Walcott: a brief introduction to his work', *Poetry Wales*, Vol.16, No.2, Autumn 1980, pp.52–63.

—'Dialect as Narrative', *London Magazine*, Vol.21, Nos.1 & 2, April/May 1981, pp.115–118.

—'Sea Memories', (Review of Midsummer), *London Magazine*, Vol.24, No.9/10, December 1984/January 1985, pp.128–130.

—'In a Green Night', *Commonwealth Essays and Studies and Essays*, Spring 1985, Vol.7, No.2, pp.103–118.

Forde, A.N.: 'In A Green Night; Derek Walcott', *Bim*, Vol.9, No.36, 1963, pp.288–290.

Fox, Robert Eliot: 'Big Night Music: Derek Walcott's *Dream on Monkey Mountain* and the "Splendors of Imagination" ', *Journal of Commonwealth Literature*, No.88, 1982, p.16–27.

—'Derek Walcott: History as Dis-Ease', *Literary Half-Yearly*, Vol.XXVI, No.1, January 1985.

Furbank, P.N.: 'In A Green Night', in *The Listener*, Vol.68, No.1736, July 5th, 1962.

Garfitt, Roger: 'Review of Another Life', *London Magazine*, Vol. 13, No.5, December 1973/January 1974, pp.124–7.

—'Resisting the Classics: Derek Walcott, The Fortunate Traveller', *Times Literary Supplement*, September 24th 1982, p.1041.

Garuba, Harry: 'Derek Walcott and Wole Soyinka', *The Literary Half-Yearly*, Vol.XXVI, No.1, January 1985, pp.63–79.

Gilkes, Michael: 'Walcott's *Midsummer*, An Outpouring of Gift', *Caribbean Contact*, March 1985, p.15.

Goldstraw, Irma: *Derek Walcott: A Bibliography of Published Poems*, Port of Spain, Research and Publication Committee, University of the West Indies, St. Augustine, Trinidad, 1979.

Gonzalez, Anson: *Self-Discovery Through Literature: Creative Writing in Trinidad and Tobago*, Diego Martin, New Voices, Trinidad, 1972.

Gowda, H.H. Anniah: 'History of Derek Walcott's Voice: A Study of his Poetry', *Literary Half-Yearly*, Vol.XXVI, No.1, January 1985, pp.92–101.

Griffith, Lynne: 'Review of *The Castaway*', *Art and Man*, Act II, scene II, June 1969, pp.15–19.

Hamner, Robert: 'Conversation with Derek Walcott', *World Literature Written in English*, Vol.16, No.2, November 1977, pp.409–420.

—'New World Burden: Derek Walcott, *Sea Grapes*', *World Literature Written in English*, Vol.16, No.1, April 1977, pp.212–214.

—'Mythological Aspects of Derek Walcott's Drama', *Ariel*, Vol. 8, No.3, June 1977, pp.35–58.

—*Derek Walcott*, Boston, Twayne Publishers, 1981.

—'Derek Walcott: His Works and His Critics — An Annotated Bibliography, 1947–1980', *The Journal of Commonwealth Literature*, Vol.XVI, No.1, August 1981, pp.142–184.

—'Caliban Agonistes: Stages of Cultural Development in Walcott's Plays', *Literary Half-Yearly*, Vo.XXVI, No.1, August 1981, pp.142–184.

—'Exorcising the Planter-Devil in the Plays of Derek Walcott', *Commonwealth Essays and Studies*, Spring 1985, Vol.7, No.2, pp.95–102.

Heaney, Seamus: 'The Murmur of Malvern', *The Government of The Tongue*, London, Faber, 1988, pp.23–29.

Holder, A. Geoffrey: 'Review of Derek Walcott', *Bim*, June 1951, p.142

Huggan, Graham: 'Opting Out of the (Critical) Common Market: Creolization and the Post-Colonial Text', *Kunapipi*, 1989, Vol. 11, No. 1, pp.27–40.

Ireland, Kevin: 'Place and Poetic Identity', *The Journal of Commonwealth Literature*, Vol.I, No.2, December 1966, pp.157–60.

Ismond, Patricia: 'Walcott v. Brathwaite', *Caribbean Quarterly*, Vol.17, Nos.3 & 4, September–December 1971, pp.54–71.

—'Naming and Homecoming: Walcott's Poetry Since *Another Life*', *The Literary Half-Yearly*, Vol.XXVI, No.1, January 1985, pp.3–19.

—'The St. Lucian Background in Garth St. Omer and Derek Walcott', *Caribbean Quarterly*, Vol.28, Nos.1 & 2, March/June 1982, pp.32–43.

—'North and South — A Look at Walcott's *Midsummer*', *Kunapipi*, Vol.VIII, No.2, 1986, pp.77–84.

—'Walcott's Later Drama: From *Joker* to *Remembrance*', *Ariel*, July 1985, Vol.16, No. 3, pp.89–101.

—'*Another Life*: Autobiography as Alternative History', in *Journal of West Indian Literature*, Vol.4, No.1, January 1990, pp.41–49.

—'Self Portrait of an Island: St. Lucia through the eyes of its Writers', *Journal of West Indian Literature*, Vol. 1, No. 1, Oct. 1986, pp.59–73.

Izebaye, D.S.: 'The Exile and the Prodigal: Derek Walcott as West Indian Poet', *Caribbean Quarterly*, Vol.26, No.1–2, 1980.

James, C.L.R.: 'Review of *In A Green Night*', *The Trinidad Sunday Guardian*, May 6th 1962, p.5.

James, Louis: 'Caribbean Poetry in English — Some Problems', *Savacou*, No.2, 1970, pp.78–86.

—'A Landscape Locked in Amber' (A review of *Another Life*), *Commonwealth Newsletter*, No.6, 1974, pp.14–15.

James, Louis (ed.): *The Islands in Between*, Oxford University Press, London, 1968.

James, Sybil L.: 'Aspects of Symbolism in Derek Walcott's *Dream on Monkey Mountain*', *Literary Half-Yearly*, Vol.XXVI, No.1, January 1985, pp.82–90.

Jeyifo, Biodun: 'On Eurocentric Critical Theory: Some Paradigms from the Texts and Sub-Texts of Post-Colonial Writing', *Kunapipi* Vol. 11, No. 1, pp.107–118.

Jones, Katie: 'The Mulatto of Syle; Derek Walcott's *Collected Poems 48–84*', *Planet*, No.62, April/May 1987, pp.97–99.

Kellman, Anthony: '*The Arkansas Testament*', in *Kyk-Over-Al* No.39, December 1988, pp.90–93.

King, Bruce (Ed.) *West Indian Literature*, MacMillian, London, 1979.

—'Derek Walcott: The Artist and Community', *Individual and Community in Commonwealth Literature*, ed. Daniel Massa, University Press, 1979, pp.84–89.

King, Cameron: 'The Poems of Derek Walcott', *Caribbean Quarterly*, Vol.10, No.3, September 1964, pp.3–30.

King, Cameron & James, Louis: 'In Solitude for Company: The Poetry of Derek Walcott', *The Islands in Between*, ed. Louis James, pp.86–99.

King, Lloyd: 'Derek Walcott, the Literary Humaninst in the Caribbean', *Caribbean Quarterly*, Vol.16, No.4, December 1970, pp.36–42.

Lamming, George: 'Caribbean Literature: The Black Rock of Africa', *African Forum*, Vol.1, No.4, Spring 1966, pp.32–52.

Lane, M. Travis: 'At Home in Homelessness: The Poetry of Derek Walcott', *Dalhousie Review*, Vol.53, No.2, 1973, pp.325–338.

—'A Difference "Growth of a Poet's Mind": Derek Walcott's *Another Life*', *Ariel*, No.9, October 1978, pp.65–78.

Liderman, Laurence: 'New Poetry: The Muse of History', *The Yale Review*, Vol.LXIII, No.1, October 1973, pp.113–123.

Lucie-Smith, Edward: 'West Indian Writing', *London Magazine*, Vol.8, No.4, 1968, pp.96–102.

Lyn, Diana: 'The Concept of the Mulatto in Some Works of Derek Walcott', *Caribbean Quarterly*, Vol.26, No.1–2, 1980, pp.49–69.

Mazzocco, Robert: 'Embracing Adversity: The Star-apple Kingdom', *New York Review of Books*, Vol.26 No.9, May 31st 1979, p.34.

McCorkle, James: 'Remapping the New World: The Recent Poetry of Derek Walcott', *Ariel*, April 1986, Vol. 17, No. 2, pp. 3–14.

McWatt, Mark: '*Remembrance*, a review', *Caribbean Contact*, December 1982, Vol.10, No.8, p.11.

Moore, Gerald: *The Chosen Tongue*, Harlow, Longmans, 1969.

—'Use Men Men Language', *Bim*, Vol.15, No.57, March 1974, pp.69–76.

Mordecai, Pamela: "'A Crystal of Ambiguities': Metaphor for Creativity and the Art of Writing in Derek Walcott's *Another Life*', *World Literature Written in English*, Spring 1987, Vol.27, No.1, pp.93–105.

Morris, Mervyn: 'Some West Indian Problems of Audience', *English*, Vol.XVI, Spring 1967, No.94, pp.127–131.

—'Walcott and the Audience for Poetry', *Caribbean Quarterly*, Vol.14, Nos.1 & 2, 1968, pp.7–24.

—'A Crystal of Ambiguities: Another Life', *Jamaica Sunday Gleaner*, Kingston, 1973, p.23.

—'Derek Walcott', in *West Indian Literature*, ed. Bruce King, pp.144–160.

Ochillo, Yvonne: 'Aspects of Alienation in the Poetry of Derek Walcott', in *Journal of West Indian Literature*, Vol.3, No. 2, September 1988, pp.39–52.

Omotoso, Kole: *The Theatrical Into Theatre: A Study of Drama and Theatre in The English Speaking Caribbean*, London, New Beacon, 1982.

Owens, R.J.: 'West Indian Poetry', *Caribbean Quarterly*, Vol.7, No.3, December 1961, pp.120–127.

Peters, Erskine: 'The Theme of Madness in the Plays of Derek Walcott', *College Language Association Journal*, Dec.1988, Vol.32, No.2, pp.148–169.

Questel, Victor D.: 'Walcott's Major Triumph — Review of *Another Life*', *Tapia*, Part 1, Vol.3, No.51, December 23rd 1973, pp.6–7; Part 2, Vol.3 No.52, December 30th 1973, pp.6–7.

—'Trinidad Theatre Workshop, a bibliography', *Kairi 76*, Port of Spain, 1976, pp.53–59.

—'Blues in Caribbean Poetry', *Kairi 78*, Port of Spain, 1978, pp.51–54.

—'The Trinidad Theatre Workshop 1966–76', *Literary Half-Yearly*, Vol.XXXVI, No.1, January 1985, pp.163–179.

Ramchand, Kenneth: *An Introduction to the Study of West Indian Literature*, Sunbury-on-Thames, Nelson Caribbean, 1976.

—'Parades, Parades: Modern West Indian Poetry', *Sewanee Review*, Vol.87, No.1, Winter 1979, pp.96–118.

—'The Fate of Writing', *Caribbean Quarterly*, Vol.28, Nos.1 & 2, March 1982, pp.76–84.

Ramke, Bin: ' "Your Words is English, is a different tree," On Derek Walcott', *Denver Quarterly*, Fall 1988, Vol.23. No.2, pp.90–99.

Ramsaran, J.A.: 'Derek Walcott: New World Mediterranean Poet', *World Literature Written in English*, Vol.21, No.1, 1982, pp.133–47.

Rodman, Selden: *Tongues of Fallen Angels*, New York, New Direction Books, 1974.

Rohlehr, Gordon: 'West Indian Poetry: Some Problems of Assessment', *Bim*, Part 1, Vol.14, No.54, January–June 1972, pp.80–88; Part 2, Vol.14, No.55, July–December 1972, pp.134–143.

—'Withering into Truth; Derek Walcott's *The Gulf and Other Poems*', *The Black I*, (Montreal), Vol.1, No.1, March 1972, pp.66–69.

—'The Creative Writer and West Indian Society', *Kaie*, No.11, August 1973, pp.48–77.

—'Afterthoughts', *Bim*, Vol.14, No.56, pp.227–232.

—'A Carrion Time', *Bim*, Vol.15, No.58, June 1975, pp.92–109.

—'Poetry, Politics and the February Revolution', Part 5, *Trinidad and Tobago Review*, May 1978, pp.8,9 & 17.

—'Songs of the Skeleton — a poetry of Fission', *Trinidad & Tobago Review*, Part 1: 'Petit Careme', 1980, pp.12,13. Part 2: 'Divali', 1980, pp.10,15,20.

—*Path Finder*, Published by the author, Trinidad, 1981.

—'Songs of the Skeleton — a poetry of Dread', *Trinidad & Tobago Review*, Part 1: 'New Year', 1981, pp.9,11. Part 2: 'Crop Time', 1981, pp.7,9,10.

—'The Problem of the Problem of Form', *Caribbean Quarterly*, Vol.31, No.1, 1985, pp.1–52.

—'History as Absurdity', in *Is Massa Day Done?*, ed. Orde Coombs, New York, 1974. pp.69–109.

Salkey, Andrew: 'Inconsolable Songs of Our America: The Poetry of Derek Walcott', *World Literature Today*, Vol.56, No.1, 1982, pp.51–53.

Stewart, Marian 'Walcott and Painting', *Jamaica Journal*, No.45, 1981, pp.56–68.

Taylor, Patrick: 'Myth and Reality in Caribbean Narrative: Derek Walcott's *Pantomime*,' *World Literature Written in English*, Spring 1986, Vol.26, No.1, pp.169–177.

Thieme, John: 'Gnarled Sour Grapes, *Sea Grapes*, Derek Walcott', *Caribbean Review*, December 1978, Vol.VII, No.4, pp.51–52.

—'A Caribbean Don Juan: Derek Walcott's *Joker of Seville*', *World Literature Written in English*, Vol.23, No.1, Winter 1984, pp.62–75.

—'Derek Walcott: *Ti Jean . . .* and *Dream on Monkey Mountain*,' in *A Handbook for the Teaching of Caribbean Literature*', ed David Dabydeen, London, 1988, pp.86–95.

Thomas, Ned: *Derek Walcott — Poet of the Islands*, Cardiff, Welsh Arts Council, 1980.

Tiffin, Helen: 'Rites of Resistance: Counter Discourse and West Indian Biography', *Journal of West Indian Literature*, Vol.3, No.1, 1988, pp.169–81.

Trueblood, Valerie: 'On Derek Walcott', *The American Poetry Review*, Vol.7, No.3, May/June 1978, pp.7–10.

Uhrbach, Jan R.: 'A Note on Language and Naming in *Dream on Monkey Mountain*', *Callaloo*, Fall 1986, Vol.9, No.4, pp.578–582.

Vendler, Helen: 'Poet of Two Worlds; *The Fortunate Traveller* by Derek Walcott', *The New York Review of Books*, March 4th, 1982, pp.23–26.

Walmsley, Anne: 'Dimensions of Song', *Bim*, Vol.13, No.51, 1970, pp.152–167.

Wieland, James: ' "Confronting His Madness": History as Amnesia in the poetry of Derek Walcott', *New Literature Review*, (Canberra) No.7, 1980, pp.73–82.

—'Finding What Will Suffice: Fictions and the Commonwealth Poet', *New Literature Review*, (Canberra), No.10, 1980, pp.18–28.

—'Making Radiant the Moment: Notes towards a reading of Derek Walcott's *Sea Grapes*', *ACALS Bulletin*, 5th series, No.3, December 1980, pp.112–121.

Willis, Susan: 'Caliban as Poet: Reversing the Maps of Domination', *Massachusetts Review*, Winter 1982, Vol. 23, No.4, pp.615–630.

Wyke, Clement H.: "Divided to the Vein': Patterns of Tormented Ambivalence in Walcott's *The Fortunate Traveller*,' *Ariel*, July 1989, Vol.20, No.3, pp.55–71.

Other Relevant Books or Essays on Caribbean Cultural Issues

Alleyne, Mervin C.: 'Language and Society in St. Lucia', *Consequences of Class Colour — West Indian Perspectives*, eds. Lowenthal and Comitas, pp.199–212.

Allis, Jeannete B.: *West Indian Literature: An Index Criticism*, 1930–75, Boston, G.K. Hall & Co., 1981.

—'A Case for Regional Criticism of West Indian Literature', *Caribbean Quarterly*, Vol.28, Nos. 1 & 2, June 1982, pp.1–11.

Ashcroft, Bill, Griffiths, Gareth & Tiffin, Helen: *The Empire Writes Back*, London, 1989.

Baugh, Edward: 'Questions and Imperatives for a Young Literature', *Humanities Associations Review*, Vol.24, Winter 1973, pp.13–24.

Brathwaite, Edward: 'Caribbean Critics', *Critical Quarterly*, Vol.11, No.3, 1969, pp.268–276.

—'Review Article: The Islands in Between', *Southern Review*, (Adelaide), Vol.3, No.3, 1969, pp.264–272.

—'The Love AXE/L: Developing a Caribbean Aesthetic', *Bim*, Vol.16, No.61, June 1977, pp.53–65; Vol.16, No.62, December 1977, pp.100–106; Vol.16, No.63, June 1978, pp.181–192.

—*The History of the Voice*, London, New Beacon Books, 1983.

Cudjoe, Selwyn R.: *Resistance and Caribbean Literature*, Athens, Ohio University Press, 1980.

Dabydeen, David (ed): *A Handbook for the Teaching of Carribbean Literature*, London, Heinemann, 1988.

Dathorne, O.R. (ed.): *Caribbean Verse*, London, 1967.

—*Dark Ancestor — The Literature of the Black Man in the Caribbean*, Louisiana State University Press, 1981.

Davis, Geoffrey & Maes-Jelinek, Hena (eds.): *Crisis and Creativity in the New Literature in English*, (Amsterdam & Antlanta) 1990.

Dawes, Neville: *Prolegomena to Caribbean Literature*, Kingston, Institute of Jamaica Pubs., Kingston, 1977.

Drayton, Arthur: 'West Indian Consciousness in West Indian Verse: A Historical Perspective', Journal of Commonwealth Literature, July 1970, pp.66–88.

Griffiths, Gareth: *A Double Exile: African and Caribbean Writing between Two Cultures*, London, Marion Boyars, 1978.

Hulme, Peter: *Colonial Encounters*, London, 1986.

Harris, Wilson: *Tradition, the Writer and Society*, London, New Beacon Books, 1967.

Kemoli, Arthur M.: 'The Theme of 'The Past' in Caribbean Literature', *World Literature Written in English*, Vol.12, No.4, November 1973, pp.304–325.

Lowenthal, David & Comitas, Lambrose (eds.): *Consequences of Class and Colour — West Indian Perspectives*, New York, Anchor/Doubleday, 1973.

McFarlane, J.E. Clare (ed.): *A Treasury of Jamaican Poetry*, London, 1949.

McWatt, Mark: 'The Preoccupation with the Past in West Indian Literature', *Caribbean Quarterly*, Vol.28, Nos.1 & 2, 1982, pp.12–19.

Owens, R.J.: 'West Indian Poetry', in *Caribbean Quarterly*, Vol.7, No.3, December 1961.

Rohlehr, Gordon: 'My Strangled City', *Canfesta Forum*, ed. John Hearne, pp.221–245.

—Introduction to *Voiceprint*, eds. Stewart Brown, Mervyn Morris & Gordon Rohlehr, Longman, Harlow, 1989.

Sleman, Simon & Tiffin, Helen (eds.): *After Europe*. Coventry, Dangaroo Press, 1989.

Wynter, Sylvia: 'We must learn to sit down together and talk about a little culture; Reflections on West Indian writing and criticism', *Jamaica Journal*, Part 1, December 1968, Vol.2, No.4, pp.23–32; Part 2, March 1969, Vol.3, No.1, pp.27–42.

Index of Works Cited

Plays

Essays

ACKNOWLEDGEMENTS

The editor gratefully acknowledges the generosity of Faber & Faber and Farrar, Straus & Giroux Inc for their permission to publish quotations from books by Derek Walcott, in particular *Selected Poems*, *In a Green Night*, *The Gulf*, *Another Life*, *Sea Grapes*, *The Fortunate Traveller*, *The Arkansas Testament* and *Omeros*.

Notes on Contributors

Katie Jones was born in Wales, where she was educated at Aberystwyth. A former Fellow at UCW Swansea, she now lectures in English at Portsmouth Polytechnic.

Nana Wilson-Tagoe was born in Ghana and educated there and in Britain and the West Indies. She is currently Senior Lecturer in Literature at Kenyatta University, Nairobi, having lectured in Ghana, Trinidad, Nigeria, America and Britain. Her most recent publication is *The Historical Imagination in West Indian Literature*.

Laurence A. Breiner is a lecturer in English at the University of Boston, where Derek Walcott also lectures during his visits to America.

Ned Thomas was until recently a lecturer in English at UCW Aberystwyth. He is the author of *Poet of the Islands*, a short study of Walcott, and of many books and articles on contemporary Welsh culture. The founding editor of *Planet* magazine, he is now the Director of the University of Wales Press.

Mervyn Morris is a West Indian poet, educated in Jamaica and Oxford. The author of three volumes of verse, he lectures in English at the UWI in Jamaica and has written widely on Caribbean literature.

Louis James lectures at Keynes College, the University of Kent and is an acknowledged expert on Caribbean literature.

Edward Baugh is Professor of English at UWI in Jamaica. Well known as a critic he is also a poet, his latest collection being *A Tale from the Rainforest*.

Lowel Fiet holds a PhD in Drama and Theatre and has lectured in Michigan and Oregon. He is now a lecturer in English and Comparative Literature at the University of Puerto Rico. An active playwright and director he is the editor of *Sargasso*, a journal of Caribbean Literature, language and culture.

Fred D'Aguiar is a playwright and poet from Guyana, now based in England. His most recent books are collections of poetry about his Guyanese background: *Mama Dot* and *Airey Hall*.

Clara Rosa de Lima is a theatre administrator, writer, broadcaster and gallery owner in Port of Spain, Trinidad. The author of several collections of verse and novels, she is an influential figure in the Caribbean arts world.

John Figueroa is a distinguished and ground-breaking commentator on Caribbean literature. A pioneering anthologist, a poet, the first indigenous Professor in the University of the West Indies, a lecturer in Britain, Puerto Rico, the Caribbean and Africa. His latest book is a history of the West Indies cricket team in England.

Stewart Brown is a lecturer at the Centre of West African Studies at the University of Birmingham. He has taught in the West Indies and in Nigeria and is the editor of *Caribbean Poetry Now*, *New Wave: Caribbean Stories of the Eighties* and *Voiceprint: poetry from the Caribbean Oral Tradition* (with Gordon Rohlehr and Mervyn Morris). His own collections of poetry include *Zinder* and *Lugard's Bridge*.